# THE INSTITUTE OF CHARTERED SHIPBROKERS

**The Institute of Chartered Shipbrokers is the only internationally recognised professional body representing shipbrokers, ship managers and agents throughout the world.**

With 24 branches in key shipping areas, 3,500 individual and 120 company members, joining ICS represents a commitment to maintaining the highest professional standards across the shipping industry worldwide.

In today's world it is essential for reasons of

- competitiveness
- efficiency and
- safety

that all key players understand the contractual relationships between themselves.

Staff with ICS qualifications subscribe to a common worldwide standard of professional competence and conduct. They have a thorough understanding of all aspects of shipping including law, insurance and economics and by doing so can communicate effectively with specialist professionals.

*"ICS is the only source of professional and vocational qualifications in shipping. Take it from us, all other things being equal, the ICS qualified candidate will get the job."*

Phil Parry, Managing Director, Spinnaker Consulting

Companies employing ICS qualified staff can be confident that they have played their part in ensuring that professionalism, industry knowledge and risk awareness are of paramount importance to their Board and management.

To find out more about ICS and membership either as an individual or company, please contact us at:

85 Gracechurch Street
London EC3V 0AA
UK
T: +44 (0)20 7623 1111
F: +44 (0)20 7623 8118
E: info@ics.org.uk

**www.ics.org.uk**

# PREFACE

## Professional education through TutorShip distance learning courses

The Institute of Chartered Shipbrokers (ICS) is the professional body for all concerned in the business of commercial shipping. Passing its examinations and being elected to membership (MICS) provides a successful candidate with the only internationally recognised qualification for shipbrokers.

## The complete syllabus covers the following subjects:

Introduction to Shipping
Legal Principles in Shipping Business
Economics of Sea Transport and International Trade
Shipping Business

Dry Cargo Chartering
Ship Operations and Management
Tanker Chartering
Ship Sale and Purchase
Liner Trades
Port Agency

Shipping Law
Financial and Management Accounting
Logistics and Multi-modal Transport
Marine Insurance

The Institute believes it is essential that a qualified shipbroker has a thorough knowledge of certain profession-specific subjects plus a sufficient knowledge of the law, insurance, economics etc so that they can communicate with a specialist professional. This results in less confusion, misunderstanding and hopefully less contractual risk. Professionally qualified personnel are consequently ideally placed to undertake the key executive roles in the shipping service sector.

*The true value of these course books is only gained if the student enrols on the TutorShip distance learning programme and all TutorShip Courses are accredited by the O.D.L.Q.C. (the Open and Distance Learning Quality Council).* We would suggest that there is nowhere better to turn to than ICS TutorShip courses for preparing yourselves for a highly successful career in the shipping profession.

We further recommend these books for practitioners and those already working in the Shipping Industry and allied trades. They will ensure you are kept abreast of developments as well as acting as useful everyday knowledge based texts for every aspect of this 'shipping business'.

Further details can be found at www.ics.org.uk

# CONTENTS

# Chapter 1

# THE BASIC TOOLKIT

## 1.1    A GENERAL INTRODUCTION TO THE TEXT

This text seeks to create in all its readers a truly critical understanding which will serve them well in all their industrial activities. It will aim to give an understanding of basic economic analysis and some of its potential shortcomings, by a development of the readers' abilities to discern why things happen, rather than simply how. Emphasis will be laid on economic analysis, success in offering a logical framework in which to appraise alternatives in a wide range of areas and exploring different courses of action. Economics is thus one of the primary methods of developing the essential professional skills of critical assessment and analysis; the development of such critical faculties in shipbroking students must be firmly grounded in a grasp of the basic fundamentals of economic analysis.

It is impossible to come to economics as a space traveller to an unknown planet, for much of the stuff of economics is familiar to everyone, like price, consumption, competition or monopoly. Similarly, the subject matter of the economics of sea transport will have much the same familiarity to those who work in the shipping industry or kindred industries. Terms for example like, freight rate, shipper, dry cargo trade or conferences, will be well known. Such familiarity has a positive and negative side. The advantages are that students possess considerable knowledge which will assist them in their study of the industry's economics and its relationship with the whole business of international trade. The disadvantages are that students come to the subject with ideas, opinions and above all, bias based on their experiences. If these ideas are rigidly held, they will inhibit any attempt to examine, or analyse what will happen under certain circumstances in a dispassionate or abstract way. In addition, the subject matter of an economic concept, for example price, in this case freight rate, is rather more complex than those familiar with the term in an everyday context may realise.

This text book will explain how some of the most useful tools in an economist's tool kit can be used. Tools serving to emphasise the practical problem solving nature of industrial economics. As the reader progresses these tools may appear to be self-evident, but, when carefully used, economic tools provide a useful means for the analysis of many market problems.

Finally, it should be pointed out that economics may be hard work, particularly in the initial stages of relating economic tools to particular shipping problems, but above all it is fun.

## 1.2    A DEFINITION OF ECONOMICS AND MARITIME ECONOMICS

At its simplest economics is concerned with improving human well-being. There are numerous definitions of economics all of which agree on it containing three elements:

*Scarcity*, unlimited or insatiable human *wants*, and *choice*.

The economic problem is that there is a *scarcity of resources* to meet the limitless human wants. This scarcity means considerable care must be taken in choosing the way resources are to be employed, as there are many uses to which they may be put. The question that needs to be asked is – What is the best use of these resources to meet people's wants and needs? Hence some authors refer to economics as the "science of choice", others "a dismal science" because its essential problem is scarcity. To attempt a tentative definition, economics is a study of the allocation of scarce resources which have alternative uses to satisfy limitless human wants.

Maritime economics is a branch of economic theory which has developed through the more established study of transport economics and uses the tools of observation, analysis and evaluation in exactly the same way as in all sectors of economic study. In seeking a definition it is essential to consider the purpose of shipping which is to move people and goods in space, that is, from place to place. In achieving this movement the dominant consideration, as in any branch of economics, is the effective allocation of scarce resources in order to reduce the real cost of this activity. Decisions about the way resources should be used are particularly important in relation to shipping, since the industry by any standard uses vast amounts of these scarce resources in the provision of services to satisfy particular human wants.

To put it another way, maritime economics is the application of economic analysis to all the functions involved in moving goods and people by sea. As one author put it "Maritime Economics is a field of study concerned with the manner in which scarce productive resources are used to bridge the spatial separation of international trading countries most effectively"[1]. Such a definition serves to illustrate how broad the subject is and how imprecise are its boundaries.

## 1.3    FACTORS OF PRODUCTION

To return to scarcity, it arises from the shortage of resources. Economists call resources *factors of production*. They are combined together in an economy to produce a range of goods and services to satisfy human wants. Factors of production are conventionally classified by distinguishing natural, human and manufactured resources, that is, land, labour and capital. Each is a generic term for a range of resources of a particular type.

To examine these categories individually:

i)   **Land** (all natural resources). The term 'land' includes all natural resources; what have been termed 'gifts of nature'. In this context natural resources include mineral deposits, such as oil, or iron ore, agricultural land, forests and building sites. Hence it comprises both the space required for production, (productive activities), and specific resource. These resources are in limited quantities at any given time. Land, therefore, can be defined precisely as the limited source of raw materials and the space in which production can be organised.

ii)  **Labour**. This is the fundamental factor of production, being the human, physical effort, skill and intellectual power which people apply to the production of goods and services. All manual workers, take for example seamen or fishermen, produce, that is, provide labour in the main by their physical effort. Top executives, managers or shipbrokers supply labour mainly by working with their minds, thinking out ways of producing goods and services. Labour, therefore, may be defined as the people's contribution to production both physical and mental.

The quantity and quality of labour will vary from nation to nation. It will be dependant on such things as the age structure of the population, the availability of educational opportunities and the political, social and cultural structure of particular societies. In a similar way to land, labour will be limited in both quality and quantity at any given time.

It should be noted here that some economic and other textbooks include a further factor variously referred to as knowledge, managerial skills, enterprise or entrepreneurship. Basically, it is the function of combining other factors in some form of enterprise. Here, for the sake of simplicity it will be included as part of labour.

iii) **Capital.** Capital or physical capital is the stock of all material goods or material resources used in production. It is a characteristic of capital goods that they are not usually

---

[1]  McConville J (1999) Economics of Maritime Transport, Theory and Practice, Witherby, London p13

wanted for their own sake, but rather for the contribution they make to production. It is the stock of machinery, equipment, buildings, roads, coal mines, oil wells, ships and so on. Capital is created by the use of resources to increase the value or productivity of land and labour resources, in economics capital is not to be confused with money. It may be expressed in terms of money but that is simply a measure or indication of value. In the same way distance is measured in miles or nautical miles. Money produces nothing. Furthermore, capital is not to be confused with such things as shares, bonds or debentures. Buying and selling such items simply changes the ownership of capital; it does not create any. They are securities, not productive capital.

The total stock of these factors of production or resources determine what an economy can produce. Each country has varying amounts of resources. This must be seen against the fact that very few productive processes require the use of factors in a strictly fixed proportion. The proportions of factors of production used in a particular process usually depends upon which factors are most abundant, i.e. the cheapest. Take for example the building of a large sea canal in North America. There, massive amounts of capital will be involved. Whereas in China or the majority of Asian countries, it will be built using large amounts of labour, the least expensive resource.

We can give a simple illustration of the meaning of factors of production by using the famous story of Robinson Crusoe, who you may recall was stranded, initially alone on a desert island. Let us make some assumptions about him. Let's say he lives on fish and catches one fish a day. He decides to forego fishing and, therefore, eating for two days. He invests this time in the making of a net. With this net he can catch five fish a day. Hence in terms of resources, he supplies the labour, land or natural resources are the sea and the fish, and the capital is the fishing net, which has increased his production of fish. It should be noted that no mention of money is made in relation to his economic capital, the net. But if the story is changed and someone came to the island and offered to exchange £10 for the net, and Robinson accepted this offer, money becomes a measure of the net's value.

## 1.4   UTILITY AND PRICE

Resources are used in production to create what economists call "utility". This is attributed to any commodity capable of creating human satisfaction. In a broad sense it is the power of a good or service to give pleasure, satisfaction or what is termed "real need fulfilment", it is a purely subjective idea incapable of direct measurement. The objective of the process of production is to increase the amount of goods and services available to satisfy human desire, that is, to create utility. Many of you will understand the concept of utility intuitively. When you buy something, and say it is "value for money", what you are really saying is that the utility you have obtained from the good or service purchased was worth at least the price you paid for it. If instead, you feel that something is a "bargain", what you are saying is that you value this product more than the price that you paid for it; you would have been prepared to pay more, but you did not need to. A "bargain" therefore illustrates the difference between *price*, what you have to pay for a product, and *utility*, what you subjectively feel that the product is worth to you.

Shipping and the maritime industry as a whole is an important element in the process of creating utility. It is involved in creating utility in a number of ways.

1.  **Place Utility.** The accessibility of goods at a certain place. For example, potatoes shipped from Egypt to a vegetable shop in a small town in Holland.

2.  **Time Utility.** The accessibility of goods at a certain time. For example, heating oil from West Africa or the Middle East in a storage tank of a small house in Northern Norway in mid winter.

Other forms of utility are also contributed to by shipping or transport, such as the act of providing a service. It is also important in the import and export of goods, that is the act of exchange. Thus shipping is a major factor in creating utility, in other words, creating "the entire amount of satisfaction obtained from consuming various amounts of a commodity in a given time period."

## 1.5 OPPORTUNITY COST

Scarcity of resources for use in production and the insatiable demand of human society forces the making of choices. Every time a choice is made something must be foregone or sacrificed. To take the example of an economy which can produce two goods, ships or rice. Shipbuilding will use a certain amount of the available factors of production which means that they cannot be used in the production of rice, that is the amount of rice that could be produced has been foregone. In this example it is being assumed that rice is the best alternative to ships using the same amount of the factors of production available. Here is one of the central ideas of cost in economics, the opportunity foregone or sacrificed by the use of resources in one way rather than another. Costs can be seen in terms of the utility of the next most attractive activity foregone. Opportunity or alternative cost doctrine gives the utility of what has been produced by measuring the utility of the best alternative production given up. Simply, the cost of producing a unit of y is the utility of the unit of x that must be given up for it. A schedule and model to illustrate this may be constructed using the above example of an economy which, instead of producing a complexity of thousands of goods, produces two types of goods, ships and rice. The production employs all the factors of production in the economy assuming the existing technological level. These optima can be illustrated by the production possibility schedule shown below:

### Table 1.1 – Production Possibility Schedule

| Showing the maximum amounts of Ships and Rice that can be produced with limited resources of Land, Labour and Capital. | | | |
|---|---|---|---|
| **Options Mn DWT** | **Ships (mn tonnes)** | **Rice of Ships* (mn tonnes)** | **Opportunity Cost** |
| (1) | (2) | (3) | (4) |
| A | 0 | 20 | |
| B | 1 | 19 | 1 |
| C | 2 | 17 | 2 |
| D | 3 | 13 | 4 |
| E | 4 | 8 | 5 |
| F | 5 | 0 | 8 |

(*) Defined as the amount of rice (in mn tonnes) given up in order to produce an extra 10mn dwt of ship. (i.e. row C col(4) = row C col (3) minus row B col(3))

At one extreme on the schedule, option A, all economic resources are involved in the production of rice. There are 20 million tons of rice produced and no ships so the country has a large quantity of rice but no ships are being built. At the other extreme (option F), it has decided to produce only ships, producing 50 million deadweight tonnes and no rice.

Note that every combination on this frontier is efficient, because each combination represents the maximum that can be achieved from the present stock of resources.

Assume for the moment, that the economy is located at point A, producing 20mn tons of rice and no ships. All of its economic resources are fully employed in this activity, so no additional output of either rice or ships can be produced at the present time. Now imagine trying to move the economy to point B. This would require shifting land, labour, and capital away from rice production, the released resources being used to start up the ship industry. Table 1.1 shows that 1mn dwt of ships will be produced at B, but only 19mn tonnes of rice. The Opportunity

Cost of the 1mn dwt of ships must therefore be 1mn tonnes of rice, since this is the amount of rice production foregone when ship production is increased. This number is shown in Column 4 of the Table. Thus Column 4 of the Schedule illustrates the concept of opportunity cost. Here movement from option A to option B shows that only 1 million tons of rice must be foregone or given up to produce 1 million tonnes of shipping. A change from point B to point C increases the sacrifice of rice to 2 million tons for an *extra* 1 million tonnes of shipping. As rice production contracts, the opportunity cost in terms of rice foregone becomes greater and greater. A larger amount of rice must be given up to build ships. Moving from option E to F means giving up a massive 8 million tons of rice to produce only an *extra* 1 million tonnes of shipping. As may be seen the opportunity cost does not remain the same throughout. This reflects the fact that some factors of production are more suited to certain uses than others. For example, land that can be flooded easily is essential for rice production, but will be of little use in building ships. Naval architects will be very productive when employed in shipping, but of little use when working in the rice fields. This means the trade-off between rice and ships varies; when resources are concentrated in ship production, the reallocation of land to rice will be the reallocation of land which is very productive in rice terms, relatively unproductive in ship terms. Ship output will not fall much, and rice output rises a lot.

### Figure 1.1 – The Production Possibility Frontier

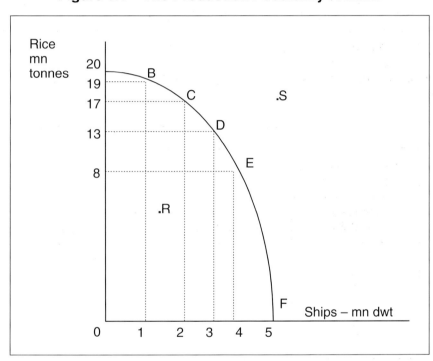

When the position is reversed, and rice production is near its maximum, the transfer of the last few naval architects will mean a large drop in ship production and a miniscule increase in rice output. This gives rise to the shape shown in Figure 1.1.

As you will see, the curve is concave to the origin, this indicates that the resources are not completely substitutable one for the other, as shown by column 3 in the Schedule. The model has rice production on the vertical axis and shipbuilding on the horizontal. The production possibility curve runs from point A to point F. The area inside the production possibility curve represents all the alternative combinations of rice and ship building which a country can just produce when all its resources are fully employed. Any point inside the curve or frontier such as that represented by R means a combination of factors of producing less than the total possible. Some factors are under or un-employed. Any point beyond the curve or frontier, for example, point S, represent combinations which are unobtainable under present conditions. Figure 1.1 shows very clearly the changing opportunity cost of producing more ships. The move from B to C yields 1 million extra tonnes of ships, at a 'cost' of 2 million tonnes of rice. The move from E to F produces the same increase in ship output (one million tonnes), but costs 8 million tonnes of lost rice production. The curve must be concave to the origin because of the assumption that factors of production are not equally effective in producing rice and ships.

The concepts of *opportunity cost*, and the *production possibility frontier* will underline much of the lessons that follow. The latter is of particular importance when considering international trade. (Lesson 9).

## 1.6    THE PRICE MECHANISM

The price mechanism is a central feature of what economists term 'price theory ' – how prices are set. An important part of economics, and indeed shipping. The two basic components of the price mechanism are demand and supply. These are governed by what are known as economic laws. These are not laws in a legal sense, they are not even rules, but serve merely to confirm a general tendency in everyday activity. The law of demand states "the demand for a good or service falls if its price increases, and rises if its price decreases, all other things being held equal or vice versa. To put it another way, demand and price are inversely related. Less quantities are purchased at a higher price, more at a lower price.

The law of supply states "the higher the price the greater the quantity which will be supplied by the producer, the lower the price the smaller the quantity that will be supplied by the producer, all other things being held equal. In other words the supply of a good increases (decreases) if its price increases (decreases). Here price and quantity supplied are directly related.

The phrase was used above 'other things being held equal'. It is used to isolate or concentrate on particular effects for it is impossible to study all economic changes at the same time. In the present case it is only possible to concentrate on the relationship between demand and supply of a commodity and its price or price changes by assuming all the influences remain unchanged. It isolates the effect of any changes that are being examined by holding all other relevant factors constant. It is a useful phrase, much used in economic literature and textbooks. (Sometimes the Latin phrase 'ceteris paribus' is used as an alternative).

Having looked at the basic law of the two sides of a price mechanism each side may be looked at in more detail.

## 1.7    DEMAND

In economics demand is not just need or desire or want. It is all of these things backed up by a willingness and ability to pay the price. This is known as <u>effective demand</u>, but is generally referred to simply as demand. It expresses the quantity of a commodity which consumers are prepared to buy over a range of prices. The two factors of primary interest are the price, and quantity demanded.

Let us take as an example the international cruise market. A demand schedule can be drawn up which records how much consumers, or in this case potential passengers, are prepared to pay for a cruise at different prices. See Table 1.2.

## Table 1.2 – Market Demand Schedule for Cruises

| Price of Cruise ($) | Quantity Demanded (passenger trips) (D) | New higher level of Demand (passenger trips) (D1) | New lower level of Demand (passenger trips) (D2) |
|---|---|---|---|
| 15,000 | 9,000 | 10,000 | 7,000 |
| 14,000 | 10,000 | 12,000 | 8,000 |
| 13,000 | 12,000 | 15,000 | 10,000 |
| 12,000 | 15,000 | 18,000 | 12,000 |
| 10,000 | 20,000 | 22,000 | 15,000 |
| 9,000 | 25,000 | 27,000 | 16,000 |

The schedule serves to illustrate the law of demand. As price falls (column 1) the quantity demanded increases (column 2) and vice versa. Columns 3 and 4 will be discussed below.

At any price, for example, $14,000, there is a definite quantity demanded of 10,000. The schedule gives the different quantities demanded at six selected price levels. The information given in the market demand schedule can be used in a 2-dimensional diagram or graph.

## Figure 1.2 – Market Demand Curve for Cruises

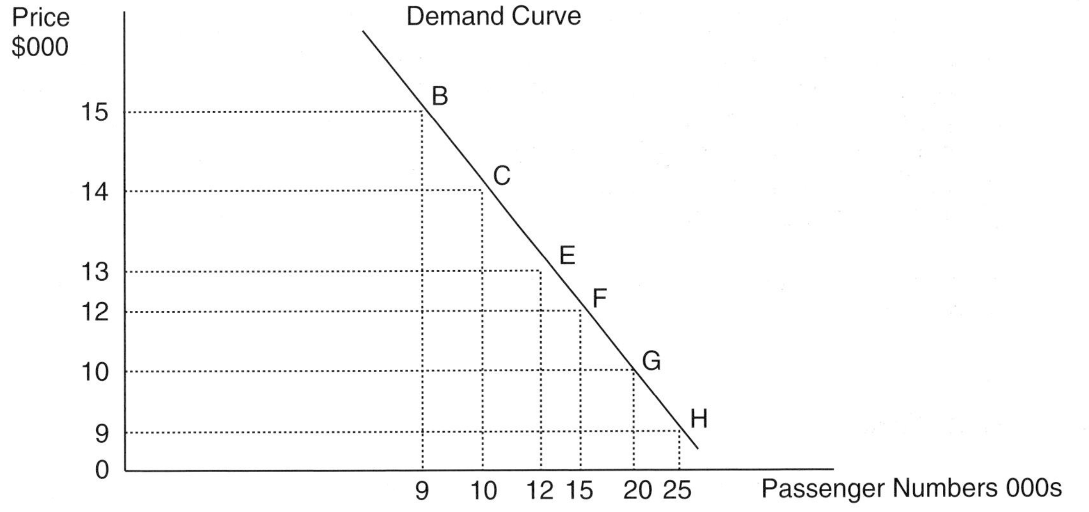

The vertical axis, as usual, shows the possible prices. The horizontal axis, as usual, shows the quantity of the commodity cruise trips that can be demanded. It should be noted that normally price is shown on the vertical axis and quantity on the horizontal axis. The negative slope for the demand curve i.e. down to the right reflects the demand and price/quantity relationships. In other words, the negative slope illustrates that a reduction in price of cruises leads to an increase in the quantity demanded. Similarly, an increase in the price results in a fall in the quantity demanded. Alternative price/quantity combinations are represented by various points on the demand curve D. An example of price $15,000 per trip the quantity demanded is 9,000 trips, point B on the curve. At point E the price is $13,000, the quantity demanded is 12,000 trips, whilst at price $9,000 the quantity demanded is 25,000 trips, point H. The demand curve shows the fundamental relationship between price and quantity demanded.

It has already been shown the higher the price, the lower the quantity demanded, and vice versa. Other factors have to be assumed to remain constant. The other factors which will affect the levels of demand are discussed overleaf:

**Income.** Normally it is expected that any change in income will create a change in demand, if people have more money to spend they will buy more, if the money they have to spend falls they will buy less. An increase in income has indeed been a factor raising the demand for cruise trips.

**Taste.** This term is used in economics to represent all other factors which influence demand. There can be many influences on taste and it can change quite suddenly. For example, a serious disaster involving a cruise vessel would change demand levels in one direction while a successful publicity campaign could change it in another.

### 1.7.1    Prices of Other Commodities

The prices of commodities are often interrelated and a change in the price of one commodity might well influence the level of demand for another commodity. This relationship exists in respect of complementary goods and substitutes.

(a) **The price of complements.** A good is said to be a complement if consumers purchase them jointly with another product. For example, milk and tea, milk and coffee, sugar and tea. In the present example assume a cruise ship entails an air flight before joining the vessel. A change in air fares, up or down, would have a positive or negative effect on the demand for cruise trips.

(b) **Substitutes.** The price of any commodity which has many substitutes is very sensitive to change. For example if the prices of other comparable forms of holiday were to change this would have an impact on the cruise market.

For students who enjoy mathematical explanations the following simple equation may serve to further enlighten the previous discussion. For those with no mathematical bent omit the following paragraph; it will have no effect on their moving to the next stage.

The discussion of demand can be summarised in symbols as follows:

$$\{Qd = f\,(P, Y, T, P_c, P_s)\}$$

This is shorthand for the demand curve where $Qd$ = the demand for cruise trips, $f$ = a function of a set of variables within the brackets. $P$ = price of a cruise trip, $Y$ = income $T$ = taste $P_c$ = price of complementary commodities $P_s$ = price of substitute goods. The equation can be used to analyse the demand of a final consumer for any good or service. It is important to distinguish between the factors price, income, taste and price of other commodities for they combine together to establish the shape of the demand curve and structure of the schedule. If apart from price they are not held constant, the demand curve will shift.

To return to the cruise example if it is assumed there is a rise in income this would create an increase in demand, all other things being equal. This is shown in column 3 of the Table 1.2, and the effect would be to shift the demand curve to the right as shown below, from D to D1.

On the other hand, a reduction in income would cause the opposite effect, a fall in the number of trips demanded at any possible price, all other things being equal. This is shown in column 4 of Table 1.2, and the corresponding leftward shift of the demand curve is shown in Figure 1.3, from D to D2.

## Figure 1.3 – Shifts in the Conditions of Demand

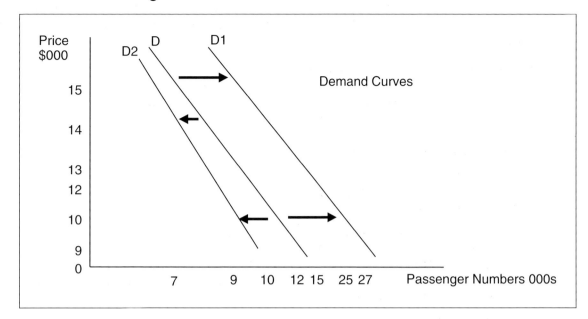

At a price of $14,000 the quantity demanded is 12,000 trips whereas only 10,000 trips were demanded before the increase in incomes. At $9,000 27,000 trips are demanded instead of the 25,000 previously demanded. Similarly, a declining income would cause the demand curve to move bodily to the left; in the opposite direction in other words. There are two distinct movements in demand.

1.  A movement along the curve in any direction known as CHANGES IN THE QUANTITY DEMANDED.

2.  A shift of the whole curve bodily to the left or the right is known as a shift in CONDITIONS OF DEMAND.


## 1.8    SUPPLY

This refers to the quantity of a product that will be offered on the market at a given price during a particular time period. To repeat the law of supply, more of a commodity will be supplied at a higher price than at a lower one[2].

A supply schedule is a table showing the different quantities the sellers are willing to offer on the market at various prices at a given time.

---

[2]  It is important to note that the supply schedule derived in this section is based upon the assumption that the market is a perfectly competitive one (See Lesson 5). Whilst accepting that the cruise industry does not fit this model terribly well, it is still a useful model to develop because it is one of the few shipping markets that impinges directly upon the final consumer.

## Table 1.3 – Supply Schedule for Cruises

| Column 1<br>Price per<br>Passenger Trip<br><br>($) | Column 2<br>Quantity Supplied<br>Passenger Trips<br><br>(S) | Column 3<br>Increase in<br>Quantity Supplied<br>Passenger Trips<br>(S1) | Column 4<br>Decrease in<br>Quantity Supplied<br>Passenger Trips<br>(S2) |
|---|---|---|---|
| 15,000 | 25,000 | 27,000 | 21,000 |
| 14,000 | 20,000 | 22,000 | 17,000 |
| 13,000 | 18,000 | 20,000 | 15,000 |
| 12,000 | 15,000 | 18,000 | 12,000 |
| 10,000 | 12,000 | 15,000 | 10,000 |
| 9,000 | 10,000 | 12,000 | 8,000 |

In a similar way to demand, the supply schedule serves to illustrate the law of supply. As price increases column 1 the producers, cruise companies, increase the amount of trips offered, as shown in column 2. (Column 3 will be discussed below). At each price there are related quantities supplied for example at a price of $13,000, 18,000 passenger voyages or trips are supplied. Once again a similar two-dimensional diagram or graph can be constructed for supply. As usual the vertical axis indicates price and the horizontal axis indicates quantity offered.

The positive slope of the supply curve i.e. upward to the right, reflects the law of supply and the direct relationship of price to quantity. In other words the positive slope illustrates that an increase in the price of a cruise leads to an increase in the quantity supplied (all other things being held equal). Similarly, a fall in the price means a fall in the quantity offered on the market. Alternative price quantity combinations are represented by the various points of the supply curve S. For example at price $9,000 per trip the quantity supplied is 10,000 trips point H on the curve.

## Figure 1.4 – Market Supply Curve for Cruises

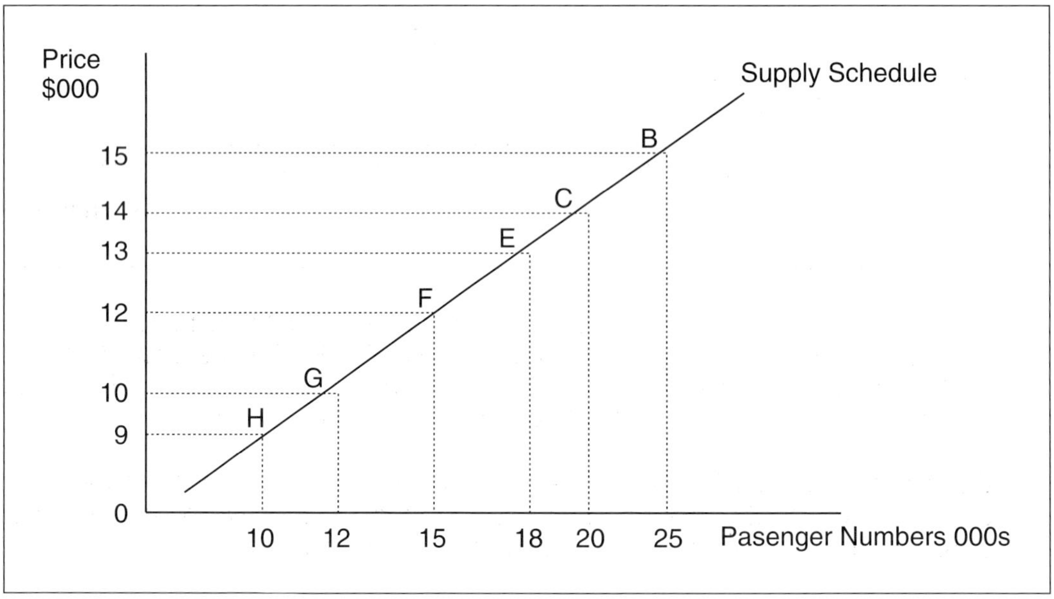

At point E the price has increased to $13,000 and the quantity offered to 18,000 trips, while at point B the price is $15,000 and 25,000 trips are offered. As with demand the supply schedule is based on the assumption that during the period under consideration the assumptions underlying the schedule remain constant. The factors affecting supply are:

1.  Costs of production. Changes in the costs of production would influence the quantity supplied at any particular price. A major modification in crew costs would have an impact on the cost of operating a ship and hence on the amount of cruises offered.

2.  Changes in the method of production. New inventions or technologies can reduce costs of production and so change producers'/suppliers' attitudes to price. In the cruise market a break-through in engine or hull design would result in a lowering of price.

3.  Inventory (stock) levels. If there is a substantial amount of tonnage laid up or under-utilised, owners of vessels might accept lower prices for their cruises. They might offer discounts, 'special offers', such as 'Two for the price of one'.

4.  Expectations of future price. If there is an expectation of a rise in price owners (suppliers) may be reluctant to sell tickets for their next cruise in the hope that the expected market price rise comes through.

To return to the cruise example, if it is assumed there has been a substantial fall in bunker prices, that is the costs of production, this would create an increase in supply, all things being equal. This is shown in column 3 of the Table 1:3 and the effect would be to shift the supply curve to the right as shown below:

**Fig. 1.5 – Alterations in Supply Conditions**

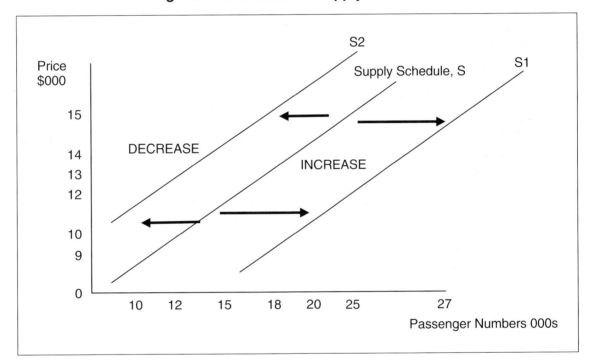

As can be seen the supply curve has moved as a whole to the right, S1. In this new situation, 12,000 trips are supplied at the price of $9,000, 15,000 trips are offered if the price is $10,000, and so on, up to the point where 27,000 trips are offered at the price of $15,000. Joining these points up on a graph generates the new supply schedule S1.

Column 4 of Table 1.3 showed the effect of a fall in quantity supplied at any possible price, and is shown as S2 in Figure 1.5 above. This schedule shows the fact that supply will be less at any possible price, compared to the original schedule S.

This brings us to two different and distinct movements in supply.

1.  A movement along the curve in any direction is known as CHANGES IN THE QUANTITY SUPPLIED.

2.  A shift of the whole curve bodily to the left or the right is known as CHANGE IN CONDITIONS OF SUPPLY.

## 1.9   THE BASIC MARKET MODEL (bringing demand and supply together)

Up until now each side of the market, in this case the imaginary cruise market, has been analysed separately. Demand, its laws and the relationship between price and quantity. Supply, its laws and the relationship between price and quantity. Neither demand nor supply can of themselves decide the market price of any product nor the quantity of the product sold. This is because individually demand and supply only indicate consumers' and producers' intentions. The next stage is to bring the intentions into reality. Hence demand and supply must be combined in a single schedule as below:

### Table 1.4 – Cruise Market. Demand and Supply Equilibrium

| Column 1 | Column 2 | Column 3 | Column 4 | Column 5 | Column 6 |
|---|---|---|---|---|---|
| Price of Cruise for Passenger ($) | Quantity Demand for Passenger Trips (D) | Quantity Supplied of Passenger Trips (S) | Passenger Trips | | Market Pressure on Price |
| | | | Shortage | Surplus | |
| 15,000 | 9,000 | 25,000 | | 14,000 | Downward |
| 14,000 | 10,000 | 20,000 | | 10,000 | Downward |
| 13,000 | 12,000 | 18,000 | | 6,000 | Downward |
| 12,000 | 15,000 | 15,000 | 0 | 0 | Equilibrium |
| 10,000 | 20,000 | 12,000 | 8,000 | | Upward |
| 9,000 | 25,000 | 10,000 | 15,000 | | Upward |

Students will recognise that the above is based on the demand and supply schedules used earlier in this Lesson. Such schedules refer of course to a particular time period. Column 1 is a list of prices a cruise passenger could be asked to pay. Column 2 is the quantity passengers would demand at those different price levels. Column 3 is the quantity cruise operators would offer at different price levels. Columns 4 and 5 highlight the differences between the two earlier columns of demand and supply. At the higher prices there is an excess of quantity supplied over passengers offering to take a trip, an excess of supply over demand. At the lower prices of $10,000 and $9,000 there is a negative difference, that is, there is a shortage; an excess of demand over supply. However, at the price of $12,000 the intention of passengers (buyers) and the cruise operators (sellers) are exactly matched. A point where there is neither an excess of supply nor demand. This is known as the equilibrium price, or the market clearing price. This is the price where the opposing forces of demand and supply are in perfect balance and there is no net tendency for market price to change. To put it another way; a point where the quantity demanded of a commodity equals the quantity supplied causing market clearance. Once obtained there will be a tendency for the equilibrium price to persist. Changes will only occur if the basic conditions of either demand or supply, or both, are disturbed (i.e. if any of the factors which have been held constant actually change). The above schedule includes the two criteria of price and quantity and therefore can be represented in a market graph or model as below.

## Figure 1.6 – Equilibrium in the Passenger Cruise Market

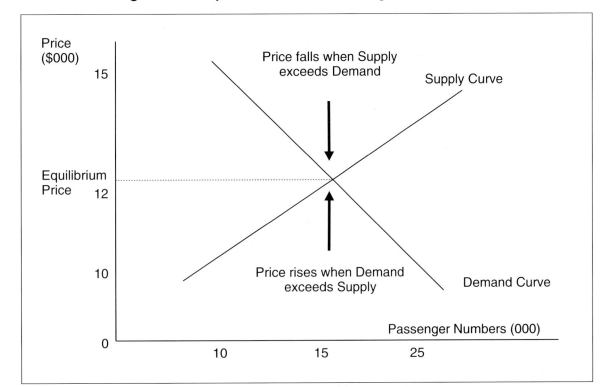

The individual demand curve and supply curve are brought together in a market model. The demand curve shows the passengers' (buyers) intentions or plans to purchase at each level or price following the law of demand. As price falls, quantity demanded increases, the curve slopes downwards from left to right. The supply curve shows the quantity cruise operators plan to sell at each level of price. Once again the law of supply is in evidence. The producers offer more at a higher price. The supply curve move upwards from left to right. Only at equilibrium price of $12,000 are the intentions of the passengers (demanders) and sellers (suppliers) exactly meshed together. At a price above $12,000 there is a surplus and market pressures for price to fall. Suppliers will withdraw from the market. At prices below the equilibrium value, there is a shortage, and market pressure develops for the price to rise. The quantity demanded will fall, whilst that supplied will increase, thus reducing the excess of demand over supply. The excess demand disappears at $12,000.

In the following diagram the above argument is retraced in a different form.

**Figure 1.7 – Simplified Model of Cruise Market**

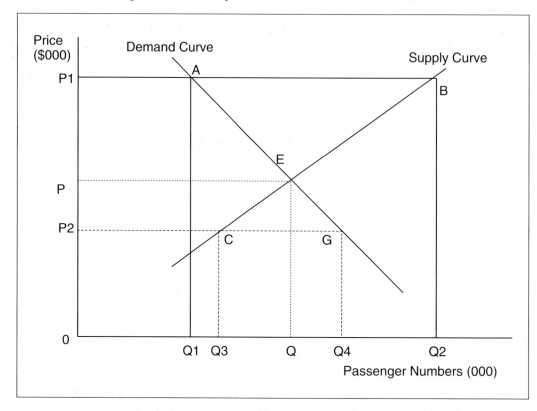

In the model, equilibrium price is P at E with quantity Q. At the higher price P1 quantity demanded stands at A and quantity supplied is B. Therefore there is an excess of quantity supplied over the quantity demanded at price P1 which creates downward pressure on the price, forcing it towards equilibrium price P. Compared to P1, less is supplied but more is consumed. These two processes both help to eliminate the excess supply that exists if the price were to remain at P1.

At the lower price P2 the quantity supplied would be OQ3 (reading the quantity from the horizontal scale from the line CQ3), while buyers wish to purchase OQ4 (reading the quantity demanded from GQ4). This means that at price OP2, there is an excess of quantity demanded over the quantity supplied. A shortage exists at price OP2, and pressure will be built up to force the price up, to return to market equilibrium P.

## 1.10   DYNAMIC ADJUSTMENT

The model described above is the simplest possible model of competitive market price determination. It is a static model, in that the effects of shifts in supply and demand on the model are not really considered. Indeed, there is an assumption that all transactions that take place in the market do so only at the equilibrium price, e.g. price OP in Figure 1.7. No transactions are permitted to take place at 'disequilibrium' prices.

Whilst a useful model in many ways, it also has some drawbacks. Perhaps the most significant is the failure to allow for the fact that there may be a considerable period of time for the required adjustments in supply to take place, when faced with a sudden change in demand conditions. For example, the shipping markets went through a crisis of severe overcapacity of tonnage in the early 1980's. This problem did not resolve itself for several years. The market model described above would therefore have to be modified to allow for this problem. This will be done in Lessons 3 and 4, when supply conditions are studied in more detail.

## 1.11   CONCLUSION

This Lesson has aimed to give students a knowledge of some of the basic concepts of economics. The key concepts of Opportunity Cost, Utility and Price have been discussed. Secondly, a model of demand and supply, and price determination in a competitive market was developed. It is very important that all students grasp these basic concepts, and the analysis of demand and supply, because they will be heavily used in the following lessons.

## 1.12   SELF-ASSESSMENT AND TEST QUESTIONS

Attempt the following and check your answers from the text:

1.   Explain what is meant by:

    a)   Demand
    b)   The inverse relationship between price and quantity.

2.   Using the information in Table 1.2 as a basis construct a schedule showing a further increase in demand and draw a graph illustrating the change in demand conditions.

3.   Explain what is meant by:

    a)   The supply schedule, or conditions of supply.
    b)   The positive relationship between price and quantity.

4.   Using the information in Table 1:3 as a basis, construct a Schedule showing an increase in supply and draw a graph illustrating the change in supply.

Having completed Chapter One attempt the following and submit your answers to your Tutor.

1.   Using the market for cruises, explain fully what would be the probable effects of equilibrium price and the quantity of the following:

    a)   A rise in incomes in the USA and Europe.
    b)   A series of well publicised unfortunate incidents on cruises.
    c)   A decrease in the price of air travel.
    d)   A substantial decrease in the cost of bunker fuel.

It is essential to illustrate your answers using demand and supply diagrams.

# Chapter 2

# THE DEMAND FOR SHIPPING

## 2.1    INTRODUCTION

The demand for shipping, like that for all forms of freight and passenger transport, results from the final consumer's demand for goods; it is not a direct demand but a derived demand. Shipping is a factor which is not in demand for its own sake but is derived from the demand for the goods that are being transported. This discussion does not include any consideration of the cruise trade. This demand is closely related to the growth in world income particularly that of the developed world, which is the major influence on the level of seaborne trade. The average distance of hauls, costs of transportation, and other factors, particularly international crises, have an important impact on the levels of derived demand for shipping. In this Lesson empirical evidence of trends in the level of seaborne trade and factors influencing it, will be related to a theoretical analysis of demand.

## 2.2    AN ECONOMIC ANALYSIS OF THE DEMAND FOR SHIPPING

The demand for shipping is dependant upon the amount of international trade generated between countries. Seaborne trade accounts for the bulk, about 75% by volume, of international movement. The level of demand is dependant on a complexity of factors the most important of which are:

i)    The level of world economic activity and particularly that of countries which are members of the Organisation for Economic Co-operation (OECD), that is, the developed market economies

ii)    The volume of seaborne trade generated and its major components.

iii)    Distance over which cargo are hauled.

iv)    Freight rates and external factors and events. These factors will be examined individually in the light of their importance in an economic analysis of shipping demand.

**World economic activity.** This is a major factor in the level of demand for seaborne trade. In the long run it is dependent upon elements such as the level of world population and changes in standards of living. In the short run a diversity of elements can be and are important.

The best guide to changes and trends in the economy of the world or that of individual countries is GROSS DOMESTIC PRODUCT (GDP) and GROSS NATIONAL PRODUCT (GNP). These will be defined thus.

**Gross Domestic Product** is a measure of the total flows of goods and services produced by the economy normally calculated on an annual basis. It is obtained by adding together the value of output, that is final consumption and investment goods, at current market prices. This explains why it is often referred to as Gross Domestic Value Added.

**Gross National Product.** This is the annual total of the current market price of goods and services produced in a country's economy. It includes incomes accrued from investments abroad less incomes earned by foreigners in the domestic economy. It is gross domestic product plus the net foreign investment earnings.

In this Chapter the main indicators of growth in all countries of the world, GDP or GNP, are simply added together and thus a crude indicator of the level of international activity is obtained. Rather than examining the whole world most analysis of shipping demand is concentrated on OECD. This is an economic organisation whose members consist of Scandinavia, most of Europe including Turkey; North America, Japan, South Korea, Australia and New Zealand. Despite the absence of such economic powers as the Russia and Central Europe as well as the smaller dynamic economies of Asia, such as Hong Kong, Taiwan and Singapore, the OECD exerts a massive influence within the international economy. This is because it includes virtually all the industrial developed countries who account for a very large percentage of world output and international trade. It has been estimated that they account for somewhere in the region of 80% of world international production, 70% of world exports by value and some 65% (by value) of the world's inter-regional dry cargo trade as well as consuming approximately 55% of oil production. This then is the primary reason for concentrating on the OECD.

### Table 2.1 – GNP Growth Rates of Major OECD Countries 1990-2003
### (Growth rate compared with the previous year %)

| Year | USA | Japan | Europe | OECD Total |
|------|-----|-------|--------|------------|
| 1990 | 1.0 | 5.6 | 2.9 | 2.6 |
| 1991 | -0.5 | 4.5 | 1.2 | 1.1 |
| 1992 | 2.2 | 2.4 | 2.0 | 2.2 |
| 1993 | 3.8 | 3.5 | 2.7 | 3.3 |
| 1994 | 3.9 | 1.0 | 2.3 | 2.8 |
| 1995 | 3.1 | 2.5 | 3.0 | 3.0 |
| 1996 | 2.0 | 3.4 | 3.2 | 2.9 |
| 1997 | 3.9 | 1.4 | 2.5 | 3.3 |
| 1998 | 3.9 | -2.8 | 2.9 | 2.3 |
| 1999 | 3.6 | -0.9 | 2.1 | 2.2 |
| 2000 | 4.1 | 1.5 | 1.7 | 1.0 |
| 2001 | 1.1 | -0.7 | 1.7 | 1.0 |
| 2002 | 0.7 | -1.0 | 1.5 | 1.0 |
| 2003 | 3.8 | 0.8 | 2.9 | 3.2 |

Source OECD "Economic Outlook" Nos. 46 Dec. 1989, 60, Dec 1996, Dec. 2002

The second reason is that statistical and other information on the OECD is more easily obtainable and comparatively more reliable.

Notes: F = Forecast values. Real GDP/GNP measures the growth in economic activity after allowing for the effects of changing price levels.

Table 2.1 presents information on the growth rates of real GNP for a number of OECD member countries for the years 1990-2003, as well as the figure for all OECD members (OECD Total).

It is noticeable that the pattern of growth is uneven. Looking at the total column, we see that in the early 1990's the OECD countries were growing very slowly. The long run average, which is 2.4% for the years 1990-2003 (sometimes called the trend growth rate). When growth is well below trend, economists say that there is a recession; when it is well above trend, there is a 'boom'. It is clear from the data that the OECD pulled out of a recession in the mid-1990's, and enjoyed a boom, which peaked in 1993 at well above trend.

Another cycle then began, with the OECD economies moving into recession in the early 1990's, with growth rates falling to 1.0% in 1991. Since then, economic growth rates have recovered somewhat, and the general outlook is for a period to 2003 is of reasonable economic growth.

It also worth noting that individual economies growth rates can differ quite markedly from the OECD's. The Japanese growth was for the years 1990 and 1991, which was very strong with a peak at 5.6% in 1990. Then decline came in late 1990-2003. Note that the fluctuation of the growth rate is more marked than that for the OECD as a whole; it is often the case that an individual country's growth rate will be more 'volatile' than that of the totality of which it is a component part. When several major economies all boom or slump together, they affect the total quite significantly; there was a well known boom in 2000, with several countries recording very high growth rates, and this is the period of the highest growth for the OECD as a whole.

### Table 2.2 – Development of world seaborne trade 2002
### (Volume in tonnes)

*In million tonne*

| Year | Crude oil | Oil products | Iron ore | Coal | Grain | Other dry cargo | Total trade | % change over prev. year |
|---|---|---|---|---|---|---|---|---|
| 1981 | 1170 | 267 | 303 | 210 | 206 | 1305 | 3461 | -4.0 |
| 1982 | 993 | 285 | 273 | 208 | 200 | 1240 | 3199 | -7.6 |
| 1983 | 930 | 282 | 257 | 197 | 199 | 1225 | 3090 | -3.4 |
| 1984 | 930 | 297 | 306 | 232 | 207 | 1320 | 3292 | 6.5 |
| 1985 | 871 | 288 | 321 | 272 | 181 | 1360 | 3293 | 0.0 |
| 1986 | 958 | 305 | 311 | 276 | 165 | 1370 | 3385 | 2.8 |
| 1987 | 970 | 313 | 319 | 283 | 186 | 1390 | 3461 | 2.2 |
| 1988 | 1042 | 325 | 348 | 304 | 196 | 1460 | 3675 | 6.2 |
| 1989 | 1120 | 340 | 362 | 321 | 192 | 1525 | 3860 | 5.0 |
| 1990 | 1190 | 336 | 347 | 342 | 192 | 1570 | 3977 | 3.0 |
| 1991 | 1247 | 326 | 358 | 369 | 200 | 1610 | 4110 | 3.3 |
| 1992 | 1313 | 335 | 334 | 371 | 208 | 1660 | 4221 | 2.7 |
| 1993 | 1356 | 358 | 354 | 367 | 194 | 1710 | 4339 | 2.8 |
| 1994 | 1403 | 368 | 383 | 383 | 184 | 1785 | 4506 | 3.8 |
| 1995 | 1415 | 381 | 402 | 423 | 196 | 1870 | 4687 | 4.0 |
| 1996 | 1466 | 404 | 391 | 435 | 193 | 1970 | 4859 | 3.7 |
| 1997 | 1519 | 410 | 430 | 460 | 203 | 2070 | 5092 | 4.8 |
| 1998 | 1535 | 402 | 417 | 473 | 196 | 2050 | 5073 | -0.4 |
| 1999 | 1550 | 415 | 411 | 482 | 220 | 2091 | 5169 | 1.9 |
| 2000 | 1608 | 419 | 454 | 523 | 230 | 2200 | 5434 | 5.1 |
| 2001 | 1592 | 425 | 452 | 565 | 234 | 2245 | 5513 | 1.5 |
| 2002 | 1565 | 422 | 475 | 575 | 220 | 2292 | 5549 | 0.7 |
| Ave.Growth Rate 1981/2000 | 1.7 | 2,3 | 2.2 | 4.9 | 0.5 | 2.7 | 2.3 | |
| Ave. Growth Rate 1991/2000 | 2.9 | 2.6 | 2.7 | 3.9 | 1.3 | 3.3 | 3.0 | |
| Ave. Growth Rate 1993/2002 | 1.6 | 1.8 | 3.3 | 5.1 | 1.4 | 3.3 | 2.8 | |

Source: Fearnleys Review, various issues

## 2.2.1  Seaborne Trade

Seaborne trade dominates international trade. It has been estimated that approximately 75% of world trade by weight moves by sea and that in terms of value approximately 65%. This despite the growth of overland traffic, particularly within Europe and the development of air freight. The table below illustrates this in terms of development over the last two decades.

The volume of trade increased by over 40% in these two decades. Against the background of this increase were changes in particular commodities' contribution to trade; crude oil and oil products declined from 44% to 37% of the total; iron ore movements in percentage terms changed a little from 9% to 8%. The most remarkable difference is in coal, which nearly doubled in importance from 5% to 9%. (Appropriate change.)

The acceleration and deceleration in world trade over the last twenty years broadly mirrors the experience of the level of economic activity. This is reflected fairly closely in the demand for shipping. What occurred was an extremely sluggish first few years of the decade, apart from 1984, until the last years of the decade. The early nineties have seen the beginnings of a recovery of world seaborne trade, especially in the oil sector, where cargo volumes have begun to reach figures last seen in the mid-1970's. Dry cargo has grown fairly steadily over the period, but note that growth did slow down in 1991-2, with the years of lowest growth being in the late 90's. Any practical economic analysis or forecast undertaken into the demand for seaborne trade needs to include the important individual components evident in <u>both</u> the above table. These were as follows:

1. The volume of oil movements.

2. Iron ore and coal shipments in particular their relationship to steel production.

3. Movements in grain.

4. Changes in other general cargoes.

5. Freight rates.

6. Other factors.

To look at each component individually:

1. **Oil Movements.** The change in the price of oil was the main influence of changes in volume throughout the decade. To look at the price movement using official Saudi Arabian light oil dollars per barrel at January 1st and July 1st of each year. The price rose from $18 in mid 1979 to a long-standing peak of $34 through 1982 and much of 1983. The impact of these prices is clearly indicated in the substantial decline in oil movements in the early years of the decade. Such price levels encouraged importing countries to curtail their consumption and seek oil substitutes, and encourage the opening of fields near the market. This dramatic rise in oil prices was matched by an equally dramatic decline in price beginning early in 1986 and continuing at a very low level until 1990. During much of this period official prices varied in the region of $17.5 to $18 per barrel. The low level of price combined with exchange fluctuations favouring consumer countries and the de-regulation of import controls on petroleum and petroleum products served to encourage oil movement from 1986 onwards.

   Iraq's invasion of Kuwait in August 1990 led to a sharp increase in the world price of oil, but other oil exporting countries, particularly Saudi-Arabia, boosted production to offset the loss of Kuwaiti oil. Prices soon came down again, reaching levels that are similar to the pre-1973 crisis values, when adjusted for inflation! World crude oil prices stabilised at around $16 per barrel in the years 1994-95. There were some decreases in the supply at the end of the decade and into the year 2000 which caused oil prices to increase substantially to over $30 per barrel.

2. **Iron Ore and Coal Shipments.** The trend in demand for steel and steel products is closely associated with other bulk cargoes. This makes demand for steel of considerable importance to the shipping industry for it does not only mean an increase in the movement of crude steel but also iron ore, coking and steam coal and other bulk products necessary for its production.

   During the period under consideration the steel industry underwent important structural changes. To simplify a complex situation production by the advanced steelmakers of Europe, America and Japan remained comparatively static. Capacity expanded rapidly in the semi-industrialised nations of South Korea, Taiwan and Brazil, etc. There was also additional expansion in the Eastern Block including China. China more than increased her steel production from about 60mn tonnes to 90mn tonnes over the period 1990-1995, an increase of 50%. The volume of seaborne movement in iron ore and coal followed the crude steel production and economic levels of activity fairly closely during the decade, with serious contractions shown in the first half and both sectors improving steadily during the closing half of the decade. The upward trend continued in the 1990's, with iron ore exports reaching 436mn tonnes in 1995, with both Australia and Brazil recording significant increases over this period. The coal trade has also experienced significant expansion in the 90's, from 340mn tonnes, in 1990 to 480mn tonnes in 1999, with Australia increasing its exports in this period. These changes have clear implications for the pattern of seaborne trade in coal.

3. **Grain.** There are numerous definitions of grain and coarse grain. Generally in maritime transport both cargoes are based on several types of grain, wheat, barley, oats, rye, sorghum and soya bean. Rice is usually packeted and therefore excluded from this discussion. Grain is a significant factor in the demand not only for bulk dry cargo tonnage but often on the tanker market.

In the long term, changes in the standard of diet and growth in world population are major factors. The balance of demand and supply is in the main covered by the production of North America. Here two points should be made. Firstly against the level of total growth grain production the percentage volume movement in seaborne trade appears to be at first sight insignificant. It has been calculated that in general the annual average total production involved in international trade is about 20% of wheat, 8% of barley, 20% of maize and 27% of soya bean. The percentage of grain amongst the five major bulk cargoes was 18% during the 1960's and increased to about 20% by the 1980's or some 200 million tons of cargo. Secondly, while the long run or decadal figures may indicate smooth movements, short run experience is totally different. To state the obvious grain production is influenced largely by weather conditions and can vary year to year. Late 1980 saw a drastic decline in the output of grain.

North America and other areas of production and this has had a major impact on shipping. In the 1990's, the grain trade has hovered around the 190mn tonne mark. USA exports recovered from a low of 80mn tonnes in 1990 to 97mn tonnes in 1995, with significant shifts in import demand occurring. In 1990 the Former Soviet Union countries imported 36mn tonnes of wheat; this had fallen to 6.1mn tonnes by 1995. Brazil, however, increased her grain imports from 1mn tonnes to over 2mn tonnes in the same period. These changes would have generated significant shifts in the trading pattern of vessels engaged in grain transportation.

4. **Other General Cargoes.** This term includes such things as the lesser bulk cargoes, general merchandise and unitised cargoes. The latter has seen multiple changes since the mid 1980's. A vast increase in container cargo handling by major ports and international trade. It has been estimated as growing at an annual rate of 10% since 1987 with approximately 36 million TEU's handled in 1988. The most conspicuous feature here has been the development of this trade in Singapore, Taiwan, South Korea and Hong Kong.

5. **Freight Rates and external factors.** Freight rates are included here merely to complete the analysis. They will be discussed in some detail below and in later lessons.

External factors include natural phenomenon, changes in technology and political events. For example, any major break-through in railways, aircraft or pipelines would have a serious impact on shipping demand. A more obvious and immediate impact would be political events. The most profound being wars which change demand criteria overnight.

Finally, natural events, especially natural disasters; for example droughts which have an impact on grain harvests, or frosts on coffee crops, result in alterations in the demand for shipping.

## 2.3    DISTANCE AND THE CONCEPT OF TONNE MILES

It has already been argued that the demand for shipping space is largely determined by the level of economic activity which is closely related to the quantity and nature of the commodities offered in seaborne trade. This is based on the number of tonnes of cargo transported. The other important factor is shipping distance. One tonne of wheat to Liverpool from Australia via the Cape will generate three times the demand for tonnage as the same tonne of wheat from Canada. Thus, a far more satisfactory measure of demand is the weight in tonnage multiplied by the distance that the tonne has travelled, this is known as tonne miles (or tonne kilometres).

For example:

> 8 tonnes of cargo are carried 500 nautical miles.
> The tonne miles will be 8 x 500 = 4,000 tonne miles.

The central importance of distance can be illustrated by the fact that between the late 1940's and the oil crisis of the mid 1970's the annual rate of growth of total tonnage was 8% whereas in total tonne miles it was 12%. During the period the average distance moved increased steadily and was in excess of that of capacity.

The reasons for this are not hard to find. The expansion of oil exports from the The Gulf and the importance of the closure of the Suez Canal, the establishment of new mineral sources in Australia, South Africa, and Japan with its basic lack of raw material combined with its rapid economic growth.

### Table 2.3 – Seabourne Trade Volume in tonne-Miles – Transport Performance

*In billion tonne-miles*

| Year | Crude oil | Oil product | Iron ore | Coal | Grain | Other cargo | Total trade | % change over prev. year |
|------|-----------|-------------|----------|------|-------|-------------|-------------|--------------------------|
| 1980 | 8319 | 1020 | 1631 | 952 | 1087 | 3720 | 16777 | -5.1 |
| 1981 | 7193 | 1000 | 1558 | 1124 | 1131 | 3710 | 15716 | -5.6 |
| 1986 | 4640 | 1265 | 1699 | 1558 | 914 | 3780 | 13856 | 5.9 |
| 1987 | 4671 | 0345 | 1761 | 1622 | 1061 | 3840 | 14300 | 3.2 |
| 1988 | 5065 | 1445 | 1950 | 1682 | 1117 | 4040 | 15299 | 7.0 |
| 1989 | 5736 | 1540 | 2012 | 1752 | 1095 | 4250 | 16385 | 7.1 |
| 1990 | 6261 | 1560 | 1978 | 1849 | 1073 | 4400 | 17121 | 4.5 |
| 1991 | 6757 | 1530 | 2008 | 1999 | 1069 | 4510 | 17873 | 4.4 |
| 1992 | 6977 | 1620 | 1896 | 2001 | 1091 | 4650 | 18235 | 2.0 |
| 1993 | 7251 | 1775 | 2001 | 1949 | 1038 | 4840 | 18854 | 3.4 |
| 1994 | 7330 | 1860 | 2165 | 2014 | 992 | 5100 | 19461 | 3.2 |
| 1995 | 7225 | 1945 | 2287 | 2176 | 1160 | 5395 | 20188 | 3.7 |
| 1996 | 7495 | 2040 | 2227 | 2217 | 1126 | 5705 | 20678 | 2.4 |
| 1997 | 7830 | 2050 | 2444 | 2332 | 1169 | 6000 | 21825 | 5.5 |
| 1998 | 7889 | 1970 | 2306 | 2419 | 1064 | 5940 | 21588 | -1.1 |
| 1999 | 7980 | 2055 | 2317 | 2363 | 1186 | 6089 | 21990 | 1.9 |
| 2000 | 8180 | 2085 | 2545 | 2509 | 1244 | 6453 | 23016 | 4.7 |
| 2001 | 8074 | 2105 | 2575 | 2552 | 1322 | 6613 | 23241 | 1.0 |
| 2002 | 7860 | 2090 | 2700 | 2570 | 1250 | 6781 | 23251 | 0.0 |

Source: Fearnleys Review, various issues

The following table illustrates the trends in terms of tonne miles over the decade since 1975. It also indicates the trends in the major bulk trades between 1980 and 1999 in terms of tonne miles, that is changes in the average length cargoes were hauled. The major point is the substantial increase, over 40% of total trade movements, against this total increase individual trades experienced different trends.

The crude oil trades has contracted some 6% due to the coming into production of sources near to the market as in the North Sea, Alaska and Mexico. As against this oil products have increased by approximately 100%, and iron ore by 40%. It is in the case of the coal trade that the most radical changes has occurred with an increase of over 160%, again this is due to the development of more distant sources from the import markets, Australia being the prime example. Grain remains comparatively stable throughout this period increasing by only some 13%.

It can be seen that the two seaborne trade indicators give importantly different information about the same trade.

Since then there has been a more or less gradual recovery but the final figure still falls considerably short of that in 1979. The table emphasises just how seriously the demand for tanker tonnage was affected with only three positive years from 1974/75 to 1985/86. This is not only indicative of the change in oil prices but of the discovery and growth in importance of new sources of oil like the North Sea and Africa.

There have been some important differences between the trend in dry cargo movements and that of oil. Following the impact of the oil shock of 1974/75 dry cargo distances recovered although they are not as buoyant as in the 1960's and early 1970's (not included in this table). While there was positive growth in the late 1970's the problem of the contraction has persisted throughout much of the early 1980's with the obvious exception of 1983/84. In the 1990's crude oil tonne miles steadily increased, reflecting the increasing relative importance of the The Gulf as an import source. By the early 1990's, crude oil tonne miles had recovered to levels last seen in the mid-1970's. You should compare Tables 2:2 and 2:3 and note the differences in the growth of demand based on tonne miles as opposed to tonnage alone. There is a clear difference in the crude oil sector; the differences are less marked for dry cargo.

## 2.4    DERIVED DEMAND FOR SHIPPING

In Lesson 1 there was considerable discussion of the concept of demand. It was argued that normal effective demand was an expression of the quantity that consumers are prepared to buy over a range of products supported by the ability to pay. This discussion examined the case of an imaginary cruise market where consumers' objective was to have an enjoyable holiday including in it a sea voyage back to the original point of embarkation. Sea cruises are the exception and not to be confused with the pure transport activity of the rest of the shipping industry. Demand for shipping is an indirect demand. Shipping is not demanded for its own sake but is derived from the demand for commodities that are to be transported. Shipping is seen as an element in the process of production, demanded not for its own sake but for the contribution it makes to the production of final consumer goods and services.

To illustrate the concept of derived demand with an example, consider the demand from the final consumer for petrol to fill his car or motorcycle in Singapore. This is related to the earlier derived demand for tankers to convey the oil from the producer in Kuwait to the refinery and then to the distribution point, or the demand for a cup of coffee at the end of a meal in a restaurant in Glasgow is part of a derived demand for tonnage to transport coffee from Brazil to the United Kingdom. Here is the essential difference from the cruise passenger whose final demand was a satisfactory holiday on a cruise ship. To re-state the definition, the derived demand for a factor like shipping is dependent on the ultimate demand for the final consumer product. The derived demand for dry cargo tonnage in conveying wheat grain comes directly from the final consumer's demand for bread. Students will have perceived that the theoretical economic concept of derived demand underlies much of the previous discussion of the importance of the relationship between increased economic activity and the level of international seaborne trade.

## 2.5   ELASTICITY OF DEMAND

Many company executives either knowingly or unknowingly use the concept of price elasticity of demand without ever being aware of the fact. Consider the managing director of an imaginary ferry company that is losing money. The central problem is what will happen to passenger revenues when fares are lowered (the opposite conclusions will hold for a fare increase). There are three possibilities to be considered.

Firstly, the situation could be that with a lowering of fares more passengers travel and total revenue increases. Total revenue is defined as price multiplied by quantity, which in this case is identical to the product of the fare charged multiplied by the number of passengers.

Secondly, the lowering of fares leaves the number of passengers unchanged; this would also serve to reduce total revenue.

Thirdly, the lowering of fares increases the number of passengers travelling with the company, but total revenues actually decline, as the increase in the number of passengers is more than offset by the fall in the average fare that each passenger pays.

An important point arises from the above analysis. The importance of being able to forecast the effect of a change in price, and whether or not the consumers (passengers) have substitute modes of travel that they can easily utilise is crucial. The kernel here is the responsiveness of buyers to a change in price. This is known as the price elasticity of

**Table 2.4 – Price Elasticity of Demand for a Ferry Service**
**(Daily trip numbers)**

| (1)<br><br>Price<br><br>(£)<br>(P) | (2)<br>Ferry<br>Passengers<br>Demand<br>(000)<br>(Q) | (3)<br>Total<br>Revenue<br>(TR)<br>(£000)<br>(P x Q) | (4)<br>Marginal<br>Revenue<br>(MR)<br>(£000) | (5)<br>% Change<br>in<br>Price | (6)<br>% Change<br>in<br>Quantity | (7)<br><br>Elasticity<br>(col 6/col5) |
|---|---|---|---|---|---|---|
| 145 | 1 | 145 | — | — | — | — |
| 130 | 2 | 260 | 115 | -10.3 | 100.0 | -9.7 |
| 115 | 3 | 345 | 85 | -11.5 | 50.0 | -4.3 |
| 100 | 4 | 400 | 55 | -13.8 | 33.3 | -2.4 |
| 85 | 5 | 425 | 25 | -15.0 | 25.0 | -1.7 |
| 70 | 6 | 420 | -5 | -17.6 | 20.0 | -0.9 |
| 55 | 7 | 385 | -35 | -21.4 | 16.7 | -1.3 |
| 40 | 8 | 320 | -65 | -27.3 | 14.3 | -0.5 |
| 25 | 9 | 225 | -95 | -37.5 | 12.5 | -0.33 |

Note: Marginal Revenue, column 4, is defined as the change in Total Revenue that has accrued following an increase in the quantity of trips sold: for example the change in q from 6 to 7 is +1, and the change in TR is 385-420=-35. So Marginal Revenue is given by -35/+1 = -35.

demand, or simply elasticity of demand. In general terms elasticity can be defined as a measure of the responsiveness of a variable to a change in another.

In the ferry service example the degree of responsiveness of passenger traffic is measured with regard to changes in fares. The ferry situation is set out in the following table from which a number of observations can be made

An important fare in the table is that of £85. Lowering fares has the effect of raising both the quantity of ferry trips demanded by consumers, and the ferry company's total revenue, until the price is reduced from £85 to £70. Further reductions beyond that point cause total revenue to contract, even though the number of ferry trips continues to increase. Thus it can be seen that marginal (extra) revenue changes from a positive to a negative (plus to a minus). Any reduction below the £85 fare, for example to £70 or £55, causes a fall in total revenues, even though passenger numbers still rise. The percentage increase in quantity demanded is now smaller than the percentage fall in fares (price), and therefore total revenue (price times quantity) falls, reducing from £420 (at a fare of £70) to £385 (at a fare of £55). The table highlights the importance of the relationship between percentage change in the number of passengers (quantity) and the percentage change in fares (price) and the effect this will have on total revenue. This can be seen as follows:

$$\text{Price Elasticity of Demand} = \frac{\text{Change in Quantity Demand}}{\text{Original Quantity Demanded}} \times \frac{\text{Change in Price}}{\text{Original Price}}$$

This rather cumbersome formula can be changed and simplified to:

$$\text{Elasticity of Demand} = \frac{\text{Percentage change in quantity demanded}}{\text{Percentage change in price}}$$

$$\text{or } E_d = \frac{\%\Delta Q}{\%\Delta P} \qquad \text{where } \Delta = \text{a small change}$$

The above formula has been used to compute the numbers shown in the final column of Table 2.5. Note that they are all negative in sign. This is due to the assumption, usually borne out in real life, that when prices of any good or service rise, the quantity demanded will fall, and *vice versa*. But this means that a fall (rise) in price will lead to a rise (fall) in quantity, so the two percentage changes must move in the opposite direction. It is a basic mathematical rule that the ratio of any two numbers will itself always be a negative value if the ratio contains two numbers which are themselves opposite in sign; hence price elasticity will never be positive, and will nearly always be negative. Assuming that this is the case, economists simplify matters by ignoring the sign and focussing on the magnitude, or size, of the calculated elasticity (this is called the absolute value).

A second point worth noting is that strictly, the elasticity formula given above is valid only for very small changes in price, whereas our example generates very large percentage changes. Our formula may then act as an approximation, but may not be as accurate as in the situation of small percentage increases.

What has emerged are two basic forms of elasticity, separated by the critical value of unity.

1. *Elastic* demand. A percentage change in the quantity demanded is greater than a percentage change in price. Price elasticity of demand is greater than unity (Ed is greater than 1. The sign normally used to indicate 'greater than' is >). A rise in price will reduce total revenue and vice versa.

2. *Inelastic* demand. The percentage change in the quantity demanded is less than the percentage change in price. The price elasticity of demand is less than unity (Ed is less than 1. The sign normally used to indicate 'less than' is <). A rise in price will increase total revenue and vice versa.

3. *Unitary* elasticity. This occurs where a percentage change in the quantity demanded equals a percentage change in price. This means that total revenue remains constant. This is of course mathematically logical, but is a situation between elastic and inelastic which very rarely occurs.

The above results are laid out in Table 2.5.

## Table 2.5 – Elasticity of Demand and Total Revenue

| If demand is | That is | This means that | Therefore, when price falls, total revenue | Presence of |
|---|---|---|---|---|
| Elastic | Ed > 1 | % change in Q > % change in P | rises | Substitutes |
| Unit Elasticity | Ed = 1 | % change in Q = % change in P | remains unchanged | — |
| Inelastic | Ed < 1 | % change in Q < % change in P | falls | No, or few, substitutes |
| Q = Quantity Demanded    P = Price | | | | |

To consider the importance of elasticity, not in the case of a passenger ferry but in relation to say dry cargo freights. A simple model can be constructed around a group of dry cargo shipowners who need to be able to calculate what effect the fall in freight rates would have on their total revenue.

Let us consider three different situations.

**Situation 1** Elasticity >1 (Elastic)

Original freight rate per ton = $10 ($F_1$)

Number of tonnes which shippers demanded = 9000 ($Q_1$)
Total revenue is = $90,000 ($OF_1 E_1 Q_1$)
Freight rate contracts to = $8 ($F_2$)
Number of tonnes shippers demand increases to = 15000 ($Q_2$)
Total revenue increases to = £120,000 ($OF_2 E_2 Q_2$)

## Figure 2.1 – Elastic Demand

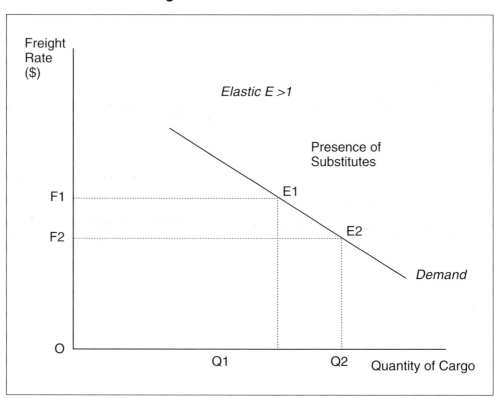

*Elastic Freight Market*
Total revenue area $OF_1 E_1 Q_1$ < area $OF_2 E_2 Q_2$. In this situation, despite the contraction in the freight rate, shippers receive an increase in the amount of total revenue.

**Situation 2** Elasticity <1 (Inelastic)

| | |
|---|---|
| Original freight rate | = $6 ($F_1$) |

Number of tonnes which shippers
demanded                                   = 20,000 ($Q_1$)
Total revenue is                          = $120,000 ($OF_1 E_1 Q_1$)
Freight rate contracts to            = $4 ($F_2$)
Number of tonnes shippers demand
increases to                               = 25,000 ($Q_2$)
Total revenue contracts to          = $100,000 ($OF_2 E_2 Q_2$)

**Figure 2.2 – Inelastic Demand**

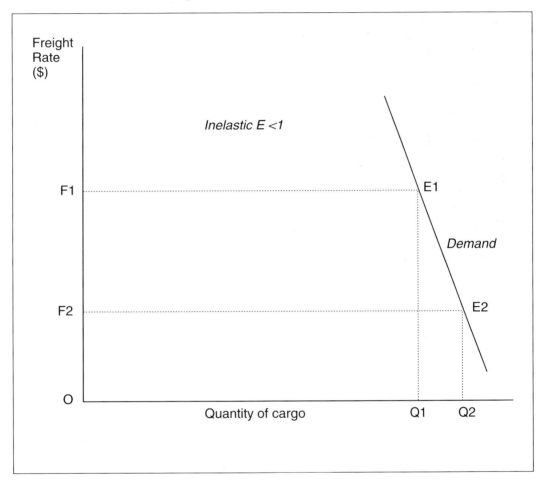

*Inelastic Freight Market*
Total revenue area $OF_1 E_1 Q_1$ > area $OF_2 E_2 Q_2$. In this situation a fall in the freight rate has engendered a contraction in total revenue despite the fact that an inelastic demand implies that there are no, or few, substitutes available.

**Situation 3** Elasticity = 1 (Unity)

| | |
|---|---|
| Original freight rate | = \$8 ($F_1$) |
| Number of tonnes shippers demanded | = 15,000 ($Q_1$) |
| Total revenue is | = \$120,000 ($OF_1 E_1 Q_1$) |
| Freight rate contracts to | = \$6 ($F_2$) |
| Number of tonnes shippers demand increases to | = 20,000 ($Q_2$) |
| Total revenue remains the same at | = \$120,000 ($OF_2 E_2 Q_2$) |

### Figure 2.3 – Unitary Elasticity of Demand

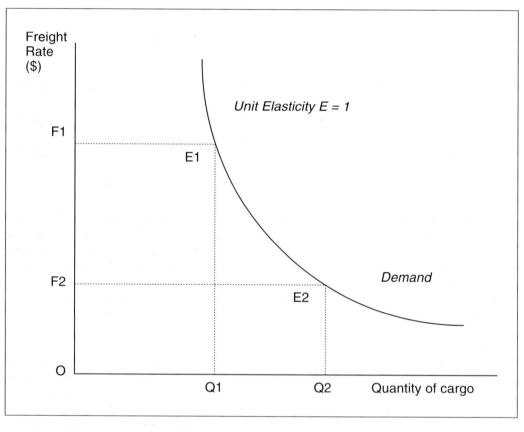

*Unitary Elasticity*
Total revenue area of $OF_1 E_1 Q_1$ = area $OF_2 E_2 Q_2$

## 2.6  DERIVED DEMAND ELASTICITY

You will have noted that in the above discussion demand was for the final or ultimate consumers as in the case of ferry passengers. This was done to develop the discussion of elasticity in a logical way. What was overlooked or ignored was that all freight shipping is an intermediate part of a process of production and the demand for shipping like the demand for raw materials or intermediate goods is a derived demand, that is the demand is derived from the consumers demand for the final product.

Derived demand has a particular set of rules relating to its elasticity. These rules, which are known as the "Marshall Rules" after Alfred Marshall, an 19th century English economist, have been adapted and modified in order to relate them to the derived demand for shipping and the factors which govern its elasticity in the short run.

**Rule 1**
There are few, if any, substitutes for shipping. The argument here is that most products in international trade require transportation by sea for which there is not normally a close substitute.

**Rule 2**
Although there may be alternative sources of the product supplied these too will normally require transportation by sea. Again it is a case of there being no substitutes. For example while coffee from Africa could be an alternative to coffee from South America, from the point of view of the European consumer, all will require sea transport. Again it is a case of there being no substitutes.

**Rule 3**
Freight rates are a small proportion of final cost. In terms of the value of cargo carried freight rates in general are a small, often insignificant, proportion of total cost, hence a relatively large increase in freight rates makes relatively little difference to the price of the product to the final ultimate consumer. The following table illustrates this point.

**Table 2.6 – Estimates of Total Freight Costs as a Percentage of Import Values**

|  | 1980 | 1985 | 1990 | 1992 | 1995 | 1997 | 1998 | 1999 | 2000 | 2001 |
|---|---|---|---|---|---|---|---|---|---|---|
| **World** | 6.64 | 5.74 | 5.22 | 5.33 | 5.32 | 5.24 | 5.06 | 5.52 | 6.22 | 6.11 |

Source: UNCTAD Review of Maritime Transport (published annually)

This table serves to confirm the general conclusion that freight rates are relatively minor proportions of the value of the final or finished commodity. The world trade ratio being in the region of 5.06% to 6.6% over the period. The interested reader might like to consult the UNCTAD review to discover that when this figure is computed for different geographical regions, a significantly higher figure is obtained for the developing countries. In 1992 the share for those countries stood at 8.5%, implying that transport costs are 60% higher, relative to import values than in the developed economies, which realised only 4.35%.

**Rule 4**
The elasticity of the demand for the final product will be an important factor in the elasticity of the derived demand for shipping. The lower (or higher) the price of elasticity of the final product, the lower (or higher) will be the price of elasticity for shipping. Since many goods transported by sea have a low elasticity this will be reflected in the low elasticity of demand for shipping. A simplified model of the whole idea can be put into words thus:

| THE DERIVED ELASTICITY OF DEMAND FOR SHIPPING | = | TRANSPORT COST AS A FRACTION OF FINAL PRICE | x | ELASTICITY OF DEMAND FOR THE CONSUMER GOODS |
|---|---|---|---|---|

The model combines the ideas of lack of substitution and confirms that in general the derived demand for cargo shipping will be inelastic.

## 2.7    CONCLUSION

This Lesson has been aimed at relating the theory of derived demand to the experience of the shipping industry over the last two decades or so. International trade was looked at both in the widest sense, and in terms of specific trades. These make up the essential components of shipping demand and assist in analysing not only what has happened, but are part of creating expectations about what will happen.

## 2.8    SELF-ASSESSMENT AND TEST QUESTIONS

Attempt the following and check your answers from the text:

1.    Compare and contrast the above tables on sea trade in tonnage, table 2.2 and tonne miles, table 2.3 and explain in detail why these are so different.

2.    "Bulk shipping demand is price inelastic, because it is a derived demand." Explain and amplify this statement.

3.    Why is the concept of substitution so important to the elasticity of demand for shipping?

Having completed Chapter Two attempt the following question and submit your answer to your Tutor.

Explain why economists describe the demand for shipping as a derived demand, stemming from international trading flows. Your answer should include real world examples of the link between trade activity and shipping demand.

# Chapter 3

# THE SUPPLY OF SHIPPING SERVICES

## 3.1    INTRODUCTION

In this lesson, the idea of the supply of shipping services is introduced. The first part of the lesson provides a broad perspective on supply; trends in the world merchant fleet are then examined. In the penultimate part of the lesson, the concepts of supply are reviewed and related to the data analysed previously. Finally, the concept of supply elasticity is discussed.

## 3.2    A BROAD PERSPECTIVE

In the long run, one would expect to observe a good correlation between the volume of world seaborne trade, measured in either tonne miles per time period, or in terms of cargo tonnes moved per year, and the stock of vessels employed in that activity.

It has already been observed that cargo volumes rose, peaked, declined and have risen again, as world trade and economic activity recovered from the recessionary period of the late 1970's early 1980's. If the shipping stock is affected by market forces, then these changes in the demand for shipping services should be reflected in the long term trends in the stock of merchant vessels, the merchant fleet.

But analysing the behaviour of shipping supply is a much more complex task than that. There is a need to be able to identify how shipowners and operators can respond to changes in demand conditions which occur on a very short term basis, as well as considering the longer term view. To do this, a clear framework within which to examine the many different facets of supply behaviour is required, along with an analysis of how supply can be adjusted to changes in demand.

Having outlined a suitable framework, the statistical evidence concerning the world merchant shipping fleet is reviewed, and then a simple theoretical model of short and long term supply responses to changing market conditions is constructed.

It is important to note, that in what follows, it is assumed that in effect, there is only one market for shipping services. This is of course a completely false assumption – there are many distinct market sectors within the shipping industry. Although the assumption is false, it is nevertheless a useful one to make at this point, and indeed can be defended up to a point; despite the existence of market segments, there is strong evidence that in the longer term at least, those markets are all inter-related, so that they tend to move 'in sympathy' with each other.

## 3.3    A FRAMEWORK FOR ANALYSING THE SUPPLY OF SHIPPING SERVICES

### 3.3.1    Measuring Output

In order to define supply properly, one needs to be clear as to what it is that the shipping industry actually produces; i.e. what is the *output* of a unit of shipping service? There are, in fact two possible answers to this question, as was implied by the earlier discussion of demand.

Firstly, shipping produces the act of moving cargo around the world, from port to port, terminal to terminal. Adding up all the tonnes of cargo moved per time period (day, week, year) gives a picture of the activity generated by the active shipping fleet. Note that output is measured in *volume* terms, and not by the *value* of the cargo. It is the cargo volume which determines how much carrying capacity is required, rather than its value. (The relationship between the weight of a cargo unit and the space that it occupies is measured by the *stowage factor*, which varies between cargo types.) Cargo volume is measured in cargo tonnes, which can be related to the two principal measures of shipping capacity, usually either by the vessel's gross registered tonne, or by the deadweight tonne; these are both (different) measures of the carrying capacity of a vessel.

Secondly, shipping produces nothing if ships do not move. This obvious point means that one can measure the output in terms of the movement of one tonne of cargo over distance in a given period of time. This measurement is called the tonne mile, the product of the volume of cargo tonnes and the distance it travels in a given period of time. Thus a fully laden 250,000dwt tanker carrying crude oil from Ras Tanura (in the The Gulf) to Rotterdam via the Cape of Good Hope, will generate 11,169 nautical miles x 250,000 = 2,792,250,000, or 2.8 billion ('000 million) tonne miles.

The distinction between the two measures of output is important for two reasons. Firstly, changes in the route will generate changes in the demand for tonne miles, even if the cargo volume appears unchanged. Consider the following example.

**Table 3.1 – Effects of changes in route volumes on tonne miles produced**

| Case A | | | |
|---|---|---|---|
| **Cargo Volume Generated** | **Route Distance** | **Time Taken (days)** | **Tonne Miles** |
| 100 | 22,238 | 93.1 | 1,116,900 |
| 100 | 10,348 | 43.1 | 517,400 |
| 200 | | | 1,634,300 |

| Case B | | | |
|---|---|---|---|
| **Cargo Volume Generated** | **Route Distance** | **Time Taken (days)** | **Tonne Miles** |
| 150 | 22,238 | 93.1 | 1,675,350 |
| 50 | 10,348 | 43.1 | 258,700 |
| 200 | | | 1,934,050 |

By simply switching cargo volume from one route to another, keeping the total constant at 200 tonnes of cargo, an increase in tonne miles has been generated. Actually, this example cheats a little, because the time taken to produce the output differs in the two cases, but the point to be made is still valid; changes in tonne miles can occur which differ from changes in the total cargo volumes moved.

### 3.3.2 A Schematic Representation of the Supply of Shipping

The supply of shipping services can be altered in two principal ways:

a) by altering the stock of vessels

b) by altering the way that the existing stock of vessels is employed.

### 3.3.3 Altering the stock of vessels

Before the data on the stock of shipping is examined, it may be helpful to lay out schematically the different ways in which shipowners can alter the output that is produced by ships, whether measured in terms of tonne miles or tonnes of cargo. Figure 3.1 illustrates the different ways of altering the present stock of vessels. This would be equivalent to the economist's concept of the 'long run' period, the period in which the capital stock tied up in a firm or industry can be varied. Such changes alter the *long run* level of output supply. This is because the items identified in the figure take a considerable period of time to implement. Vessel newbuildings need to be designed, constructed and commissioned before coming into service, and this can take two years. Scrapping a vessel, takes less time, but if the vessel is still trading, or on a time charter, it may not necessarily happen quickly.

### Figure 3.1 – Altering the Stock of Vessels

```
                    ┌─────────────────┐
                    │ Altering the Stock
                    │        of
                    │     Vessels
                    └─────────────────┘
                             │
             ┌───────────────┴───────────────┐
   ┌─────────────────┐             ┌─────────────────┐
   │   Scrapping     │             │  Newbuilding    │
   │     Rate        │             │   Deliveries    │
   │                 │             │     Rate        │
   └─────────────────┘             └─────────────────┘
```

The net change in the stock of vessels is clearly the result of the relative sizes of these two factors; in good times, deliveries will be at a high rate, and scrapping rates will be low; in bad times, the flow of deliveries will falter, whilst the level of scrapping will tend to increase. In the first case, the stock of vessels will rise; in the second, it will fall. Note that the stock can fall *even if* there are some deliveries; it is the difference between the two that alters the stock.

Formally, the above statement can be written as

$$S_{t+1} = D_t - SCR_t + S_t$$

where $S_{t+1}$ is the stock at the beginning of the next period, $D_t$ the volume of newbuildings delivered during the period, and $SCR_t$ the tonnage scrapped. It is clear that the difference $S_{t+1} - S_t$ measures the change in the stock over the period, and is equal to the difference between the rate of delivery and the rate of scrapping.

### 3.3.4 Altering the way that the existing stock of vessels is used

Figure 3.2 illustrates the principal ways in which the output from a given stock of vessels can be varied, even if the present stock is unchanged. Imagine, for the moment, that no new ships are delivered, and none are scrapped or lost. It may appear that the supply of shipping services is therefore fixed, but this is an incorrect assumption.

### Figure 3.2 – Altering the supply with a fixed stock of vessels

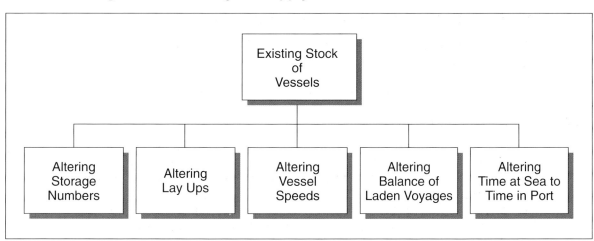

As can be seen from Figure 3.2, there are in fact a number of ways in which the output of the shipping stock can be varied, *even when the stock of vessels is unchanged.*

One method is to convert the vessel to alternative use, as a floating storage facility. This was unheard of 25 years ago, but during the period of overcapacity, a number of different methods of using that capacity were developed. Large tankers were (and still are) adapted for use as floating oil stores. Large bulk carriers can be used to store grain, acting as floating silos. In October 1996, the UK government explored the possibility of chartering refrigerated ships, to be used as floating stores for the carcasses of beef destroyed under the BSE culling programme. The ships would be moored in British ports, and linked to a mainland electricity supply. This option is being explored because existing cold store capacity on the mainland will be full before the culling programme is completed; it is therefore a short run method of temporarily increasing storage capacity.[1] Note that such a decision is not always readily reversible, as the ship may suffer significant corrosion or other long term damage, which reduces her ability to be re-employed at sea. Nevertheless, this is a method of *reducing* the active stock of vessels; once a stock of storage vessels exist, they can be added to and subtracted from over time.

The second method of altering the active stock of vessels is by 'laying up'. The vessel is usually put in a safe anchorage, a skeleton crew retained to keep up essential maintenance, and is left unemployed. In parts of the world there are in effect, managed 'car parks', where ships are left for considerable periods, with a company providing management and maintenance services. It should be clear that there are in fact additional costs to be met when preparing a vessel for lay-up; and there are usually costs involved in making her fully operational again. But these costs are relatively small compared with the large losses than might be made if the vessel trades at very low rates for any sustained period of time. Shipowners will have due regard for the present and futures state of the market when deciding on lay-up.

When demand conditions are very poor, and the outlook is not good for the next few years, one would expect to see a rise in the proportion of the vessel stock which is laid up. When demand conditions improve, these vessels can be re-activated fairly rapidly, so that supply can be expanded quickly. Once all available vessels are back in the active fleet, there is no possibility of further increases in supply from this source.

The third method of altering the short run supply of cargo tonnes or tonne miles per year or per day is by altering the *speed* of the vessel. By altering speed, journey times can be reduced, so the same stock of vessels can generate a larger throughput of cargo volume moved in a given period of time. The limits to this variation will be explored in a later chapter. The range of speed variation that is possible depends upon the technical design of the engines, and is limited at the top end by maximum speed limits, and at the lower end by considerations of engine efficiency and balance. There is usually a range of speeds that are available, although the ship is often designed/optimised for a particular speed.

Fourthly, it may be possible to alter the amount of cargo throughput generated by the *fleet overall* by altering the proportion of laden to ballast voyages. Many seaborne trades are 'unbalanced', in the sense that the cargo volumes delivered in one direction may well be larger than the flow in the opposite direction. An extreme case exists in the tanker trade, where most journeys are laden in only one direction. This implies that 50% of the potential cargo carrying space is wasted. If a 'backhaul' cargo can be found, cargo throughput can be increased without any alteration in the vessel stock.

However, it should be noted that the ability to achieve improvements in this area is driven by the nature of demand conditions, rather than supply. As demand patterns change, with new sources of production coming on stream, or new sources of consumption becoming more important, supply has to respond; the changing utilisation of the fleet reflects these changes.

---

[1]  Source: Buckingham, L. "Fridge ships to store culled cows", TheGuardian, Friday, Oct 11th 1996

On the other hand, ship management must always be on the alert for new ways of using vessels, ways which may raise the average utilisation rates achieved.

Finally, altering the proportion of time that vessels spend in port relative to time spent at sea can affect supply. If port turnround times are reduced, ships can sail more frequently in a given time period, and produce a larger output in a given time period. If they lengthen, or if significant port congestion occurs, shipping supply is reduced. If the proportion of trade on long haul rises relative to short haul routes, the ship stock can be used more efficiently, as it can spend more of its time at sea. Again, this factor is partly driven by elements outside the shipowners' control; many ports are operated independently of shipowners, so decisions affecting port efficiency and organisation are made by bodies separate from the shipowners themselves.

## 3.3.5    Supply in the very long run

So far, a number of ways in which the supply of shipping can be altered have been discussed. Section 3.2.2, discussed what could be done even when the stock of vessels was unchanged, a position that economists' would describe as 'the short run'. In 3.2.1 we considered how supply is altered when the stock is allowed to change, which is defined as 'the long run'. In both these cases, economic theory still keeps certain elements fixed, at least in the imagination! These factors are the *level of technology* available to the suppliers, and *the prices of the inputs used in providing those services.*

*The level of technology.* This phrase is the economist's shorthand to describe the prevailing set of technical know-how, organisational knowledge, and management structures which are currently available to the industry. Technical progress is the name given to the idea that, over time, new things are discovered, and these new ideas are implemented to improve the products and services produced. New, stronger steels can be employed to reduce weight without reducing tensile strength; new engine designs generate the same power output from a smaller engine with lower fuel consumption; new ways of organising cargoes, from pallets to containers, revolutionise the structure of general cargo trades. Some of these changes occur suddenly; others are gradual, but incessant; they all add up to the ability to deliver more output with less input. The most dramatic example of this process in shipping was the container revolution; each container vessel could generate the equivalent output of 2-3 general cargo vessels of equivalent size; thus output can be maintained with less input.

*Changes in the Price of Inputs*
Supply can be influenced by alterations in the cost of key inputs. Recall the exercise you were asked to do in lesson one. A large increase in bunker fuel prices leads to an upward shift in the supply schedule; this is the same thing as saying, that at the given freight rate, suppliers can offer less output than before.

To expand on this a little further; if fuel prices rise significantly, fuel expenses rise sharply. One way of offsetting this is to reduce the speed of the vessel; this leads to lower fuel consumption, but *it also leads to lower output, given our discussion above.* Thus one might expect to observe, in those trades where it is feasible to do so, a reduction in vessel speeds when fuel prices are high, and a restoration of speed when prices fall again. The proviso is important; in the liner trades, keeping to a timetable is important; the option of changing speed is not available; so suppliers have to find other methods of 'insuring' themselves against the fluctuations of the bunker fuel price.

To recap: the supply of shipping services can be varied in many different ways. In the short run the principal means of doing this is to alter the proportion of the stock laid up, or to alter the vessel speed, where possible. In the longer run the stock of vessels can be altered by delivering newbuildings or scrapping some of the present stock. Finally in the very long run the efficiency of supply can be altered by technological change and input price movements.

## 3.4     TRENDS IN THE WORLD MERCHANT FLEET, 1970-1999

It is assumed that the numbers published by Lloyds' Register provide a reasonable basis for an examination of trends in the total stock of merchant vessels over the past 25 years. Note that defining 'the fleet' is itself not an easy task. Firstly, what is the smallest size of vessel that should be included? Lloyds uses 100 grt, but other industry analysts use different criteria; for example bulk market analysts use 10,000dwt as the minimum size of vessel that fits into this category. Secondly, the United States has a stock of vessels held in reserve for strategic purposes. There are also vessels that trade exclusively on the US/Canadian Great Lakes. Often these are excluded from the analyses of the world fleet, since they are effectively limited in their purpose or their scope of operations. Nevertheless, Lloyds' Register includes them.

Table 3.2 below illustrates the development of the World Fleet, as defined by Lloyds, over the period 1970-99. The table shows the stock in both gross registered ton and deadweight tonnage, and the annual percentage change in that stock. These two measures reflect slightly different aspects of a vessel's carrying ability, as noted earlier. Both measures will be referred to in the following discussion.

The average annual growth rates for both series are 3.4% per year for grt. and 3.5% per year for dwt, a close correspondence. Such a growth rate has more than doubled the total stock over 30 years, and the table reveals this to be the case.

Although the long run trends of capacity and demand growth appear to be quite closely related, the short term variations tell quite a different story. The strongest growth rates of the entire period are to be found in the 1970's, averaging nearly 7% per year for the period 1970-79 in grt terms, and more than 7% for dwt. This itself hides the extraordinary 'boom' period of expanding supply in the early 1970's, which tailed off to a mere 2% growth in 1979.

In the 1980's the stock of ships actually declined. In 1982, a peak of 4226 mn. grt. or 702mn. dwt. was reached, followed by several years of decline; the newbuilding rate of delivery was lower than the scrapping loss rate in this period, which was one of crisis, both in shipping and shipbuilding, for obvious reasons. This process continued throughout the eighties, coming to an end in 1988, a year of recovery. The average annual growth rate in the period 1980-89 was -0.2% for grt and -0.3% for dwt, generating a small, but cumulatively significant decline in the ship stock by the end of the decade. By contrast, the 1990's have been years of relatively steady expansion. The 'boom' and 'bust' cycles have not yet reappeared, although this does not mean that they never will!

How can the process of rapid expansion, overcapacity, decline, and recovery be understood?

## Table 3.2 – Development of the World Merchant Fleet 1970-2003

|  | Mn GRT | % Change | Mn DWT | % Change |
|---|---|---|---|---|
| 1970 | 227.5 | 7.5 | 338.8 | n.a. |
| 1971 | 247.2 | 8.7 | 376.2 | 11.0 |
| 1972 | 268.3 | 8.5 | 414.1 | 10.1 |
| 1973 | 289.9 | 8.1 | 452.5 | 9.3 |
| 1974 | 311.3 | 7.4 | 494.0 | 9.2 |
| 1975 | 342.3 | 10.0 | 553.4 | 12.0 |
| 1976 | 372.0 | 8.7 | 608.3 | 9.9 |
| 1977 | 393.7 | 5.8 | 648.8 | 6.7 |
| 1978 | 406.0 | 3.1 | 670.4 | 3.3 |
| 1979 | 413.0 | 1.7 | 681.5 | 1.7 |
| 1980 | 419.9 | 1.7 | 690.5 | 1.3 |
| 1981 | 420.8 | 0.2 | 697.2 | 1.0 |
| 1982 | 424.7 | 0.9 | 702.0 | 0.7 |
| 1983 | 422.6 | -0.5 | 694.5 | -1.1 |
| 1984 | 418.7 | -0.9 | 683.3 | -1.6 |
| 1985 | 416.3 | -0.6 | 673.7 | -1.4 |
| 1986 | 404.9 | -2.7 | 647.6 | -3.9 |
| 1987 | 403.5 | -0.3 | 640.8 | -1.1 |
| 1988 | 399.5 | -1.0 | 638.0 | -0.4 |
| 1989 | 404.9 | 1.4 | 658.4 | 3.2 |
| 1990 | 426.0 | 5.2 | 681.5 | 3.5 |
| 1991 | 436.3 | 2.4 | 694.7 | 1.9 |
| 1992 | 445.2 | 2.0 | 710.6 | 2.3 |
| 1993 | 457.9 | 2.9 | 710.6 | 0.0 |
| 1994 | 475.9 | 3.9 | 719.8 | 1.3 |
| 1995 | 490.7 | 3.1 | 734.9 | 2.1 |
| 1996 | 507.9 | — | 758.2 | 3.2 |
| 1997 | 522.2 | — | 775.9 | 2.3 |
| 1998 | 531.4 | — | 778.7 | 1.6 |
| 1999 | 543.6 | — | 798.9 | 1.3 |
| 2000 | 558.1 | — | 799.0 | 1.3 |
| 2001 | 574.6 | — | 825.6 | 2.1 |
| 2002 | 585.6 | — | 825.6 | 2.1 |
| 2003 | — | — | 844.2 | — |
| Average Growth |  | 3.4 |  | 3.2 |

Source: UNCTAD Maritime Review 1989, 1993; 2003 Lloyd's Statistical Tables 1995 N.B. Estimates are Mid-Year until 1992. Lloyd's data has been adjusted to end-year measures from 1992 on. DWT data for 1993 to 1995 is not consistent with the earlier series, hence the gap in percentage growth. No GRT figures for 1996 onwards.

One answer is that most shipping markets operate in a cyclical fashion. The greatest increase in capacity occurred in 1970-75, where three factors were at work. Firstly, trade had boomed in the late 60's, and continued to do so until October 1973, when the Arab-Israeli conflict triggered a 400% increase in the price of crude oil. This boom led to very optimistic expectations about the future, and large numbers of vessel orders were placed. Secondly, the closure of the Suez Canal in 1967, following the six-day war between Egypt and Israel, had generated a large increase in the demand for tankers. Coupled with this was the significant increase in tanker sizes that occurred from 1970 onwards, and in large bulk carriers. A huge wave of 'optimism' engulfed the shipping world; in 1973 for example, the total number of orders for new tankers was equivalent to about 20% of the existing world tanker stock! This rather fanciful view of the market was shattered by the rise in the price of crude oil. The effect was to slow down the growth of all major world economies, and hence, the growth of world trade. So large increases in supply arrived at the time when demand growth faltered; a combination which generated depression in the shipping markets.

But ships are long lived assets; they have technical lives of 30 years or more. A few bad years can always be expected. Owners and operators found ways of matching supply to demand, as discussed earlier; scrapping was still seen as a 'last resort'.

Trade demand began to pick up in the early 1980's, and has recovered steadily since. Trade volumes have only recently exceeded those last seen in the mid 1970's, and as the fleet statistics show, the world fleet is now larger than it was at that previous peak, both in grt. and in dwt. terms.

One final point worth noting from Table 3.2 is the implication of the different rates of growth of grt and dwt on a year to year basis. Vessels such as bulk carriers and tankers have a much larger carrying capacity when expressed in dwt terms than when it is expressed in grt; other vessel types have a closer link. The expansion in the early 1970's is accompanied by dwt growth rates that are higher than those of grt[2]. This is the period in which the average size of tankers and bulk carriers grew rapidly, and it is this fact which explains the difference. In later years, the difference has not been so marked.

## 3.4.1 Newbuilding Trends

It has been shown that the change in the vessel stock is given by the net position of newbuilding and scrapping rates. Table 3.3 shows trends in Newbuildings by Vessel Types for the period 1980-2002. The annual number of vessels delivered falls until 1988, then begins to rise. It appears that the rate of deliveries is also affected by expectations about the future, conditioned upon market knowledge at that time. The individual figures are not in themselves terribly useful, as year to year variations can be quite large.

It has been suggested that the continuously high levels of newbuildings which occurred in the early 1980's was despite prevailing market conditions. Japan and South Korea maintained relatively high levels of production, owing to their ability to charge low prices because of government subsidies and favourable credit arrangements for overseas purchasers. Some have claimed that these vessels were sold at prices which failed to cover their true costs of production, which, if true, would worsen market supply conditions overall. However, it should be noted that vessels have a long life; it is equally possible that owners were taking a very long term view of their investment decisions, with a horizon of 5-10 years; some may recognise the cyclical nature of the business.

Deliveries peaked in 1993 and 2000 for all ship types, reflecting a peak in orders some one to three years earlier. The recent strong performance of the dry bulk sector is reflected in the sharp increases in deliveries of these vessels in 1994 and 1995, with numbers of deliveries approaching those last seen in the early 1980's. The strong growth of the container trades is also reflected in the rising numbers shown in Table 3.3, although it should be noted that UNCTAD have not published separate data for this ship type until comparatively recently.

The cyclical pattern of the shipping industry is clearly brought out in the Table, as the numbers and dwt delivered declines from 1980 until 1988. By close of the 1990s, deliveries were running considerably lower in terms of numbers, and substantially higher in terms of dwt. This generalisation does not hold for bulk carriers and containers at the end of the decade.

---

[2] Ship capacity is measured in three main ways. A ship's deadweight tonnage (dwt) is the total weight of cargo, bunkers, water and extra items (expressed in metric or imperial tons) which it can lift when loaded in salt water to maximum draught under winter, summer or tropical loadlines. Gross register tonnage (grt) measures the internal volume of all enclosed spaces in the ship and is equal to the tonnage below the tonnage deck plus the tonnage of all enclosed spaces above deck. Net register tonnage (nrt) is the residual tonnage after various allowances for propelling power, crew spaces and navigation spaces etc. have been allowed for. GRT is often used as a basis for payments, such as to P and I clubs, whilst nrt is used to assess port and terminal dues. Dwt is the best measure of cargo capacity. (Source B N Metaxas, The Economics of Tramp Shipping, Athlone Press, 1971, pages 13-19.)

## Table 3.3 – Developments in Newbuilding Deliveries 1980, 1985 to 2002

| | 1980 | 1985 | 1990 | 1991 | 1992 | 1993 | 1994 | 1995 | 1996 | 1997 | 1998 | 1999 | 2000 | 2001 | 2002 |
|---|---|---|---|---|---|---|---|---|---|---|---|---|---|---|---|
| **Tankers** – No | 235 | 105 | 142 | 169 | 251 | 278 | 185 | 163 | 310 | 223 | 291 | 305 | 446 | 550 | 447 |
| Dwt | 6.7 | 2.5 | 5.0 | 6.7 | 9.0 | 9.8 | 7.1 | 6.3 | 13.8 | 8.7 | 15.5 | 20.7 | 41.8 | 34.3 | 24.0 |
| **Bulk Carriers** – No | 131 | 276 | 123 | 79 | 77 | 101 | 194 | 257 | 293 | 311 | 225 | 185 | 344 | 165 | 275 |
| Dwt | 5.1 | 12.4 | 5.5 | 3.1 | 3.3 | 4.3 | 8.4 | 11.1 | 17.5 | 18.2 | 11.3 | 12.4 | 20.1 | 95.0 | 20.8 |
| **General Cargo** – No | 266 | 186 | 288 | 310 | 360 | 441 | 324 | 320 | 380 | 379 | 324 | 307 | 255 | 142 | 136 |
| Dwt | 2.8 | 1.6 | 3.1 | 3.3 | 2.0 | 1.5 | 1.1 | 1.1 | 2.0 | 2.4 | 3.0 | 2.9 | 25.3 | 12.2 | 16.0 |
| **Container Ships** – No | — | — | — | — | 88 | 93 | 142 | 166 | 20.7 | 256 | 263 | 125 | 373 | 180 | 135 |
| Dwt | — | — | — | — | 2.2 | 2.0 | 3.3 | 3.9 | 5.3 | 6.9 | 7.3 | 3.4 | 15.0 | 65.6 | 62.2 |
| **Other Ships** – No | 1642 | 837 | 1089 | 998 | 766 | 875 | 585 | 612 | 107 | 116 | 107 | 98 | 136 | 101 | 111 |
| Dwt | 3.8 | 3.2 | 2.1 | 2.8 | 2.1 | 2.8 | 1.7 | 1.8 | 0.2 | 0.1 | 0.2 | 0.2 | 30.8 | 80.0 | 13.0 |
| **Total** – No | 2274 | 1404 | 1642 | 1556 | 1506 | 1788 | 1430 | 1518 | 1297 | 1285 | 1210 | 1020 | 1554 | 1138 | 739 |
| Dwt | 18.4 | 19.7 | 15.7 | 15.9 | 22.0 | 43.0 | 42.1 | 43.2 | 37.3 | 57.2 | 42.4 | 49.6 | 80.1 | 51.6 | 19.0 |
| **% of World Fleet** | 4.5 | 4.7 | 3.9 | 3.7 | 4.3 | 4.5 | 3.0 | 3.3 | — | — | — | — | — | — | — |

Source: UNCTAD Maritime Reviews, 1988, 1993, 1995 and 2003

Notes:

1. % World Fleet defined as Delivery Dwt divided by Dwt of the World Fleet in the previous year (from Table 3.1)
2. Dwt measured in millions. 'No' measures number of vessels
3. UNCTAD figures for 1994 and 1995 are given in GRT, not Dwt. They have been converted so are not directly comparable with data for previous years
4. Separate Container ship figures not available for years prior to 1992
5. 'Other Ships' are Passenger ships from 1996 onwards

## 3.5 FACTORS AFFECTING THE SHORT RUN SUPPLY OF SHIPPING SERVICES

The previous section examined data relating to the elements of Figure 3.1 above. Attention is now turned to the trends in factors that affect the supply, even when the stock of ships might be fixed.

### 3.5.1 Use of Vessels for Storage

Certain vessel types can readily be turned into storage facilities. The obvious ones are the use of crude oil tankers for oil storage, and bulk carriers for grain storage. The UK government's proposal for using reefers for storing cow carcasses has already been noted; a few years ago the same government considered a proposal that some vessels be modified and used as floating prisons!

Using ships as floating storage devices does have a 'cost', however. The vessel will suffer increased corrosion, and it is a relatively expensive way of storing something compared to dedicated ground based equivalents. But if land is scarce, and therefore expensive, and ships are oversupplied, and therefore relatively cheap, it may be feasible. Japan in fact holds a strategic stockpile of crude oil in just such a fashion. Useable land is very scarce in Japan. B.P. regularly monitors the numbers of tankers used in this way, and classifies them into 'semi-permanent', and 'temporary'. In 1985 6.5% of the tanker stock was employed in this way; by 1993 the figure had fallen to 3.5%.

These tankers are not necessarily immediately available to move cargoes, as they may be hired out on long term contracts. Nevertheless, they are still a potential source of extra supply if demand grows more rapidly than anticipated.

### 3.5.2 Laying up/Reactivating Vessels

A vessel which temporarily stops trading is said to be laid-up. This happens when the shipowner or manager can no longer justify trading at the prevailing levels of freight rates and demand conditions, and presumably, sees no sign of any future improvement. By laying-up, some of the operational costs of a vessel are avoided, and provided that engines and other sensitive equipment are maintained in good condition, there is no damage or deterioration of the vessel. The basic idea is simple. The vessel is brought back into trading when rates recover and market conditions improve, so that the vessel can trade as a 'going concern'.

Essentially, this can be viewed as an 'investment decision' by the operator or owner. On the one hand, the owner can carry on trading, presumably at a loss, if they are considering laying up their vessel. If they carry on trading at unprofitable rates, a series of losses will be generated over a number of trading periods.

On the other hand, certain expenses are incurred in the act of laying up. Against this is the *reduction in losses* which would have been incurred if the vessel continued to trade. Whilst the cost of capital has to be met, other operational costs are clearly avoided in lay-up. The owner has to evaluate the net cost or benefit to them of deciding one way or the other. The decision is clearly influenced by two principal factors;

1.  The expectations that the owner holds of the future levels of freight rates; and

2.  The actual cost of running the vessel as a 'going concern'.

If the owner runs a 'high operating cost' vessel, and has very pessimistic expectations about the future levels of rates, then lay-up may be considered.

As one might have realised by now, Lay-Ups vary over time, and are a good barometer of market conditions. They are best expressed as a percentage of the vessel stock, in the same way that many countries publish their statistics on unemployed labour. The absolute number is affected by trends in the labour force, so using percentages compensates for this. In fact most published shipping data concentrates on the absolute numbers of vessels and dwt, and this can be misleading. Table 3.5 presents data expressed in this way, for the period 1981-1994. The lack of demand, relative to capacity emerges quite clearly from the data. Lay-Ups reached 12% of the stock in 1982-83, then decline to very low levels indeed. Note too, the difference in behaviour of tankers from other vessel types. Tanker Lay-Ups were 18% in 1982, falling sharply during the decade. But they rise again in 1992-3, albeit to a much lesser extent than they have down in the past.

**Table 3.5 – Lay Up Rates, 1981-94**
**(% of vessel stock)**

| Year | Tankers | Non-Tankers | World |
|------|---------|-------------|-------|
| 1981 | 7 | 1 | 4 |
| 1982 | 18 | 7 | 12 |
| 1983 | 18 | 6 | 12 |
| 1984 | 16 | 4 | 9 |
| 1985 | 13 | 3 | 7 |
| 1986 | 6 | 2 | 4 |
| 1987 | 4 | 2 | 3 |
| 1988 | 1 | 1 | 1 |
| 1989 | 1 | 0 | 1 |
| 1990 | 1 | 0 | 1 |
| 1991 | 1 | 1 | 1 |
| 1992 | 3 | 1 | 2 |
| 1993 | 2 | 1 | 1 |
| 1994 | 1 | 1 | 1 |

Source: Merchant Fleet Statistics, Department of Transport, 1994. Numbers are for Mid-Year.

On the other hand the 'other ship types' experienced very low levels of lay-ups, even in 1992-3. It should be clear from this that different market sectors may face different market conditions, even if they are often treated as a complete whole. This point will be returned to later.

### 3.5.3    Variations in Vessel Speed

It was pointed out earlier that output can be increased by the simple device of making vessels go faster or slower. The range of speed that can be used depends on engine design; as noted earlier the limits are given by the maximum speed of the vessel and the speed below which the engines can be damaged or the vessel is unsteerable.

This range can still be important however. Small changes, if applied to every vessel in a fleet, can bring about significant alterations in its cargo carrying capability.

Following the collapse of oil demand in the mid 70's, and the four-fold increase in the price of bunker fuel, a large number of tankers started to 'slow-steam'. Prior to 1973, most tankers ran at their design speed, usually around 14 knots. By 1975-6 a large proportion of tankers were sailing at 10 knots, effectively reducing their cargo moving capacity by about 20% (since half of the journey was in ballast).

This is a very effective way of reducing supply in the short term, as well as being a sensible response to the rise in fuel input prices. This change can happen very quickly, provided of course, that one starts at full employment and a negative shock is experienced! Once a portion of the fleet is 'slow-steaming', changes in output can be generated by speeding up again! (However, if the new, lower vessel speed is in fact optimal for the higher fuel price, it may need a very large increase in demand to generate this result).

### 3.5.4    Variations in Port Time

Short run supply can also be altered by varying the proportion of time that a vessel spends in port. A vessel that reduces port and idle time to a minimum will produce a higher volume of output in the same time period than one that does not. When demand is low relative to existing capacity, port turnround times and waiting times may lengthen; the *productivity* of the system (output relative to total input) will fall and rise accordingly.

One way in which Port Time is affected is by the changing composition of demand. When long distance routes become more important in a trade, the vessels employed in that trade will spend proportionately more of their time at sea, and the overall productiveness of the vessel stock can rise. When the opposite happens, productivity will be reduced, as ships will spend a greater proportion of their time in port.

## 3.6    PRODUCTIVITY TRENDS AND SUPPLY CONDITIONS

Table 3.6 provides details of some simple measures of the productivity of the world merchant fleet. Before the table is discussed in detail, it should be pointed out that these productivity measures are the result of the interaction of the present level of demand and the current stock position; they should not be taken as simply measuring the *efficiency of supply on its own.*

Recall that changes in fuel input prices can affect vessel sailing speeds; it was noted earlier that a large increase occurred in 1973. If demand remained unchanged, the optimal vessel speed would tend to be reduced, (in markets where this is feasible), and output per dwt will fall. So some of the reduction that occurred in the 1970's can be linked to this change; *it does not imply a fall in efficiency.* In fact, it was an optimal response! If the price of fuel goes in the other direction, one might expect the trend to be reversed; and fuel prices have fallen quite dramatically in the past decade, following the fall in crude oil prices.

Table 3.6 therefore needs to be interpreted with some care; ideally, one should compare years in which demand levels are similar, ship stock levels are similar, and fuel prices are similar before we make any comparisons. These remarks notwithstanding, the broad trend of the figures are still worth commenting on.

Firstly, ship productivity appears to be lower than it was 25 years ago, when expressed in terms of tons of cargo carried per dwt. or by ton miles per dwt. The 1970 figure is never surpassed in the Table; but 1970 was a boom year, and a year in which capacity was stretched to meet prevailing demand. It is only in the last few years that productivity levels have reached similar levels; but the 1993 figure is still only 75-80% of those achieved in 1970, and only marginal higher at the end of the decade, but have risen substantially since 1999 (to 2002).

Secondly, a broad cycle appears to emerge, with the data in columns 4 and 5 showing the same trend; cyclical decline until 1983, then a recovery, peaking in 1989 and levelling off. The bottom of the cycle appears to be in 1983; note that this is the same year in which lay-ups were running at 18% for tankers, and 12% overall. This is no accident; the two series are reflecting different aspects of the same basic relationship.

**Table 3.6 – Productivity of the World Merchant Fleet 1970-2002**
**(selected years)**

| | World Fleet (M dwt) 1 | Total Cargo (M Tons) 2 | Ton Miles Performed (000 mn) 3 | Tons of Cargo Per dwt 4 | Ton-miles Per dwt (000) 5 |
|---|---|---|---|---|---|
| 1970 | 326.1 | 2,605 | 10,654 | 7.99 | 32.67 |
| 1980 | 682.6 | 3,704 | 16,777 | 5.42 | 24.47 |
| 1985 | 664.8 | 3,382 | 13,160 | 50.9 | 19.80 |
| 1986 | 639.1 | 3,459 | 13,856 | 5.41 | 21.68 |
| 1987 | 632.3 | 3,505 | 14,298 | 5.54 | 22.61 |
| 1988 | 628.0 | 3,692 | 15,299 | 5.88 | 24.36 |
| 1989 | 638.0 | 3,891 | 16,385 | 6.10 | 25.68 |
| 1990 | 658.4 | 4,000 | 17,121 | 6.09 | 26.00 |
| 1991 | 683.5 | 4,120 | 17,783 | 6.03 | 26.15 |
| 1992 | 694.7 | 4,220 | 18,228 | 6.07 | 26.24 |
| 1993 | 710.6 | 4,330 | 18,994 | 6.09 | 26.73 |
| 1994 | 719.8 | 4,485 | 19,600 | 6.23 | 27.23 |
| 1995 | 734.9 | 4,651 | 20,188 | 6.33 | 27.47 |
| 1996 | 758.2 | 4,758 | 20,678 | 6.28 | 27.27 |
| 1997 | 775.9 | 4,953 | 21,672 | 6.38 | 27.93 |
| 1998 | 788.7 | 5,064 | 21,425 | 6.42 | 27.16 |
| 1999 | 799.0 | 5,129 | 21,480 | 6.42 | 26.88 |
| 2000 | 808.4 | 5,871 | 23,016 | 7.30 | 28.50 |
| 2001 | 827.7 | 5,840 | 24,241 | 7.10 | 28.00 |
| 2002 | 844.2 | 5,888 | 23,251 | 7.00 | 27.50 |

Source: Review of Maritime Transport, UNCTAD, 1987, 1995 and 2000.

## 3.7 SURPLUS TONNAGE AND THE CONCEPT OF THE ACTIVE FLEET

Some shipping economists have produced estimates of the tonnage which is 'surplus' to demand requirements in a particular year. They do this by allowing for those vessels that are idle, laid-up, or 'slow-steaming'. This is a crude way of measuring the degree of 'slack' in the system, in the sense that it measures the amount of 'spare capacity' that is readily available to meet unexpected increases in demand. The data is shown in Table 3.7. The key statistic to note is the measure of the surplus tonnage measured as a proportion of the world fleet. It peaks at 29% in 1983, and then falls away, declining to 10.1% in 1993, and to 6.9% in 1995, to approximately 3% over the last three years.

Will this number ever fall to zero? It seems very unlikely. Underlying this calculation is the implicit assumption that somehow, the volume of demand in any one year must match the volume supplied, in terms of shipping capacity. Since demand has to be forecasted, it seems extremely unlikely that this would ever occur except occasionally. Now consider the 'costs' of always being short of capacity; the inability to move cargoes in sufficient volumes in the right time periods would generate large losses of sales further up the supply chain; whereas having some surplus means that unexpected variations in demand can (usually) be met.

An analogy might be useful here. The 'normal' level of output from a factory is not 100% of capacity; it is usually set at 85-90%. The 'spare' can be used to meet unexplained variations in demand. Remember, also, that the output of shipping *cannot be stored*. Once lost, it is lost forever. In a sense, a surplus of ships is one way of creating an inventory of available extra ship output if it is needed.

Of course, this argument can be taken too far. Ships represent capital investment. Too many idle means too much capital tied up in non-income earning assets; so there is probably some range which is optimal, balancing the costs of lost output against the costs of idle capital.

One final point to note about this concept; the amount of surplus tonnage may well be affected by the underlying unit costs of labour, capital, and fuel. It has already been noted that slow-steaming is related to high fuel prices, and it may be that slow steaming is an *optimal response.* To assume that vessel speeds are constant, and compute the required tonnage balance accordingly, might well be a mistake.

## 3.8    SEGMENTED SUPPLY

Until now, the data for the world merchant fleet has been examined as a whole, and apart from the comments about the tanker market, it has been assumed that conditions are similar in all sectors. Whilst this is a convenient simplification, it may give the reader a false impression; quite significant differences exist in market supply behaviour between the shipping sectors. Essentially the shipping stock can be divided into seven broad categories:

1.    Vessels employed in serving the wet trades,

2.    Vessels employed in the dry bulk trades,

3.    Vessels employed in the unitised trades (container ships),

4.    Vessels employed in non-unitised liner trades (general cargo),

5.    Vessels employed in the short sea trades, such as short sea ferries,

6.    Vessels employed in the cruise trade, and

7.    Specialised or dedicated vessels.

Since certain vessels are better adapted to certain trades, and not to others, local demand conditions can generate quite different supply behaviour between the segments. Most of the 'surplus tonnage' referred to above is in fact, concentrated in the tanker market. For example, in 1986, the relevant percentages for the different segments were 26.3% for tankers, 14.3% for dry bulk, 6.2% for general cargo, and 4.8% for unitised trades (container vessels). By 1993, the respective figures had altered to 15.3%, 9.9%, 4.5%, and 1.5% respectively[3]. Tankers' share of surplus tonnage rose between 1992 and 1993, whilst dry bulk carriers fell; this illustrates the point that, whilst the markets appear to be tied together by common long term trends, there are often quite important variations from this trend in the shorter term.

In what follows, it is assumed that the supply schedule that is under construction relates to the major bulk markets, such as oil and the dry bulk trades. It is far less straightforward to construct such schedules (*if indeed, it is at all possible!*) for the liner trades and the short sea shipping sectors. This is for reasons that lie beyond the scope of this chapter, but are well known in mainstream economic analysis.

## 3.9    RELATING THEORY TO EMPIRICAL EVIDENCE

How can one make sense of the changes that have been discussed in the earlier sections?

One way is to use the basic framework of supply and demand. Demand has already been discussed, but the supply curve of shipping services has yet to be defined. To do this, a distinction will be made between the *short run,* which is defined as the period in which the stock of vessels is unchanging, and the *long run*, in which the stock is allowed to alter.

### 3.9.1    The Short Run Supply of Shipping Output

It might be imagined, that, since the stock of vessel tonnage has been held fixed, there can be no variation in the supply of output. But this is incorrect, for the reasons discussed earlier.

---

[3]  UNCTAD Review of Maritime Transport, 1993

**Table 3.8 – Estimates of Tonnage Over Supply in the World Merchant Fleet, 1970-1999**

| | 1970 | 1975 | 1980 | 1985 | 1990 | 1991 | 1992 | 1993 | 1994 | 1995 | 1996 | 1997 | 1998 | 1999 | 2000 | 2001 | 2002 |
|---|---|---|---|---|---|---|---|---|---|---|---|---|---|---|---|---|---|
| **World Fleet** | 360.21 | 546.3 | 682.2 | 664.8 | 658.4 | 683.5 | 694.7 | 710.6 | 719.8 | 734.9 | 758.2 | 775.9 | 788.7 | 799.0 | 808.4 | 825.6 | 844.2 |
| **Surplus Tonnage** | 0.6 | 46.3 | 97.1 | 161.5 | 63.7 | 64.2 | 71.7 | 72.0 | 63.4 | 50.8 | 48.8 | 29.0 | 24.7 | 23.7 | 18.4 | 21.5 | 21.7 |
| **Active Fleet** | 325.5 | 500.0 | 585.1 | 503.3 | 594.7 | 619.3 | 623.0 | 638.6 | 656.4 | 684.1 | 709.4 | 746.9 | 746.0 | 775.3 | 790.0 | 804.1 | 822.5 |
| **Surplus Tonnage as % of World Fleet** | 0.2 | 8.4 | 14.2 | 24.3 | 9.7 | 9.4 | 10.3 | 10.1 | 8.8 | 6.9 | 6.4 | 3.7 | 3.1 | 3.0 | 2.3 | 2.6 | 206 |

Source: Maritime Transport Review, UNCTAD, 1987, 2000 and 2002

Note: Fleet Estimates are Mid-Year until 1990; End – Year for 1991 on

If output is measured in terms of tonne miles of cargo moved per time period (day, month, year), then output can be varied, literally from zero (all ships idle), to a maximum value, determined by the present size of the ship stock, its productivity, and vessel speeds.

Imagine, for the moment, that all the necessary information needed to work out each vessel's cost per tonne mile of cargo was available. One could rank these in order of low cost to high cost. Then, supply could be permitted to increase.

What is the cheapest way of producing the supply? The obvious answer is to use the low cost vessels first, as this is the most profitable. Now imagine raising rates a little – many more vessels will become profitable to operate; this process can continue until all vessels are utilised. Once they are all in use, the only way of producing more output is to make them go faster; but this requires higher rates still, as fuel consumption is increased. At some point, all possibilities are exhausted, and, no matter how much further the rate is increased, there is no possibility of supplying more tonne miles of output from the given stock of ships.

The general idea can be illustrated with the supply curve drawn in Figure 3.3 below. It has been drawn as a broad ' backward L – shaped' curve, because for much of its range, the availability of a large stock of under-utilised vessels means that tonne mile supply can be increased rapidly in response to a small increase in rates; but when demand approaches full capacity, further increases in rates do nothing to stimulate short term supply increases. They do, however, act as a signal to encourage further investment in shipping. When the rate (expressed as dollars per tonne mile of cargo carried) rises from $1 to $1.50, there is a considerable expansion in supply. But when the rate rises again, to $2, there is no further increase in the quantity supplied.

**Figure 3.3 – Hypothetical Supply Curve for Shipping Output, derived from a fixed stock of ships**

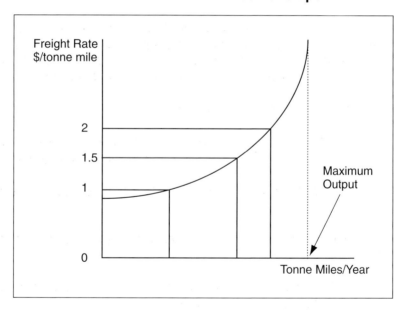

## 3.9.2    The Long Run Supply of Shipping Output

In the longer term, the supply of tonnage will be increased, if deliveries exceed scrappings and losses, or reduced (if the reverse is the case). The new vessels will be more efficient, and hopefully, cheaper to run than the scrapped ones; this will make the entire schedule *shift* to the right in the case of an expansion, or to the left in the case of a contraction.

The shift is unlikely to be parallel; the efficiency gain is on average, likely to be no more than 2-3% per year; so the 'flat' section of the supply schedule will not shift down by much. The real difference lies in the vertical section, which can shift out to the right quite sharply, if for example, increases are 10% of the existing vessel stock.

Such a situation is shown in Figure 3.4, below.

**Figure 3.4 – Effect of an Increase in the stock of ships on the Supply Curve**

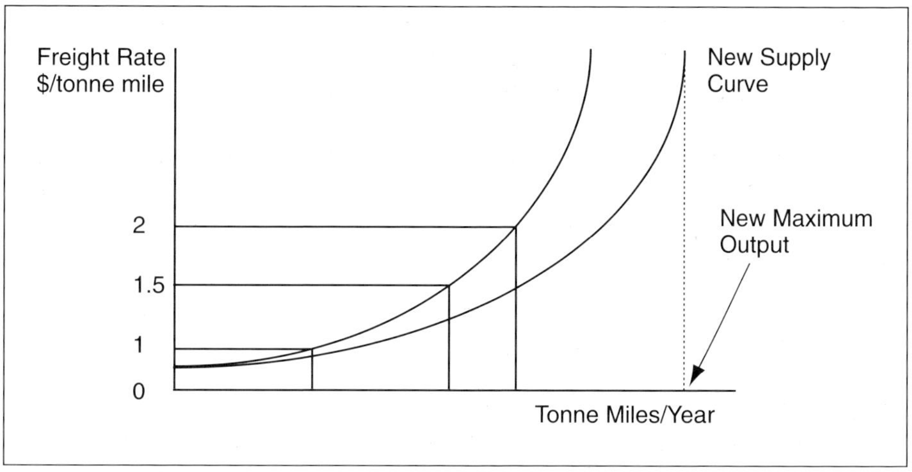

The model of supply which has now been constructed will be combined with assumptions about demand, and used to analyse the behaviour of the major bulk markets in the following chapters. It is very important that you grasp the concept of the supply curve, because it has already been implicitly used when the empirical evidence was discussed in earlier sections.

## 3.10 MEASURING SUPPLY RESPONSIVENESS: THE CONCEPT OF ELASTICITY OF SUPPLY

It was pointed out that the response of supply to a change in demand conditions, as measured by an increase in the freight rate, differs, depending upon the amount of 'slack' in the system. Just as the responsiveness of demand to a change in price, or the freight rate, can be formally measured, so, too, can the responsiveness of supply.

The formal definition of supply elasticity is

Own Price Elasticity of Supply = $\frac{\% \text{ change in the supply of shipping services}}{\% \text{ change in price (freight rate)}}$

The number that is obtained from this calculation is expected to be *positive* or *zero*, but never negative.

It will be positive if the supply of tonne miles or cargo tonnes moved per unit time period increases with an increase in the freight rate.

It will be zero if, despite the increase in the freight rate, there is no observable increase in tons of cargo moved or tonne miles performed.

Examples:
If the freight rate was to rise from $10 per ton of cargo moved to $12, (20% increase in price), and cargo tonnage lifted rose from 48,000 to 56,000 (a 16.6% increase), then the elasticity of supply would be about 0.83, or *inelastic*, because the number is less than unity.

If, on the other hand, the same rise in the freight rate were to bring forth an increase in cargo liftings from 48,000 cargo tonnes to 96,000, (100% increase), the computed elasticity would be 100/20 = +5, which is very elastic.

Figures 3.3 and 3.4 illustrate both types of responses. A very price elastic supply curve appears relatively 'flat', nearly parallel to the axis that measures output; a highly inelastic supply schedule has an almost vertical appearance, being almost parallel to the price (vertical) axes. The short run supply of shipping possesses *both* of these properties over different ranges of output supply.

### 3.10.1 Supply Elasticity and Time

The above discussion has implied that the responsiveness of supply to changes in freight rates is influenced by the time period allowed for that response. By permitting the stock of vessels to alter, supply is more flexible than it is in the period when the stock of vessels is fixed.

One extreme case of this is to imagine how the shipping markets respond in an even shorter time frame. Supply might even be perfectly inelastic, i.e. have a supply price elasticity of zero. Suppose a charterer wants a vessel to transport a particular cargo at very short notice from a particular port. It must be moved within 24 hours, say. Contacts with brokers establish that there is only one vessel available for this cargo in the time available. If the shipowner knows this, he or she can extract the maximum price that the charterer is prepared to pay. But 24 hours later, other vessels arrive in the area, free of contract; immediately the balance shifts towards the charterer as vessel owners compete for the business. This potential to exploit the market is thus very transient, given the mobility of vessels. Nevertheless, the supply responsiveness is more or less zero in the first 24 hours, but getting progressively larger as more time for greater supply reaction is allowed.

### 3.10.2 Empirical Evidence

Beenstock and Vergottis' masterly study of the world tanker and dry cargo markets, estimated that the short run supply elasticity of tonne miles with respect to the freight rate was 0.24 for tankers, a number which implies an *inelastic* response. They pointed out that this number would be much greater when large numbers of laid up vessels were present. This finding is consistent with the shape of the short run supply curve of shipping services shown in Figures 3.3 and 3.4 above.

They also found that the *long run elasticity* with respect to the stock of ships was *unity*:– in other words, in the long term, a broadly proportional response of supply tonnage to long term trends in demand is to be observed.

## 3.11 CONCLUSION

This lesson has exhaustively analysed the basic idea of the supply of shipping services. Data on supply trends over the past 20 years was analysed, and the idea of a supply curve for shipping was introduced. Finally, the term, 'own-price elasticity of supply' was introduced.

## 3.12    SELF-ASSESSMENT AND TEST QUESTIONS

Attempt the following and check your answers from the text:

1.    List all the factors that influence the supply of shipping. What does (1) an increase, and (2) a decrease in the average age of vessels indicate?

2.    What are the advantages and disadvantages of dead weight tonnage, gross tonnage and net tonnage as a measurement of vessel size?

3.    The stock of vessels will change over time. List the factors which will influence this change.

Having completed Chapter Three, attempt the following and submit your essay to your Tutor.

What factors help explain the shape of the short run supply of shipping services? Why can the short run price elasticity of supply alter from being very elastic to being very inelastic? Why will supply elasticity be higher in the longer run than in the short run?

Where relevant, illustrate your answer with real world data.

# Chapter 4

# SHIPPING COST ANALYSIS AND ECONOMIES OF SCALE

## 4.1 INTRODUCTION

This lesson discusses the important area of ship costs. One common theme that occurs in shipping is the role of economies of scale in influencing important commercial decisions such as the most suitable size of ship to use, or company mergers. The determinant and structure of shipping costs is the focal point of this lesson.

## 4.2 AN OUTLINE OF BASIC COST CONCEPTS

Economic theory discusses cost determinants with specific reference to a firm which produces just one type of output. In the shipping business, the output can be measured either by the volume of tonnes of cargo moved per day or per trip or per year, or by the volume of tonne miles produced by the vessel, either per day, per trip, or per year. The nature of the cargo carried is really immaterial to cost analysis; the focus is on measuring either the *total cost* of moving a given quantity of output, or on the *average total cost (total cost divided by the volume of cargo carried),* which is sometimes referred to as *unit cost,* or *average cost*. Costs measured per tonne of cargo are very useful, since the freight rate is usually expressed per ton of cargo in the bulk trades. In the container business, costs are often expressed per TEU (Twenty foot equivalent unit), again, because rates are expressed per 'box'. It is clearly very important to be able to express prices and unit costs in the same way, so that profitability can be measured!

### 4.2.1 Short Run costs

In the short run, the ability of any firm to vary production or output is limited, because some of the inputs which are used in producing that output are fixed in quantity. (Recall the definition of the short run, in chapter 3).

Economists define two categories of costs in the short run period. They are

a)   *Fixed Costs, or Overhead Costs*, and

b)   *Variable Costs, or Direct Costs (Sometimes called avoidable costs)*

*Fixed Costs* are defined as all those expenses which have to be met when producing the output of goods or services, *but which do not vary* with the level of production of that output. Accountants and Marketing people often call these 'Overheads'. Basically, they are costs which are necessarily incurred, but their level is unaffected even if production fell to zero.

*Variable Costs* are defined as those items which do vary with the production of output. These may be quite a small proportion of the total cost of production, depending upon the business that one is examining.

It is important to note that this distinction is only valid in the short run. Indeed, it defines the short run, since its definition is not determined by a period of calendar time.

For example, the short run time period for a tramp ship operator may in effect be a matter of a few months. In most shipping situations, the largest cost item is the capital tied up in the ship or ships themselves. Whilst the firm is committed to owning that ship, it has to meet the implied capital cost of ownership, the opportunity cost. The firm expects to receive a return on the capital invested in the vessel, and this return can be viewed as a *fixed cost*. The reason is simple. The return is needed to keep the company in the tramp shipping business, but it is a cost that does not vary with the output that the ship produces. It does not matter whether the ship sits at Lay-Up for six months, producing no output, or is actively trading; the daily capital cost has to be recovered. This cost is clearly fixed, as long as the tramp operator stays in the business.

On the other hand, it is clear that fuel consumption, and hence bunkering expenses, are directly related to producing output, (tons of cargo moved, or laden tonne miles produced). Such items are therefore defined as variable costs.

### 4.2.2    Behaviour of Total Costs and Output in the Short Run

Describing the link between total costs and output in the short run is not at all straightforward.

Fixed Costs are unaffected by the change in the level of production. Hence it can be argued that they can be treated as a constant, independent of the level of output.

Figure 4.1 below shows such an example, in the context of shipping. Assume for example, that the daily overhead costs attributed to a 50,000dwt dry cargo vessel have been calculated by her owners as being $10,000 a day. The vessel is to be used to trade from the UK to Montreal and back, a journey of 3000 nautical miles. The output produced by this journey can vary between zero and 150 million tonne miles, assuming it is laden one way. Assuming the round journey takes 17 days, the total fixed cost attributed to the trip is $170,000.

### Variable Costs

The principal variable costs will be *voyage related* costs. Fuel consumption, both at sea, and in port, must be accounted for. In addition, there will be port and canal dues (where appropriate), and stores and provisions for the crew. In addition, there may be loading and discharge costs to consider. Fuel consumption will rise as the laden weight of the vessel rises (this effect will be very marginal), but port and cargo handling charges will increase with the volume of cargo being moved). If these increase at a constant rate per ton, a line showing the relationship between total variable costs and cargo volume produced can be drawn, as in Figure 4.1 below.

### Total Costs and Output

Adding the total fixed cost to the total variable cost generates total cost, for any given volume of cargo delivered, from zero to a full load, under our assumptions. This diagram assumes that the relationship between variable costs and output is a simple, constant proportional one.

### Figure 4.1 – Total Costs and Output Relationships in the Short Run

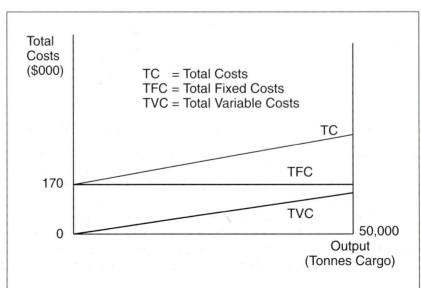

Figure 4.1 will be used as the basis for a breakeven analysis, introduced in chapter 5.

## Average Costs

Whilst examining total costs may be useful, market prices are not expressed this way. Market rates are expressed per ton of cargo delivered; passenger fares are quoted per person. It is therefore useful to translate the total cost or producing output into its unit cost equivalent, or average cost. Average costs are easily defined. The total cost of producing output is simply divided by the output being produced. In the example above, the average total cost per ton of cargo delivered can be found by dividing the total costs of delivering the cargo by the quantity of cargo delivered.

Similar calculations can be made for average fixed costs and average variable costs. But now, their behaviour will be quite different. In the example, average fixed costs will decline steadily, from $170,000 per tonne when only 1 ton of cargo is delivered ($170,000/1), to $3.4 per tonne when 50,000 tonnes are delivered (($170,000/50,000).

This implies that the average fixed cost value declines steadily, and is always minimised when the maximum output is produced.

The behaviour of average variable costs is quite different in this case. With a fixed journey length, and fixed vessel speed, plus the assumption of a fixed cargo handling charge per ton of cargo delivered, average variable costs will be constant. They are the same whether one ton or 50,000 tons is discharged. Note that *Total Variable Costs* will increase. *It is the unit cost, or average variable cost, that is constant.*

Adding the constant average variable cost with the average fixed cost yields average total cost. In this case, it reaches its minimum at the maximum cargo volume which can be carried. This is inevitable, given the assumptions, but is not always the case in shipping, and it is definitely not the case in many other industries.

### Figure 4.2 – Average Cost and Output Relationships

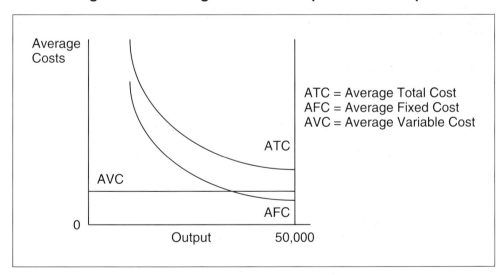

### 4.2.3    The General Relationship Between Short Run Costs and Output

In many circumstances, the linear relationship developed between output and costs is not an accurate one. Indeed, it is possible to find a more complex interrelationship in shipping, which we will come to later in this lesson. In general terms, economists do not expect total variable costs to rise proportionately with output. This is because of the fact that inputs into the production process which are variable, (such as the quantity of fuel in shipping), are combined with a fixed quantity of another input (capital, or the ship itself, in shipping). The law of variable proportions states that there is an optimal combination of these inputs. This implies that if the 'mix' of inputs is not optimal, efficiency is reduced, and average variable costs are higher than can be achieved at a different level of output. There will be, for any given size of capital, a most efficient level of output. Efficiency here is being measured in terms of the lowest average total cost.

In this situation, average variable cost *falls at low levels of output* and then *begins to increase at higher levels of output*. Since average total cost is the sum of average fixed and average variable cost, this generates a 'U' shaped average total cost curve. The reason is simple. At low levels of output, fixed costs are a very large share of total costs. They are falling sharply. When combined with a falling average variable cost curve, average total costs must fall. As output continues to increase, two things happen. Firstly, the relative importance of the fixed cost element declines, and its rate of fall declines. Secondly, average variable costs, which are now a larger and larger share of overall costs, start to rise rapidly. This makes average total costs rise.

If average costs have this U shape, there must be a range of output over which unit total costs are at their lowest. This range, or specific level of output, is the most efficient level of output associated with the quantities of capital, labour and the other inputs used in the production process.

Figure 4.3 shows the typical cost relationships that are expected.

## Figure 4.3 – Traditional Cost Output Relationships

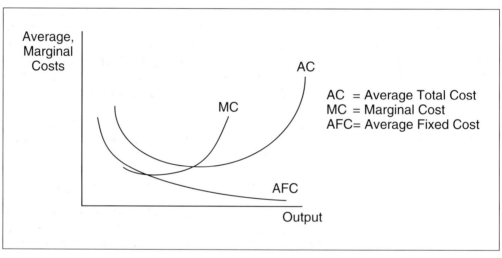

### 4.2.4    The Concept of Marginal or Incremental Cost

The last cost concept to be introduced is very important for decision-making. This is the concept of *marginal, or incremental cost*. Marginal cost is defined as the change in total costs generated by the production of an extra unit of output. In the short run, marginal cost must be related to variable costs, since, fixed costs cannot be altered, by definition. The only changes in total costs that can be generated are generated through the change in total variable costs associated with the change in output.

In the example used above, marginal cost is in fact the same value as average variable cost, because of the assumption that the cargo related costs are independent of the volume of output carried. But this is not always the case. When average variable costs rise, marginal costs will be rising even faster; when average variable costs fall, marginal costs will be lower than average variable costs.

The measurement of marginal cost itself can vary; it has to be defined very carefully. For example, what is the marginal cost of carrying an extra passenger on a bus or a train, or of taking an extra tonne of cargo on a vessel about to depart? If the carrying units are not already fully laden, the answer is usually an extremely small number. But this example is rather extreme. Now consider the same situation, this time assuming that the bus, train, or ship is fully loaded. The answer to the question is now quite different, since the costs incurred will constitute those associated with an providing extra train, an extra bus, or an extra ship. In effect, assuming, on average, in the long run, that capacity utilisation is close to 100%, the latter type of marginal cost is a measure of the long run total cost of meeting that extra demand. On the other hand, if capacity is idle, the same 'marginal cost' can be measured as a very small number, relative to the total costs involved.

It is often the case that the change in output which is being considered is not just one extra unit. It may be several thousand tonnes of cargo, which forms a consignment which a charterer wishes to move. In this case, the appropriate measure is the extra (incremental) costs associated with accepting that consignment. This may be converted to a per ton measure by dividing the estimated additional total costs related to the movement of the consignment by the tonnage of the consignment, to arrive at a per tonne figure for the incremental cost of accepting the business. This figure can then be compared with the extra revenue that the cargo brings. It should be clear that if the consignment generates additional revenues which exceed the extra costs incurred, the shipowner/operator will be better off by accepting the business.

## 4.2.5    Long Run Costs in Economic Theory

The *Long Run* is defined as the period of time in which it is possible to vary all the input quantities used in producing a given level of output. It is assumed that the unit prices of those inputs remain unchanged. Thus, the amounts of capital, land, fuel, labour required to produce a given level of output can all be varied.

In the long run, by definition, *fixed costs do not exist*. This is because every element used in the production process can be varied. In shipping, one of the key determinants of the output produced by a vessel trading on a particular route at a given speed is its size. Other things equal, the larger the size, the larger the cargo volume, cargo tonne miles, or passenger numbers carried per time period. The long run period for a shipping operator is therefore the period long enough for the size of vessels to be considered as a variable.

Given that there are no fixed costs. Long run costs are simply described. The *long run average cost* measures the total unit cost of producing a given level of output, given the prices of the inputs employed in the production process.

Long run average costs can be related to output in three different ways.

1. Long run average costs may fall, as output levels rise. When this occurs, Economies of Scale are said to exist. Put bluntly, their existence implies that the larger the volume of output that can be achieved, the lower the unit or average cost of production.

2. Long run average costs may remain unchanged as output levels change. In this case, Constant Returns to Scale are said to exist. Average costs are the same, irrespective of the level of production.

3. Long run average costs may rise as output levels rise. This situation is defined as one in which Diseconomies of scale are present. Basically, this implies that it may be more efficient to produce lower levels of output, because unit costs will be less.

These categories are illustrated in the long run cost curve shown in Figure 4.4 overleaf.

**Figure 4.4 – Long Run Average Costs and Returns to Scale**

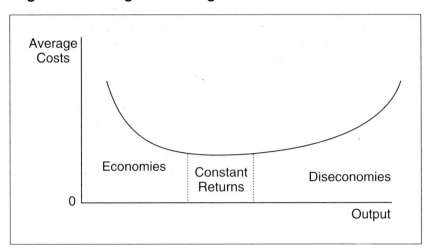

## 4.3    THE CONVENTIONAL ANALYSIS OF VESSEL OPERATING COSTS

Vessel costs are often classified into three distinct categories, defined for a particular vessel size. In a sense then, the trade analysis is a short run framework, but when several different sizes of vessel are considered, the information could be related to the 'long run' period discussed earlier.

The three distinct categories that are employed are:

### 4.3.1    Capital Related Costs

These are the cost items incurred by the shipowner which can be attributed to the ownership of the ship itself. The principal items are:

a)    Repayments of the Loan Principal, if a mortgage or other financial instrument has been used to purchase the vessel.

b)    Payment of interest on the outstanding balance of any loan/mortgage

Both of the above would be cash payments, usually occurring on a six monthly basis.

c)    The interest payments needed to generate an annual return to the shipowners equity invested in the vessel. These are not necessarily cash payments, but they are a legitimate cost item because they measure the opportunity cost of the shipowner's capital which is tied up in the ship itself.

Many shipping consultants include a notional 8% on the capital value of the ship to represent the return that the shipowner should obtain on the investment.

### 4.3.2    Direct Operating Costs

These are items which are necessarily incurred in the running of the vessel, but which do not vary with the vessel's use. They include such items as hull and machinery insurance, P and I, cargo insurance, crew costs, lubrication costs, repairs and maintenance expenditures, stores, etc. Table 4.1 lays out the major cost items.

### 4.3.3    Voyage Related Costs

Voyage related costs are those items which can be avoided if a voyage is not made. The major component is fuel costs, which are determined by the fuel consumption of the vessel on a particular journey, and of course, the price of bunkers. Fuel consumption is often computed at a particular vessel speed. However, variations in vessel speed can have significant effects on the rate of fuel consumption, so assumptions about speed have to be made.

Other components of voyage related costs include Port and Canal Dues, Pilotage and Towage, and Cargo loading and discharging charges. The relative importance of these two cost components will be affected by the journey distance. Short haul trips will mean a large proportion of vessel time spent in port, with a greater weight for Port Dues etc. Long haul trips, will mean a larger sea time, smaller port time, and a greater weight for fuel consumption at sea.

**Table 4.1 – Typical Cost Structure**

| Capital Cost | Direct Operating Costs | Voyage Related Costs |
|---|---|---|
| Interest on Loans<br>Repayment of Loan<br>Interest on Equity<br>Taxation | Insurance<br>   Hull and Machinery<br>   Protection and Indemnity<br>   War Risks<br>Crew Costs<br>Repairs and Maintenance<br>Stores<br>Administration Expenses | Fuel Costs<br>Canal Dues<br>Port Dues<br>Cargo Handling Costs<br>Crew Provisions |

Recalling the discussion of the economic theory of costs, it is clear that columns 1 and 2 of the above can be viewed as consisting of *fixed costs*; they are given no matter what the level of output produced by the vessel. The voyage related costs thus become the variable costs, in the model developed earlier.

**A hypothetical example**

A ten years old 50,000 dwt dry cargo vessel, operating 350 days a year, is estimated to require $10,000 per day to cover its direct and capital costs. The capital requirements are estimated at $900,000 per year (it has been assumed that a return of 10% of its present capital value of $9mn. is required), or $2571 per day. The remaining $7229 daily cost represents the costs incurred in crewing, insuring, and maintaining the vessel. The voyage costs would clearly depend on the journey length and ports involved. If the vessel traded to Montreal from the UK, the voyage related costs could be computed, and the total cost of delivering the cargo computed. The total cost could be converted into $ per cargo ton basis (which is an *average cost concept*), so that comparison with the freight rate could be made.

## 4.4 SPECIFIC FACTORS AFFECTING THE RELATIONSHIP BETWEEN COSTS AND SHIPPING OUTPUT

A number of assumptions have been made in Section 2. Firstly, vessel size has been taken as fixed. All the costs are calculated with that assumption in mind. Secondly, the total and average cost of delivering the cargo to a specific port requires additional assumptions about:

a) The cargo load factor

b) Vessel speed at sea (affects time spent at sea relative to in port)

c) Voyage distance (affects time spent at sea relative to in port)

d) Cargo handling rates (affects time spent in port relative to time at sea)

e) The proportion of the journey spent in ballast

f) The size of the vessel itself.

These items interact with each other; if speed is increased, fuel consumption rises, but on the other hand, time spent at sea will fall, so the amount of overhead allocated to a specific cargo trip will fall. Whether the cost per ton of cargo delivered falls or rises becomes an interesting question.

One way of analysing the effects of these changes is to allow only one factor to change, keeping all the other possible changes constant. This is what is done in the following sections.

### 4.4.1    Changes in the Vessel Load Factor

Variations in the vessel's average load factor will affect the average cost per ton of cargo delivered. Increases in load factors will lower unit costs, decreases will raise them. Attempting to increase a load factor may be one of the key goals in certain sectors of the shipping business. As we have seen, industries with very high fixed costs and low variable costs will experience sharply falling average unit costs in the short run, because the overhead can be spread over greater output volumes. The containerised liner trades are a good example. Shipping lines sail according to published timetables. The short run average cost is minimised at a 100% utilisation rate. The lines are continuously striving to raise the load factor of their vessels, as this generates more revenue *and lowers unit costs*.

In the tramp trades, the load factor is not really an issue. Tramp operators will be seeking cargoes that match their capacity, and usually they sail with full cargoes. In the oil trades, the cargo flows are very unbalanced; usually one leg of the journey is carried out in ballast. Until the mid 1970's, all tankers sailed fully laden. During the 1973 oil crisis and immediately after, part-cargoes became much more common, being a means of employing tanker tonnage that would otherwise be idle. As the tanker market recovered from this shock, part-cargoes have again become relatively uncommon.

### 4.4.2    Changes in Vessel Speed

Shipping output can be altered by varying the speed of the vessel, as noted in Lesson 3. Indeed, it has been argued by some authorities[1] that speed variations are effectively *the only way of varying short run output in the tramp and bulk trades*.

Ships are usually designed to run at a particular speed. The speed chosen is determined by the vessel's size, technical characteristics (Catamarans travel faster than single hulled vessels), and engine power. When designed, vessels are often optimised for a particular trade, so once built, the flexibility is reduced. But there is still some room to vary speed, and thus output.

Making a ship go faster does two things. Firstly, it alters fuel consumption. Indeed there is a well-known approximate relationship between speed and fuel consumption; known as the cube rule, it says that a 1% increase in vessel speed will lead to a 3% increase in fuel consumption. (This formula is calibrated for deviations from the vessel's design speed.) If fuel consumption rises, the amount of fuel required for a journey will rise. Because the speed increase is less than proportional to the consumption increase, fuel consumption will rise, even if the journey time has been reduced. (A more accurate relationship between speed and fuel consumption, called the 'J-curve', has been developed by P. Alderton[2]).

However, the reduction in journey time brings a second consideration into play. Recall that a vessel's costs include a daily overhead, covering capital and direct costs. Reductions in journey time means a reduction in the allocation of overheads to this trip, so that there are two opposing forces at work on costs.

Modelling these effects is best carried out with a simulation; taking particular vessel characteristics, a particular journey, and most importantly, assumptions about the price of bunker fuel and freight rates available for any extra cargo carried in the time saved by speeding up the vessel.

It can be shown that the average cost per ton of cargo delivered falls, and then rises, around the vessel's design speed. The range of vessel speeds over which this variation is often limited; at the top end, by the discomfort of the crew as the vessel shakes itself to bits, and at the bottom

---

[1]  Evans, J.J and P. Marlow (1990) *Quantitative Methods for Maritime Economics* Fairplay Publications:Coulsdon, UK.
[2]  Alderton, P. M. (1995) *Sea Transport: Operations and Economics*

end, by the loss of vessel manoeuvrability and steerability. A 14-knot vessel may have an effective speed range of 10 to 16 knots say; this is still a range of -30% to +12% relative to the design speed.

It is important to note that this relationship is derived for a given price of bunkers. An increase in the bunker price will shift the entire relationship up and to the left, thus reducing the least cost speed. A decrease in bunker prices will do the reverse.

Note, too, that when freight rates are high, the profit rate increases, and it becomes worthwhile to increase vessel speed. This assumes that the short run situation exists, since an even more profitable response may be possible in the long run – buy and operate another vessel!

**Figure 4.5 – Average Cost and Vessel Speed**

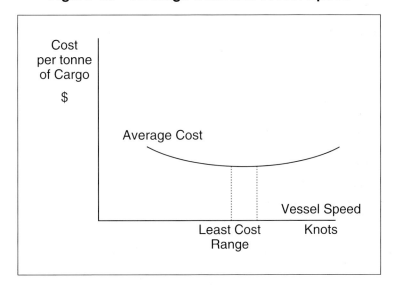

There is good evidence to back up the link between rates, bunker prices and speed in the bulk trades. After the 1973 oil price crisis, the price of bunkers rose by 400%. At the same time, oil movement volumes grew less rapidly, and indeed, declined in the late 1970's. These two effects, coupled with low rates for tankers, led a significant number of vessels to 'slow steam'. Market observers noted that tanker speeds fell from around 14 knots to about 10 knots. Market behaviour was in line with the model described above.

There are however, some trades in which speed variation is only used to maintain the published sailings timetable. The liner trades, in particular, have to meet deadlines in order to satisfy their contractual obligations to their customers. They have far less room to respond to variations in bunker prices. Indeed, they behave quite differently, inserting into their contracts a clause that permits them to pass on the effects of unexpected movements in bunker prices to the customer. This response is needed because of the different nature of the service offered in these trades.

### 4.4.3 Changes in Distance Travelled

Altering the voyage length will automatically increase the total costs incurred by a vessel of a given size, and with the other factors held constant. There are two obvious reasons. With vessel speed held constant, longer voyage lengths mean larger fuel bills. But it also means a longer journey time, and hence the direct operating and capital costs which accrue to that journey also increase.

Again, the relationship between costs and distance can be graphed, as in Figure 4.6 below. The relationship is drawn for a given vessel size. The vertical distance OX represents the fixed overhead that would be incurred if the vessel sailed no miles at all. After that, each extra mile requires fuel, plus additional time costs. These will rise proportionally with distance, assuming a fixed vessel speed.

## Figure 4.6 – The Relationship between Average Cost and Distance

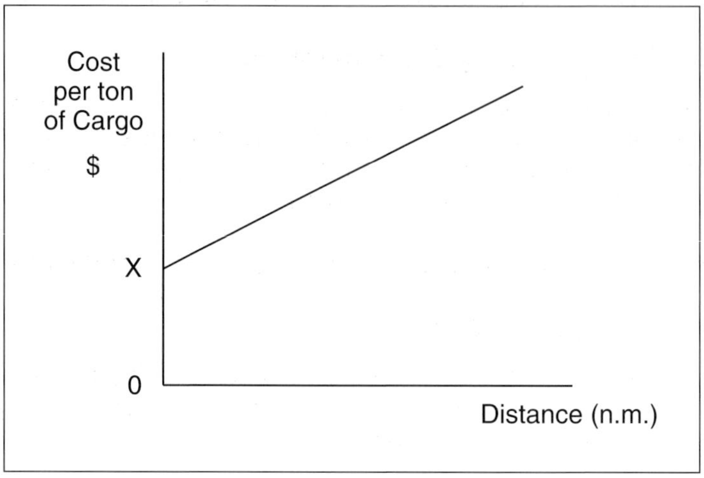

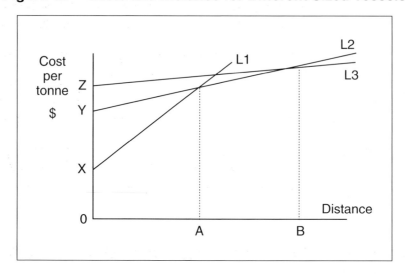

This relationship can be developed by graphing the relationship between cost and voyage distance for successively larger sizes of vessels, measured in dwt. Let $L_1$, $L_2$ and $L_3$ represent three successively larger sizes of vessel. The fixed overhead element will tend to get larger as the vessel gets bigger, because larger vessels have larger daily direct and capital costs. On the other hand, the increase in fuel required to travel further will be lower, because fuel consumption (at a given vessel speed) rises less than proportionately with vessel size. This means that the slopes of the lines become flatter as vessel size increases.

Over the distance range OA, it is clear that the smallest vessel size is the most economic. Over the range AB, it is vessel size $L_2$, whilst the largest vessel becomes more efficient as the voyage length increases. For voyage distances around OA, vessels $L_1$ and $L_2$ will be in competition, whilst around OB, it will be $L_2$ and $L_3$. There are thus a series of links created between vessels of differing sizes.

## Figure 4.7 – Costs and Distance for Different Sized Vessels

Figure 4.7 illustrates another interesting point. As the voyage distance increases, and the time spent at sea increases relative to the time spent in port, the preferred, or optimal size of the vessel increases. This point will be considered in more detail below.

### 4.4.4    Changes in Cargo Handling Rates

Changes in the rate of cargo loading and discharge will lower the amount of time the vessel spends in port. Other factors being held equal, this will reduce the constant terms (vertical distances such as OX in Figure 4.6) shown in the earlier figures, but will not alter their slopes. The reduction in the constant terms will alter the critical distances at which one vessel size becomes more efficient than another; in general, higher cargo handling rates will reduce the distance at which the larger vessel becomes more economic than the smaller.

### 4.4.5 The Proportion of Journey Spent in Ballast

It should be clear that reducing the proportion of the journey that is spent in ballast will lower the average cost per ton of cargo delivered. This is because the vessel is carrying more cargo, producing more output, with more or less no change in total voyage costs. (Fuel consumption will increase slightly, but not significantly).

The effect is exactly the same as raising the vessel's load factor.

### 4.4.6 Changes in the Vessel's Size

Vessel size can be altered! There are two ways. Firstly, vessels can be 'jumboized', or reduced in cargo capacity, by the 'simple' device of inserting or removing sections of the hull! This is clearly an expensive process.

Secondly, the vessel size can be altered on the drawing board! Prior to commissioning, the shipowner will have to consider the most appropriate sized vessel that best suits the market that it is to serve.

Both of these are *long run* decisions however. For the sake of completeness, it should be noted that the cost-distance relationship for different sizes of ship can be calculated, which was shown in Figure 4.7 above. It should be clear that, for greater distances, the preferred size of the ship increases. But the full examination of the relationship between average costs and vessel size leads into an analysis of long run costs, and this issue is discussed in the next section.

### *Addendum* Time Spent in Port relative to time spent at Sea

Two of the factors discussed above have a direct effect on the relative proportion of time spent in port and at sea by a vessel. It should be fairly clear that port time costs will be affected by vessel size. There are two reasons for this. Firstly, the larger vessel will incur greater port charges, as they are often based on either g.r.t. or n.r.t., so larger vessels will be charged more. A related factor is of course, the opportunity cost of the vessel itself. The larger the vessel, the greater the value of capital tied up in the vessel, and the greater the opportunity cost of idle port time.

However, large vessels are often able to discharge their cargoes more rapidly than smaller ones, so that the time they need to spend in port need be no longer than that expected for a smaller vessel. The reason is simple; larger vessels lose more revenue than smaller ones when they do nothing, so it is often the case that they are equipped with higher capacity loading and discharging on board facilities – oil tankers are a good example.

One implication of this is that, other things being held equal, the larger the proportion of time that a vessel spends in port per year, the smaller its preferred size. The reason is that less capital is tied up doing nothing! Multi-port operations also tend to reduce the optimum vessel size, for similar reasons.

## 4.5 LONG RUN VESSEL COSTS: ECONOMIES OF SCALE AND OPTIMAL SHIP SIZE

It was noted at the end of section 3 that vessel size could be varied in two ways; by altering the dimensions of an existing vessel, or by ordering a new one. Information from shipbuilders about the costs of building different sizes of vessel, together with estimates of their running and voyage costs, can be used to estimate the average cost of delivering a ton of cargo (or passenger) between two ports for different sizes of vessels. This is the *long run* situation that was defined earlier in section 1, particularly section 1.5.

It is important to note that this long run relationship between average cost and vessel size, which is taken to measure output, is constructed with a number of underlying assumptions. Firstly, *input prices* are assumed to be constant. In the long run context, this means the price of capital (interest rates), the price of labour (crew wage rates) and the price of fuel (bunker prices) are assumed to take the same values when comparing average costs at different sizes. Secondly, voyage characteristics, load factors and the other items mentioned in Section 3 would also need to be kept constant.

In Section 1.5 above three different relationships between long run average costs and output were identified. They were

a)   *Economies of Scale*

b)   *Constant Returns to Scale*

c)   *Diseconomies of Scale*

Economies of scale exist in two principal areas of shipping. The ship itself, and port facilities, such as container terminals. This section discusses the reasons for the presence of scale economies in general, and then for their existence in shipping.

Economies of scale are essentially of two broad types. Those which are enjoyed by a single firm through that firm's individual policy. These are known as internal economies. There are also external economies which result from the expansion in scale of the whole industry or a number of firms within the industry and cause a decline in costs to all the firms in the industry. In the present discussion there will be a concentration on internal economies but students should be able to see for themselves the effects these economies have on the wider external economies of the industry.

Professor E.A.G Robinson[3] classified internal economies under five convenient headings – Managerial, Commercial, Financial, Risk Bearing and Technical. While much of the remainder of this lesson will concentrate on the latter category, before proceeding it is important to look briefly at each of the former categories.

**Managerial Economies:** These are concerned with the control of the organisation. This is part of the important process known as the division of labour where individuals increase their productivity by specialising in a specific task. Management becomes increasingly specialised in a particular aspect of the function of a large firm. Senior management can concentrate on general policy delegating subsidiary, often specialised tasks to others, usually within a divisional structure.

A small shipping firm with only one or two ships may find it cheaper and more efficient to have their ships managed by a specialist management company instead of employing its own staff. Thus the small shipowner will benefit from the economies of scale gained by a large management company.

This will apply to the point where the expansion of the fleet makes management expenses greater than the firm employing its own management staff. As with any business larger shipping firms will be able to have their own specialist legal and insurance departments for example thus saving fees and making more informed management decisions.

Such economies are also applicable to the major conference/liner companies, which have offices all over the world. As part of their company policy, they transfer staff to other places in the world in order to create an all round management.

**Commercial Economies:** Sometimes referred to as marketing economies. Large production allows bulk buying at a discount. In selling the marketing cost per unit of output and advertising is cheaper in larger volumes. The shipowner or operator can achieve economies of scale by placing regular orders in respect of say maintenance or bunkering.

---

[3]  Robinson, E. A.G. (1958) *The Structure of Competitive Industry* Cambridge University Press, Cambridge, UK.

**Financial Economies:** Large companies have advantages in raising finance for expansion either through banks or by going to the public through the sale of shares. It is much more difficult for the small company to convince potential lenders of their financial stability.

**Risk Bearing Economies:** There are three types of risk. Firstly those risks which can be insured against. Often large companies can insure at low premiums simply because of the size and the limitation of risk. For the same reasons some large companies will insure themselves internally rather than give their business to insurance business. Secondly, large businesses can usually bear their own risks by say introducing a new commodity because they will have secured the confidence of their customers. Thirdly, there are risks which cannot easily be insured against, usually referred to as uncertainties. Such uncertainties can, and often do cause the bankruptcy of small companies, whereas larger concerns can diversify their product industrial section or market thereby compensating for the difficulties in one area by the buoyancy in another. This is one of the basic strengths of the large multi-national company. Increasingly shipping companies are diversifying their interests and investing in related services, such as through transport and leisure services. Larger shipping companies can more easily switch vessels from one trade to another trade should the need arise; if for example a certain vessel has to undergo major repairs, then the services of that vessel can be taken over by another vessel of their fleet and so save the cost of having to charter a vessel. Conferences, of course, also offer the opportunity to spread risk.

### Ability to exploit large, indivisible investments:

An important reason for falling long run costs is the fact that certain technologies may require very large throughputs before they become worthwhile investments. These are sometimes called indivisible, or lumpy, investment. Inventories are a good example. A small shipping company will not find it economic to hold inventories of spare parts for its vessels, but a company running and maintaining a fleet of several ships may. The inventory will reduce the fleet's downtime, raising overall efficiency. Inventory stocks increase less than proportionately with output, thus permitting large fleets to gain cost savings.

*Crew size* does not increase with vessel size; it is largely independent of it. Crew costs per dwt will fall as the vessel size enlarges. A number of operating costs *fall per dwt* as vessel size increases, including fuel, lubes and spares.

It must be remembered that shipping is a **business** and may benefit from internal economies of scale in the sphere of management and administration just like any other type of business organisation, as well as through the technology specific to shipping.

**Technical Economies:** These are basically concerned with the nature of production; in the present context the production of shipping services and what some authors refer to in a limiting way as the economies of ship's size. To examine it first from this point of view, a ship is to all intents and purposes essentially a large box and will act accordingly as volume increases faster than surface area. To look at this using a simple model. Assume a box either side of which measures 1 metre. Each side of the box has an area of 1 x 1 equalling 1 square metre. Since there are six sides including the lid, the total area is 6 x 1 = 6 sq. m. The volume is, however, 1 metre x 3 that is 1 x 1 x 1 = 1 cubic metre.

If the size of the box is now doubled, the side is now 2 metres. The surface area is 6 x 4 equalling 24 sq. metres, but the volume has increased to 2 x 2 x 2 equalling 8 cubic metres. Hence the surface area has quadrupled but the volume has increased eightfold. If this simple sum is translated in terms of bulk carriers a small increase in vessel size (surface area) will bring a substantial increase in the carrier capacity (volume).

Obviously the increase in the size of the ship will result in increases in the total construction costs, but these increases will be less than the proportionate increase in size. A brief example of this point is given in table 4.2 below.

As can be seen, there is a decrease in average construction costs (cost per dwt or cost per TEU), with increases in vessel size, for all three vessel types. However, it should be stressed

## 4.12    SELF-ASSESSMENT AND TEST QUESTIONS

Attempt the following and check your answers from the text:

Close the book, and write short notes on the following concepts:

a)    fixed and variable costs

b)    average fixed and average total cost

c)    long run average costs

d)    how internal economies of scale could affect your place of work.

e)    What are the principal factors influencing the relationship between costs and output in the short run?

Having completed Chapter Four attempt the following and submit your essay to your Tutor.

What are the economic reasons for the existence of large disparities in the observed average size of vessels employed in the dry bulk, tanker, container and general cargo trades?

# Chapter 5

# COMPETITIVE SHIPPING MARKETS:
## Bulk Dry Cargo

## 5.1    INTRODUCTION

The dry bulk trades have been transformed over the past 25 years. The average size of the vessel engaged in these trades has doubled in size, as was shown in Chapter 4. There is now a large range of vessel sizes, with vessels of 10,000dwt being regarded as rather small and insignificant.

The dry bulk trades have in fact evolved from the Tramp market. Traditional tramp markets were served by small, general purpose vessels, essentially scouring the world's ports in search of business. That business was primarily undertaken on the spot markets, with owners using the global network of shipbrokers to seek business for their vessels. At the same time, charterers would contact the same set of brokers to inform the market of their chartering requirements. Brokers thus perform a fundamental function, in providing information to both sides of the market place, to enable contracts to be made.

Nowadays, as vessel sizes have increased so much, there is a tendency for really significant charterers to use consecutive voyage charters and contracts of affreightment. Owners have to be able to offer several vessels to fulfil these types of contracts, but if the company operates large vessels, such contracts provide greater continuity of employment.

Despite the growth in these types of contracts, there is still a large volume of spot charters. This market is widely regarded, by both practitioners and observers alike, as being very competitive. In this lesson, the focus is on the development of a simple model of the competitive process that will then be used to analyse market behaviour in these trades. The centre of attention will be the tramp vessel throughout this lesson.

## 5.2    DEFINITION OF THE DRY CARGO SECTOR

The dry cargo sector can be defined using two basic methods. Firstly, it could be defined on the basic unit which provides the service, the tramp ship. Alternatively, a broader based approach could be adopted, defining the sector in terms of its major market characteristics. These two approaches will overlap to a considerable extent.

### The Tramp Ship

The first approach, used by several authors, is to define the sector in terms of the vessel itself. Gripaios[1] defines the tramp ship as follows:

> "A deepsea tramp ship is prepared to carry any cargo between any port at any time, always providing that the venture is both legal and safe". Gripaios, p. 7.

This definition focuses upon the nature of the market that the vessel serves. During the 1960's, vessel size increased, and a more recent definition, by the late Professor B. N. Metaxas[2], is given overleaf.

---

[1] H. Gripaios (1959) Tramp *Shipping*
[2] B. N. Metaxas (1971) *The Economics of Tramp Shipping* Athlone Press:London

"Any vessel with a tonnage of 4,000 deadweight or above, which in the long run does not have a fixed itinerary, and which carries mainly dry cargo in bulk over relatively long distances and from one or more ports to one or more ports is an ocean or deepsea tramp". Metaxas, p. 6.

Notice that both definitions emphasise the fact that the vessel has no fixed pattern of employment; it is this feature that has been labelled 'tramping'. But Metaxas' definition differs in several respects from the earlier one. Firstly, a minimum vessel size is introduced, in order to exclude small vessels from the market. Secondly, attention is drawn to the term "relatively long distances", which is a way of focussing on the deepsea nature of the tramping operation. Finally, Metaxas also states that the vessel trades mainly in the dry cargo sector.[3]

## Market Characteristics

The problem with defining a market in terms of a set of specific vessel characteristics should be obvious to anyone who thinks about it a little. By including a specific vessel size, Metaxas has 'dated' his definition. The growing average size of most vessel types over the past 25 years, (as we saw in Lesson 4) means that 4000dwt appears to be a rather small vessel nowadays.

In the past two decades, dry bulk vessels have increased their size range, varying from 10,000dwt up to 120,000dwt (Capesize), through the 50-80,000dwt (Panamax size) categories. These vessels are more specialised than the old tramps, as some are clearly too large to trade 'from any port to any port'; indeed the very largest cannot transit the major canals of Panama and Suez, hence the term Capesize.

In addition such vessels are often employed on contracts of affreightment, which permits the shipowner to meet the charterer's requirements by using more than one vessel, or by consecutive voyage charters, which oblige the shipowner to commit the vessel to several voyages in a row for a particular charterer. These longer term commitments from both sides of the market do not fit neatly with the definitions of either Gripaios or Metaxas.

A modern definition would need to include the development of these longer term commitments, which have been brought about by two major trends.

Firstly, cargo volumes, and average lot sizes, have increased, thus creating the 'bulk dry trades' sector. Secondly, the most efficient way of meeting these trends is to use larger vessels. But, as we have seen, larger vessels require larger capital requirements from the owners; they are only prepared to risk the commitment to such large vessels if they have a better guarantee of employment; and this is what the above contracts provide them with.

However, it should be clear that the freight rates arrived at for these contracts are still influenced by the spot market. The analysis that follows focuses on this sector of the market, noting that there are other contract types available.

A definition that was based upon market structure might be more generally applicable, as it would be less affected by changes in the size of vessels which were used to serve it.

· One of the key features of the dry cargo markets is the fixing of many contracts in an 'open market' situation. What is meant by this is the fact that most contracts between charterers and shipowners/ship managers become well known to all the market participants, through the activities of the essential market intermediaries, the shipbroking companies. This openness means that all 'agents' in the market know the prevailing levels of freight rates, and can make their own decisions accordingly.

The markets publish details of all types of contracts, from `spot' contracts, to be started in a matter of days or weeks, through consecutive voyage and contracts of affreightment, to time

---

[3] For further detailed discussion see J. McConville (1999) The Economics of Maritime Transport, Theory and Practice, Witherby, London Chapter 10

charters of varying duration. (It is important to note a major difference between time charter contracts and the other sort: – they are expressed in terms of $ per summer dwt per month or $000 per day, and are effectively the 'hire' rate for a vessel, independent of its place of operation. Spot contracts also include port and voyage expenses. In the former case, these are paid for by the charterer in addition to the time charter hire; in the latter case, the price paid by the charterer includes all expenses.)

What exactly are 'open market fixtures'? The basic elements of the spot market are as follows:

i) The provision of a vessel to load cargo for a specific destination at short notice

ii) To offer a vessel for hire for a single voyage usually with a time limit of up to one year. The market for long term and short term fixtures is intimately related for open market fixtures and will have an important influence on the other fixtures. UNCTAD defined an 'Open Market' as follows:

"The open market embraces the aggregates at any given time of *tramp ship* owners seeking employment for their vessels and shippers requiring the services of tramp ships for a limited period. The keynote of the open freight market is the quick and easy communication of information. The basis is an international network of shipowners, shipbrokers and charterers, closely and continuously linked by telecommunications. Thus, any charterer needing a ship of a certain size and type available at a specific port on or about a specific date can be assured that his needs will be made known to shipowners in all countries which possess merchant fleets."[4]

Hence for the purposes of this course the clearest definition may be found in the market characteristics rather than in the particular specification of the vessel.

## 5.3 ECONOMIC CHARACTERISTICS

The economic characteristics of the dry cargo bulk freight markets has led some authors to argue that it is a very competitive one, close to the *perfectly competitive model* used by economists. There are a number of important features of this model, which have to be satisfied in real life if it is to be usefully applied to the analysis of the dry cargo market. The assumptions are listed below:

1. Every supplier in the industry seeks to maximise their profits, which are defined as the difference between their total revenues and total costs. Put differently, profit maximisation requires that firms (shipping companies) sell only that output level which maximises the total profit they make.

2. There are numerous buyers and sellers in the market.

3. The service offered by each shipping company is exactly the same as every other company on the market. In the dry cargo market, what is being provided is cargo space, which can be argued to be exactly the same, no matter what ship or what company. After all, grain or iron ore are indifferent to their surroundings, unlike human cargoes, such as passengers.

4. There is easy exit from and entry to the market.

5. There is full information, in the sense that all participants in the market place know the same as everyone else; market rates are known to all, and cost information is also widely available.

---

[4] UNCTAD (1988) Freight Markets and the Level and Structure of Freight Rates UNCTAD, Geneva, para. 39 (Italics added).

Under these circumstances, a perfectly competitive market is said to exist.

The dry cargo market fulfills all of the above conditions. Charterer's and shipowners are both driven by the profit motive, although this is difficult to prove directly.

Assumption Two is clearly satisfied. There are a large number of charterers and shipowners in the market, and even the very largest shipowning company owns a tiny percentage of the total dry cargo tonnage business; the largest charterer is responsible for a small percentage of turnover. This means that no single supplier or single user of the market can influence the behaviour of freight rates in the market; they cannot be 'fixed', but are driven by overall demand and supply conditions.

Assumption 3 is also easily satisfied. The basic service being provided is the safe transportation of cargo in a timely manner. Provided that all ships trade with the relevant classification certificates, that their crews are properly trained, and the vessels are well maintained, and that loading and discharging procedures are carried out correctly, it makes no difference as to the ship used. The one area of concern, raised in Lesson 4, must lie in the presence of substandard ships. If these have a greater risk of foundering, of cargo damage or loss, or of unreliability, then the cargo space in these vessels is not quite the same quality as in those vessels that do meet the requirements listed above. With that proviso, it will be assumed that the analysis is based on ships of an acceptable standard.

Assumption 4 is also easily satisfied. If a shipowner earns unsatisfactory profits from the ship, and sees no long term prospects for recovery, then they can put the vessel up for sale. This may take a few months, providing there are willing buyers. If it is loss making, the capital value will be low, but at least the owner has exited. The new owner may be able to make a profit because of the fact that his capital investment is lower than the previous owners. If many owners cannot make profits, and buyers are few, they can either lay-up or scrap the vessel. Exit occurs if the vessel is scrapped, since less tonnage is now available for supply.

Entrance is the opposite. One can enter the market by buying a second-hand vessel, or by ordering a newbuilding. It is the newbuilding component that alters the supply of tonnage in the long term.

Entry and exit is 'easy' in this market, because existing shipowners have no way of preventing such a process. This is in contrast to other types of markets, where existing firms may have several different ways of preventing new firms from entering and competing. Note that 'easy' does not mean 'costless'; it is an expensive process to set up a shipping company! What is meant, however, is that economists do not expect the operating costs of a new entrant to be any higher than those of companies already in the business; *they would not suffer a cost disadvantage from entering*.

Assumption 5 is best justified by two words; Baltic Exchange. Although little direct trading is now done on the floor of the Baltic, it symbolises the fact that there is a meeting place at which charterers can find ships and shipowners can find charterers, and at the same time learn what current market rates are. Nowadays, many transactions take place on computer screens in shipbroker's houses; the effect is the same. The brokers act as information transmitters, ensuring that all players are kept fully informed of any event that might affect the market.

An important characteristic of a competitive market is that shipowners *have no* individual *influence over market rates*. But since profit is made in the margin between revenues and costs, the only element that they have control over is costs. Competitive markets tend to be driven by cost trends, rather than by demand features. In other words, continuous attention to all aspects of costs, keeping them as small as possible, is a hallmark of a competitive industry.

The assumption of a competitive industry permits the use of a simple model of industry behaviour, which will be developed in section 6 below. Before that, the structure of the dry cargo fleet, and the use of breakeven analysis in tramp operating decisions, will be explored.

## 5.4 DRY BULK MARKET DEMAND STRUCTURE AND TRENDS OVER THE PAST 25 YEARS

Table 5.1 provides annual data on the growth of dry cargo demand over the past 25 years. Column 1 reveals that the total volume of cargo, measured in cargo tonnes, has nearly trebled in that period. This works out at an annual average compound growth rate of 4% per year. This rate of growth is quite a respectable one; the UK's growth rate has been around 2.5% per year for the same period, although of course, other developed countries have grown faster.

The average growth rate hides two points worthy of note. Firstly, demand growth is much more uneven on a year to year basis. Column 2 shows the annual growth rate over the previous year's level of demand. This column reveals many interesting features. It is clear that the highest rates of growth to be observed occurred in the period 1968-73. In that period there is only one growth rate that is less than the 4% average, while there are several at two to three times greater than that. Secondly, it should be noted that growth rates seem to go in 'spurts'; the rate peaks, declines, and in some years becomes negative (i.e. demand falls), before recovery again. In other words, demand growth tends to move in 'economic cycles', of good years, medium years, poor years, and back again. These cycles exist around a rising trend in the total volume of cargo moved.

### Table 5.1 Dry Cargo: Seaborne Trade, Fleet and % Surplus 1968-1995

| Year | Dry Cargo Trade Mn Tonnes | Annual Increase Percent | Dry Cargo Ton Miles bn. miles | Average Length of Haul (n.m.) | Ore and Bulk Carrier Fleet M.n. GRT | Annual Increase Percent | % Surplus in World Dry Bulk Fleet |
|---|---|---|---|---|---|---|---|
| | 1 | 2 | 3 | 4 | 5 | 6 | 7 |
| 1968 | 930 | 8.0 | | | 34.9 | 20.0 | |
| 1969 | 990 | 6.5 | | | 41.8 | 19.8 | |
| 1970 | 1125 | 13.6 | | | 46.7 | 11.7 | |
| 1971 | 1140 | 1.3 | | | 53.8 | 15.2 | |
| 1972 | 1216 | 6.7 | | | 63.5 | 18.0 | |
| 1973 | 1346 | 10.7 | | | 72.6 | 14.3 | |
| 1974 | 1440 | 7.0 | | | 79.4 | 9.4 | |
| 1975 | 1373 | -4.7 | | | 85.4 | 7.6 | |
| 1976 | 1471 | 7.1 | | | 91.7 | 7.4 | |
| 1977 | 1515 | 3.0 | | | 100.9 | 10.0 | |
| 1978 | 1602 | 5.7 | | | 106.5 | 5.6 | |
| 1979 | 1731 | 8.1 | | | 108.3 | 1.7 | |
| 1980 | 1833 | 5.9 | | | 109.6 | 1.2 | 11.4 |
| 1981 | 1866 | 1.8 | | | 113.1 | 3.2 | 19.8 |
| 1982 | 1921 | 2.9 | | | 119.3 | 5.5 | 23.5 |
| 1983 | 1878 | -2.2 | | | 124.4 | 4.3 | 25.6 |
| 1984 | 2065 | 10.0 | | | 128.3 | 3.1 | 23.4 |
| 1985 | 1923 | n.a. | 7908 | 4112 | 134.0 | 4.4 | 22.5 |
| 1986 | 1945 | 1.1 | 7951 | 4088 | 132.9 | -0.8 | 14.3 |
| 1987 | 1999 | 2.8 | 8282 | 4143 | 131.0 | -1.4 | 13.1 |
| 1988 | 2105 | 5.3 | 8795 | 4178 | 129.6 | -1.1 | 10.6 |
| 1989 | 2199 | 4.5 | 9126 | 4150 | 129.5 | -0.1 | 7.5 |
| 1990 | 2253 | 2.5 | 9340 | 4146 | 133.2 | 2.9 | 8.5 |
| 1991 | 2330 | 3.4 | 9586 | 4114 | 135.9 | 2.0 | 8.8 |
| 1992 | 2360 | 1.3 | 9638 | 4084 | 136.8 | 0.7 | 10.6 |
| 1993 | 2385 | 1.1 | 9828 | 4121 | 140.9 | 3.0 | 9.9 |
| 1994 | 2478 | 3.9 | 10271 | 4145 | 143.3 | 1.7 | 8.4 |
| 1995 | 2601 | 5.0 | 10870 | 4179 | 149.3 | 4.2 | 7.1 |

Sources: Columns 1 and 3: O.E.C.D. Maritime Transport Review 1994, UNCTAD Review of Maritime Transport 1995
Column 7: UNCTAD Review of Maritime Transport 1995

*Notes*:
1. % Active Fleet series breaks in 1986; data not comparable between 1985 and 1986
2. Dry Cargo measured in metric tons until 1984. It is in imperial tons afterwards. See Tables 1 & 2 of UNCTAD Review

The above analysis examined demand measured in tonnes of cargo moved. This may well give an incomplete picture if the journey distance alters, since the basic unit of output is the 'cargo tonne mile'. Column 3 provides information on the volume of tonne mile movements over the past 10 years. In this period, tonne mile demand increased by 3.2% per year compound, whereas cargo tonnes moved grew by 2.6% per year. This finding implies that journey distances have increased, as column 4 indeed reveals. The average haul has not increased by much though; it has moved from 4112 nautical miles in 1985 to 4179 nautical miles in 1995.

Column 5 provides information as to the growth of the dry bulk fleet, which has averaged 5.5% per year over the period, in GRT terms. Note that this growth is higher than that of tonnage demand; however, it is not clear as to whether or not tonne mile demand has grown by a similar amount, so it would not be fair to conclude that supply capacity has outstripped demand just on the basis of these figures.

Interesting points emerge in the detail. The highest annual growth rates of GRT are seen in the 1968-73 period, with figures reaching 20% in 1968. Expansion never exceeds 6% after 1978, and there are several years, (1986-1989) in which the fleet capacity shrinks. Notice that these occur a few years after the peak levels of unemployed tonnage, which reached 20% or more between 1982 and 1985 (see column 7).

The decline in the lay-up rate coincides with a small increase in the fleet size, and a recovery in demand growth.

## 5.5 AN ANALYSIS OF THE COST STRUCTURE OF TRAMP SHIP OPERATORS

Lesson 4 introduced the basic concepts of cost analysis employed by economists. In the short run, Tramp Operators will have to identify their costs in terms of those items which are affected by the amount of output that the company produces, and those that are independent of any variation in that output, i.e. splitting their costs between *fixed* and *variable*. In the cost model presented in Lesson 4 above, it was argued that in the shipping context, most 'variable costs' related to those items specifically related to producing output, which of course implies those cost items related to undertaking a voyage, and the speed at which that voyage is undertaken.

The other way of viewing short run costs is to ask yourself a simple question. What costs are avoided if I do not carry out a particular activity? The distinction between *avoidable* and *unavoidable* costs is also useful when making operational decisions.

### 5.5.1 The Lay-up Decision

Here is an example. What costs should be considered relevant in the decision of a Tramp Ship operator to lay up their vessel, or to continue to trade?

A 'common sense' answer might be to estimate the total costs incurred if the ship were to continue to trade, undertaking another journey that takes six weeks, say, and compare that to the freight revenue obtained from the trip. If the trip loses money, in the sense that freight revenues are less than the total costs, then the vessel could be laid up.

There are in fact, two things wrong with this analysis. Firstly, it assumes that lay-up is a costless activity. Lay up costs money; the vessel has to be maintained, it has to be provided with some power, and it may have to be moved to a safe lay-up position. On the other hand, the vessel will no longer have a full crew, provisions and maintenance etc. will be less, so that the costs associated with owning the vessel will be reduced.

The second error is that the analysis includes costs that will be incurred by the owner whether the vessel trades or not; but if these costs are common in both situations, they cannot affect the outcome of the decision; they can in effect, be cancelled out.

Suppose that the owner estimates that daily operating costs are $10,000 for a vessel in a trading condition, and $4,000 in lay-up. $3,000 of this cost is assumed to be the capital cost of owning the vessel; it is not avoidable, whatever one does with the vessel. It therefore can be cancelled out. The relevant costs become $7,000 per day when trading, and $1,000 per day when laid up.

Suppose the owner is now offered a charter which takes 42 days, and will incur voyage related costs of $380,000 in the period. On a total cost basis, the owner will require $800,000 revenues; if the vessel has a 50,000dwt carrying capacity, this implies a rate of $16 per ton of cargo delivered. But suppose the market rate is only $14. Should they lay-up the vessel?

If they lay up the vessel, he faces extra costs of $42,000, (42 days x $1000)

If they take the charter, they gain $700,000 in extra revenues ($14 x 50,000), and spends ($7,000 x 42 + $380,000 = $674,000). The owner therefore gains $26,000, compared to the loss of $42,000 resulting from lay up. They should take the charter, even though the rate is less than the 'full cost' of the trip.

The same conclusion would of course be reached if the capital costs of $3000 per day had been included. The total costs of lay up would be $42,000 + (42x$3000) = $168,000, whilst the total profit (loss) from trading would be $700,000 – $420,000 –$380,000 = ($100,000). This is of course, a loss making situation, but it is in fact the best that the owner can do in the circumstances. The $100,000 loss is in fact *smaller* than the loss made by the owner if the lay-up option were chosen, which is $168,000. Note that the difference between the losses, $68,000, is exactly the sum of the cost saving from not laying up ($42,000), and the net revenue (extra revenue minus extra costs resulting from continuing to trade ($26,000).

The hypothetical example ignored any additional costs incurred with the lay up itself; including these would of course only serve to emphasise the fact that trading will often take place at market rates which are less than the long run costs of providing the service.

At what point will it become worthwhile to lay-up? One way of answering this is to develop a model of the 'breakeven level of freight rates' needed to maintain trading. This will be explored in section 5.6 below.

The analysis carried out so far has implicitly assumed that the basic unit of analysis is the vessel itself; i.e. the firm is a one ship operation. Whilst this assumption may be reasonable for many small dry cargo companies, it is not true for a large number of dry cargo firms who operate several vessels, maybe hundreds. As the number of ships operated by companies increases, the role of ship management, of planning and communications, all become more significant. It might be expected that these costs, which are generally unrelated to the level of output produced by the company's vessels (although they may be related to the number of vessels operated and controlled) will increase as a share of total costs, as the company size expands. On the other hand, the discussion in Lesson 4 also indicated that larger firms may experience lower unit costs for a number of reasons; there are two forces at play here which can work in opposite directions.

It is widely argued that Tramp Operators tend to have a higher proportion of their costs as variable costs when compared to other market segments. S. A. Lawrence[5] points out that:

> "Tramp companies operate with smaller overheads than liners and have no commitment to maintaining a regular service, enjoying greater flexibility in the use of their ships."

As a final point in this section, it is worth emphasising that the distinction between short run fixed and variable costs is not clear cut. It depends on the nature of the problem being considered, and on the type of vessel under analysis, as well as the time period involved. In our discussion of the lay-up problem, some items of daily operating costs could be avoided, so were treated as variable. But if the owner was considering between two trading options,

---

[5] S.A. Lawrence (1978) *International Sea Transport*

the entire daily running cost would become fixed, because all those elements could not be avoided. Time is also an important factor. The shorter the time period under consideration, the greater the proportion of costs that will be fixed. Once a vessel is at her loading berth or a voyage is commenced practically all costs become unavoidable.

## 5.6 THE USE OF BREAKEVEN ANALYSIS IN DETERMINING MINIMUM FREIGHT RATES

A well-known method in both economics and management is to present information on revenue and costs in the form of a break-even analysis. The normal procedure is to calculate the load factor or level of utilisation required to break-even. If actual load factors or utilisation levels exceed the calculated number, it is clear that profits are being made. If, on the other hand, the target load factor figure does not materialise, losses will be made.

Whilst defining the load factor may well be significant in the liner trades, whose vessels operate to a timetable, whether or not they are fully loaded, this is not normally the case for dry cargo shipping, where full cargo loads are usually the rule, rather than the exception.

Instead of applying the model to working out the breakeven load factor, it can instead be employed to work out the 'break even rate' i.e. the freight rate which will ensure that a full cargo load will generate sufficient revenue to cover costs. This is a very plausible use to put this model to, because freight rates in the dry cargo trades are quite volatile; it is therefore quite useful to work out the minimum rate required to break even.

The model is based on the following assumptions:

1. The vessel is taken as the basic unit of analysis.

2. Costs and revenues are assumed to be linear (i.e. total variable costs rise in constant proportion to output, and total revenues also rise in constant proportion to output. This implies that the average revenue, or unit price, of freight rate per tonne of cargo, is constant over the volume of output being examined, and the average variable cost is also constant as output changes.)

3. The market contains many sellers (shipowners) and many buyers (charterers) who cannot influence the market rate on their own.

4. This means that the actual freight rate is taken as fixed, since no individual has any ability to alter it. Each individual is said to be a price taker.

Figure 5.1 overleaf shows the standard breakeven model, drawn for the current market rate. The *slope* of the line OF represents the market price; since total revenues rise in line with volume carried, the price is constant all the way along OF.

At cargo quantity OQ3, which represents a full cargo load, total revenue is given by the vertical distance Q3F. On the other hand, if no cargo is carried at all, total revenue is zero. Total fixed costs are OP, which is the same value as Q3V. Total fixed costs are the same, no matter what cargo quantity is loaded. Total variable costs are the difference between total costs and total fixed costs; at zero cargo quantity, they are zero, so total costs equal OP. When the maximum cargo quantity is loaded, total costs rise to Q3T, and the distance VT represents total variable costs at that level of output.

## Figure 5.1 – Break Even Model

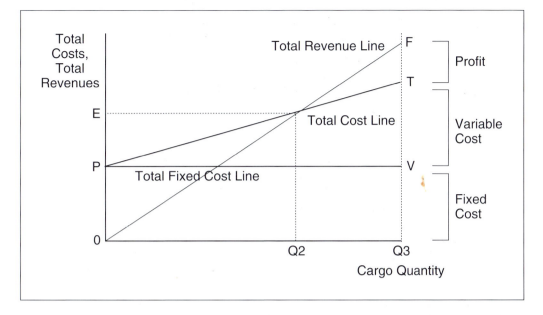

It is clear from Figure 5.1 that total revenue equals total cost at cargo quantity level OQ2, with associated total cost = total revenue = OE. This cargo quantity is called the *breakeven* quantity, because it is at this point that total revenues cover both variable and fixed costs. The figure is often expressed as a percentage of the maximum quantity that can be carried or produced, a number which is found by measuring the ratio of OQ2/OQ3. Then multiplying by 100.

### 5.6.1    Finding the Breakeven Rate

The above analysis was outlined in Lesson 4, so it should be familiar to you by now. In the tramp shipping context it is perhaps more useful to use this model in a slightly different way. Instead of asking the question "What cargo quantity do we need to load in order to break even?" the question is changed to "What freight rate do we need to break even?"

The assumption that is needed for this analysis is that the vessel will always trade at or very near its full cargo carrying capacity for the voyage being considered. Figure 5.2 shows the new situation.

## Figure 5.2 – The Break Even Freight Rate Model

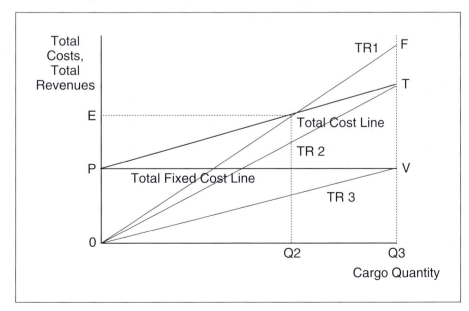

Two additional total revenue lines have been added to the diagram. Each represents the behaviour of total revenue at *different freight rates.* The slope of TR2 represents a lower level of freight rate than TR1, and TR3's slope corresponds to a lower rate than TR2. In other words, the flatter the slope of the total revenue line, the lower the freight rate per tonne of cargo.

Given the assumption that the vessel is always fully laden, it is clear that the break even rate must be given by the line TR2. If OQ3 tons of cargo are carried, a total revenue of Q3T is obtained, and total costs of OQ3T are incurred.

It follows that, if the freight rate is above that implied by the line TR2, then the tramp operator will make a profit. On the other hand, at a rate of TR3, he will make a loss.

Again, the question that can be put is; What is the lowest rate which the owner should accept? Or put another way, will the owner ever accept a rate lower than TR2?

The answer to the latter question is *yes.* The minimum short run rate that is acceptable depends on whether the losses incurred from accepting the business are smaller than the losses incurred from being idle. As long as total variable costs are covered, it is worthwhile accepting the business, if the loss so incurred is smaller than the loss arising from the vessel doing nothing.

In fact TR3, which represents that rate, must also reflect the slope of the total variable cost curve. Under the special assumptions of this model, it is the same as the *marginal cost*[6] of moving one more ton of cargo. Put another way, the price must never be below the marginal cost or producing the output, and *must never be less than the average variable cost of production.* This is in fact a general rule that always applies, no matter what the relationship is between costs and output.

Recall the discussion of lay-up. It is clear that the lower the proportion of variable costs to fixed costs in a shipowner's company, the greater the scope for the freight rate to fall *below* the long run total cost of producing that output, or of maintaining the ship. This is an important point to note, because it is one of the factors that helps to explain the sharp fluctuations that are observed in freight rates in the dry cargo trades, especially when contrasted with those set in the liner trades. Owners, in depressed markets, may well accept short run trip charters at rates well below those required to cover their long run costs, if the proportion of variable costs are low.

## 5.7   MODELLING THE DRY CARGO MARKET

A very simple cost model of a tramp ship owner has been discussed, in which freight rates were taken as given. In what follows, it is assumed that the market can be separated into specific segments, one of which is being modelled. The bulk dry trades is taken as an example, leaving the segment of smaller vessels and the markets that they serve to one side for the moment. The analytical framework developed here can still be applied to these other segments as well, provided that they satisfy the following assumptions:

1.   Each shipowner/ship management company is seeking to maximise their profits, (or minimise their losses).

2.   Each charterer is seeking the cheapest rate consistent with an acceptable quality of service offered by the shipowner.

3.   There are a large number of fixtures, the details of most of which are readily available to all market participants.

4.   The model of perfect competition is assumed to be an appropriate framework for analysing market behaviour. The assumptions underlying this model have been discussed in Section 2 above of this lesson.

---

[6] The concept and definition of marginal cost was discussed in Chapter 4

### 5.7.1    Modelling Demand

Readers may like to review their knowledge of demand from their study of Lesson 2. The individual shipper's firm requiring transport/shipping services regards the freight rate as a given value which they cannot alter through their own individual action. It is assumed that there is a downward sloping relationship between the cargo volumes required to be moved and the level of freight rates, other things held equal. The higher the rate, the smaller the demand for cargo movements, and vice versa.

Will market demand be very responsive, or very unresponsive, to a change in the freight rate? Both are possible and consistent with a downward sloping relationship between rates and cargo quantities. The discussion in Lesson 2 helps us to an answer to this question.

The demand for dry cargo tonne miles is a *derived demand.* Lesson 2 reviewed the basic principles underlying the estimation of price elasticities for derived demands.

The principal factors were:

1. The value of the own price elasticity of demand for the final good.

2. The existence of close substitutes

3. The proportion of the total final price which transport constitutes.

Take grain as an example. Grain movements are driven by production and consumption trends in different regions, by local weather conditions and crop yields, and by changing patterns of food consumption. Grain is itself an input; it is used to make bread or pasta, or fed to animals to produce meat. But bread, meat and pasta all *have low price elasticities* of demand. Most empirical evidence suggests that they are price inelastic.

Grain movements from major exporting regions such as North America have to go by sea. Air transport, whilst feasible for small volumes, is a very expensive alternative.

Freight rates are now about 5% of the final price of most traded commodities in West Europe (See Lesson 2 for more details).

The conclusion is that, taken as a whole, market demand is likely to be extremely inelastic with respect to changes in freight rates. The demand curve can be represented as an almost vertical line, as in Figure 5.3 below.

Note that this conclusion is for *the market as a whole.* It does not follow that demand conditions on any one trade route are also necessarily inelastic. It could be the case that the possible sourcing of demand from other countries and other routes makes the demand on each route much more sensitive to changes in the specific route's freight rate; indeed, owners will always be seeking out trades/routes which are more profitable than others. But the ability to switch vessels' from one route to another at relatively short notice implies that rates should not get too out of line with each other (allowing for genuine differences in costs between routes of course); and indeed, the behaviour of individual freight rates suggests that this is indeed the case.

## Figure 5.3 – Inelastic Freight Demand Schedules

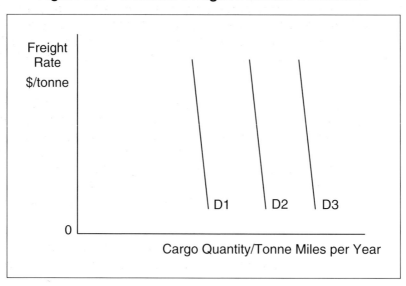

Freight rates are measured on the vertical axis and quantity of the commodity (or cargo tonne miles) are measured on the horizontal axis. D1, D2, and D3 show three different demand schedules, each further out to the right. These represent different volumes of demand, generated by higher and higher levels of economic activity, industrial production, or world trade volumes. A fall from D2 to D1 would represent a decline in tonne miles demanded, or cargo tonnes moved, as we saw happen in Table 5.1 in 1986 for the tonnage data. A rise, or shift of the demand schedule from D2 to D3, would represent the long term expectation.

Recall that there are cycles of demand growth. In some periods the demand schedule will be shifting rapidly out to the right, reflecting boom conditions; in other years, it will be hardly shifting at all, and perhaps even declining.

Over a long time period, it is anticipated that the trend will be a shift out to the right.

### 5.7.2 Supply

Given the discussion of short run costs in Lesson 4, and the discussion of short run supply in Lesson 2, it is time to try to integrate these two. Under competitive conditions, it was pointed out that the shipowner should never accept a freight rate that is less than the average variable cost of the ship's output. It has also been pointed out that different ships have different costs, because either they are of different ages, or because they operate under different flags, or face different wage costs.

Imagine that all these costs were known, and that a ranking could be organised, starting with the dry cargo bulk vessel with the lowest average variable cost, moving up to the next, and so on until the last, most expensive vessel is brought in. If the freight rate were high enough, and cargo volumes large enough, all these vessels will be employed. Now imagine the rate is steadily reduced. Which vessels will cease trading first?

The answer should be clear; those with the highest variable, or avoidable costs. As the rate is remorselessly lowered, more vessels are forced into idleness, until none are trading. Furthermore, it was earlier demonstrated that capital costs should play no role in the lay-up decision in the short run, since these costs have to be met whether or not the vessel is being traded. Older vessels will tend to have higher operating costs than newer vessels, partly because they will be designed with older, less efficient equipment in place, partly because they will require greater crew numbers than modern ships, and partly because they may have older, more fuel inefficient engines. It is not surprising then, to observe that the majority of laid up vessels are the older ones of the fleets.

The discussion to date has ignored the fact that, in the short run, vessel variable costs can themselves be altered by varying the operating speed. Lower speed means lower output and lower costs. If freight rates are low because demand is low, the loss of output is more than offset by the benefits of slower steaming. Thus it is possible to expect the supply of tonne miles, the supply curve discussed in Lesson 3, to be directly related to the cost considerations discussed in Lesson 4, and here.

The shape of the supply schedule drawn in Figure 3.3 of Lesson 3 is repeated below. It is drawn so that it becomes steeper in slope as maximum tonne mile production is attained. There are two reasons for this. Firstly, the additional tonne miles being created near 'full capacity' are being created by the more inefficient vessels in the fleet, the ones with higher variable costs. These vessels add a lot to costs without adding that much extra to output. Secondly, speed increases are a limited way of raising output, as seen in Lesson 4. The extra costs of fuel consumption increase more rapidly than the extra output, so the required supply price increases.

The curve eventually becomes vertical, representing the notion of full capacity utilisation. *No more output can be obtained from the existing fleet, in the short term.*

In the language of economics, the supply curve represents the additional, or marginal costs, of meeting the extra output required. This proposition is only valid if the market is itself competitive.

### Figure 5.4 – Short Run Shipping Supply Curve

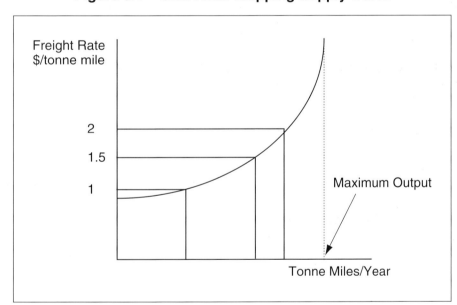

## 5.8    DETERMINING THE EQUILIBRIUM FREIGHT RATE

The market is defined as the interaction of supply and demand, which both together determine the equilibrium freight rate and quantities sold at that rate. Figure 5.5 overleaf shows several different possible short run market equilibria, each determined by different demand conditions. The key factors that make demand conditions alter relate to the volume of world trade, which is driven by overall economic activity, and changing degrees of openness towards trade by individual nations. Demand curves further to the right represent larger trade volumes.

Demand volumes increase from D1 to D4. Between D1 to D3 there is a relatively small rise in the market freight rate and a large rise in tonne miles produced. But between D3 and D4, the increase in demand is translated into large increases in rates, because supply becomes very inelastic, and the scope for increases in supply become increasingly limited.

## Figure 5.5 – Short Run Market Interaction

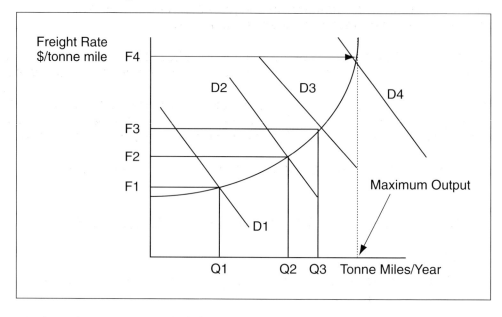

The above model can be used to examine short run fluctuations in market conditions, but not long run ones. This is because the supply schedule represented in Figure 5.5 is drawn for a given stock of ships, as discussed in Lesson 3. It is a useful framework to explore fluctuations in freight rates in the short term however.

Consider the shift in demand from D3 to D4. Rates move up very sharply, and supply does not increase much. This creates large profits for existing shipowners, who will be encouraged to order new vessels. The value of existing vessels will also rise, reflecting the markets' expectation that profits are going to be healthy in the future. The increased number of orders will translate into a rightward shift in the supply curve in the long term, and this will lead, to a fall in rates if demand remains at D4.

On the other hand, a fall in demand from D2 to D1 means a fall in supply and a rise in vessel lay-ups. Remember that in the short run, some vessels will be trading at rates which do not cover their full costs. While this is acceptable in the short term, it is not the case in the longer term. Some vessels will be laid up, or scrapped. The scrapping of vessels, as shown in Lesson 3, leads to a leftwards shift of the supply curve. This process will help raise rates if the supply shifts far enough.

### Extending the model

More detail can be incorporated into the basic model by considering, first, how the increase (decrease) in short run supply can be implemented. A rise (fall) in demand generates the rise (fall) in rates. The higher (lower) rates create incentives to increase (decrease) tonne miles supplied through the following mechanisms:

a)   The higher (lower) rates encourage a higher (slower) speed, where possible in terms of sailing timetables.

b)   The higher (lower) rates will encourage owners with high variable cost vessels to bring them out of (out them into) lay-up.

In the long term, higher (lower) freight rates and low (high) rates of lay-up will encourage owners to order newbuildings or delay scrapping (cancel existing orders/stop ordering or increase scrapping). These processes will shift the supply curve out to the right in the case of an increase in demand, or to the left in the opposite case.

A key factor influencing this decision is the *expectations* of shipowners. The expectations of future levels of freight demand, and freight rates, will be critical in determining how the market reacts to short term changes in demand and rate levels.

If owners are fundamentally optimistic about the future, falling rates in the short term may not lead to a longer term reduction in shipping capacity. If that expectation is false, however, it will be revised, and those changes will take place.

On the other hand, pessimistic expectations about the future will reinforce any short term downturns, and may lead to a shortage of capacity if demand grows unexpectedly rapidly.

Expectations can be very volatile, and their volatility helps explain the sudden increases and equally sudden falls that have been observed in rate movements, particularly when political events, wars or other events which have strategic impacts on dry cargo markets.

The analysis of how expectations are formed is beyond the scope of this lesson.

## 5.9    CONFRONTING THE MODEL WITH THE EVIDENCE

The above model implies:

1.  That freight rates should be sensitive to short run market conditions, reflecting both present and expected future situations.

2.  There will be a strong positive correlation between demand growth and new orders, provided that the present stock of vessels are highly utilised (low levels of lay-ups)

3.  There will be a strong positive correlation between freight rates and new orders, with periods of high rates associated with higher than average orders, lower than average lay-ups and scrapping.

4.  Exceptional events will generate significant increases in rates, if they occur when existing shipping capacity is being fully stretched. These are usually anticipations or outbreaks of war, or strategically important changes, such as the closure of the Suez Canal in 1967, re-opened finally in 1975. This closure, was of course, war related.

**Figure 5.6 – Freight Rates from 1860 to 1975**

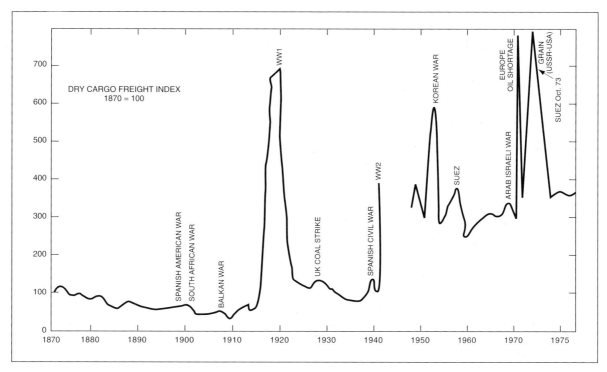

89

Figure 5.6 shows the freight rates for just over 100 years from 1870 to 1975. From this graph, we can suggest that:

- freight rates are low for longer periods than they are high. This low plateau should in theory be the 'equilibrium freight', or break-even freight, where the Shipowner's revenue is only just slightly above that point where he would consider laying up.

- the high freight rates are not caused by high demand as such, but where some unexpected 'disaster' creates a temporary need for more ships. If you were cynical, you might observe that strikes, famines and wars were good for Shipowners (though note the exception of the Arab-Israeli war in October 1973.

- the high rates in the First World War were due to the high insurance premiums charged at this time[1].

Note that there are substantial periods of demand growth in which freight rates do not fluctuate all that dramatically. In these periods, either there is plenty of capacity available to meet any increase in demand, or the expansion of demand is matched by the correct expansion of capacity, brought about by accurate expectations generating the correct level of ordering. The 'spikes' are generated by events which are not completely anticipated by the market – and as noted earlier, tend to be wars or war related events which impact on the shipping markets.

A clear example of such a boom is that of the early 1970s. Growth in demand for shipping services was very high in the late 60's early 70's, with one peak observable in 1970. World commodity prices rose sharply in the period up to 1973, and shipowners fell over themselves to order new vessels. Many of these were of the new large designs, as this was the period of rapid increases in the sizes of dry bulkers. In September 1973 this all came to a halt with the six day Arab-Israeli war ending with the closure of the Suez canal and the Arab oil embargo on countries seen as pro-Israel. The 400% rise in the price of crude oil delivered a huge shock to the Western economies that had been previously growing quite rapidly. Their economic growth faltered (the UK's real income fell in 1974), and has never really recovered. But lower growth means lower growth in the demand for shipping movements.

The change in the rate of demand occurred precisely when ship orders were very high. So, in the rest of the 1970's, owners had to grapple with the problems of slower demand growth and much larger levels of shipping capacity. In fact recovery has only occurred in that past decade or so.

It is worth re-examining Table 5.1 in the context of the above comments, and relating the data to the information contained in Figure 5.6. The rate peaks of 1970 and 1973 correspond to the years of highest annual growth of tonnage carried, of 13.6 in 1970 and 10.7 in 1973. Note that demand actually declined by nearly 5% in 1975. In 1970 and 1973, there was very little laid up tonnage. In 1984, as can be seen from Table 5.1, over 20% of the fleet was laid up. The increase in demand was easily met from existing capacity, and no peak in the rate is observed.

These observations are consistent with the demand/supply model discussed above; in the first two peaks, demand is at or near full capacity – so further increases help generate large rate increases as supply response is very small. But in the 1984 case, there is plenty of spare capacity and similar sized increase in demand is met with no corresponding rise in freight rates.

---

[1]  P. M. Alderton – *Reeds Sea Transport: Operation and Economics* (5th Edition) 2004. Page 142/3.

### 5.9.1    Historical Developments

**Figure 5.7 – Shows the behaviour of certain dry cargo rates over
the period 1989-1996**

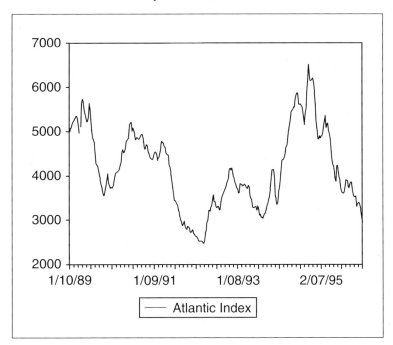

Source: SS&Y Research Department

The SS&Y Atlantic index tracks the movements of freight rates on 9 major routes which Capesize (120,000dwt) tramp vessels operate on, and reflects their behaviour in index number form. The marked volatility of the index reveals just how sensitive rates are to current demand and supply conditions. The recent boom in the dry cargo sector is clearly reflected in the peak values of the index in the 1994 to 1995 period. Rates are clearly very responsive to changes in market conditions.

## 5.10    DYNAMIC CONSIDERATIONS

The model employed so far has concentrated primarily upon current demand and current supply conditions. The only additional factor which has been discussed is the role of expectations – they help determine owners' ordering, scrapping and operational decisions, because ships are long lived assets, and owners need to form a view about future market conditions as well as considering the present.

The question arises then, just how are these expectations formed? What shapes them?

One possible answer is that they are shaped by our knowledge of the past. Past data, recent trends, can be projected forward to help shape our guess as to future demand conditions. There is a lot to be said in support of this. The huge wave of ship ordering in the early 1970's can be seen as a response to the widely held view that the market was going to continue to grow as rapidly in the second half of the 1970's as it did up until late 1973. If one anticipates good times, one needs to order new vessels early, as they may take 18 months to 2 years to be built. If these expectations are correct – no problem – demand grows as everyone expects, and the capacity is there to meet it.

But suppose the expectations turn out to be incorrect – the unexpected happens. The vessels have been ordered, and a large number of them are delivered. Market conditions in the late 1970's become a nightmare for owners (but wonderful for charterers). The market is left in turmoil, with large numbers of vessels and little growth in demand.

Trying to understand demand and supply conditions in 1978 would therefore make very little sense if one just examined 1978's demand and 1978's supply. The supply available in 1978 is itself the consequence of *past* decisions by owners. It is this fact that leads to the conclusion that the market will generate its own dynamic behaviour over time, as it continually readjusts to new demand conditions as best it can.

The poor trading conditions of the late 1970's early 80's influenced newbuilding. Orders became relatively scarce. But if demand conditions alter for the better, this lack of new investment may itself generate another 'cycle' in the market.

The fact is, dry cargo markets appear to move through 'cycles' of boom, recession, slump, recovery, and back to boom again. These cycles are partly generated by the cyclical growth in demand, but are also a result of the fact that supply adjustment is a slow and often painful process in markets where the assets are long lived, as they are in shipping. Thus it may be more sensible to modify our demand and supply model to allow for the presence of such cycles of economic activity.

Some observers have suggested that there are cycles of different periods observable in the market, overlaying each other. For example, one might observe a seasonal pattern of demand as being the shortest cycle. On top of that, world demand growth appears to cycle over 5-7 years. Ship supply cycles are longer reflecting the average age of 13 years. Finally, some observers (Kondratieff), have suggested very long cyclical patterns, of around 50 years.

Whether or not one accepts the presence of all of these, it is undeniable that viewing the market as a dynamic one, as a process in which demand conditions and supply responses change over time, gives a much richer picture of the way the market operates. Unfortunately, it is also a more complex idea to grasp. But realising that ship supply response to a change in demand is often spread out over several periods, years even, is a step in the right direction.

## 5.11    CONCLUSION

This lesson has examined the Dry Cargo Market for Tramp Shipping in some detail. After examining the changing definitions of a Tramp, and the changing nature of the market, various aspects of the costs of operating as a tramp were explored. It was argued that the dry cargo market could be viewed as a highly competitive market structure, close to perfect competition. A model of the market was developed based on this assumption. Demand was always price inelastic, but supply elasticity depended upon the present level of fleet utilisation. The behaviour of market rates was examined, and the data related to that provided in Table 5.1. Finally, the dynamic nature of the market was emphasised.

## 5.12   SELF-ASSESSMENT AND TEST QUESTIONS

Attempt the following and check your answers from the text.

1. Why has the definition of the Tramp Shipping Industry moved from a definition based on vessel type to one based on market characteristics?

2. Write out, in your own words, the main characteristics of a competitive market.

3. Write your own definition of:
   i)   Fixed Costs
   ii)   Variable Costs

   and illustrate how these costs will change for a particular vessel type over different periods of time.

4. What additional costs might be incurred if a vessel is to be laid up? What *demand* factors also affect the Lay-Up decision?

Having completed your study of Chapter Five, attempt the following and submit it to your Tutor.

Why is the dry cargo market regarded as being perfectly competitive? Relate your explanation to the empirical evidence.

Illustrate your answer with the use of diagrams or models.

# Chapter 6

# COMPETITIVE SHIPPING MARKETS:
# Tankers

## 6.1    INTRODUCTION

What is a tanker vessel? A tanker may be defined as a vessel which is specifically designed to carry liquid cargoes. The most common types of cargo carried in such vessels are chemicals, wine, vegetable and other food oils, refined oil products and crude oil. This lesson will concentrate on the market for crude oil tankers, as it is by far the largest. The markets for crude oil and refined products are often referred to as the tanker trades.

The tanker trades are a subject that can be written about at great length; they are a fascinating subject in their own right. The principal reasons for studying them are:

1.    The oil trades have grown enormously over the past 30 years; but they have also grown very unevenly. The problems of the 1980's tanker markets cannot be understood without some knowledge of earlier periods.

2.    Tanker average sizes grew dramatically, especially in the early 1970's. Although there has been a small decline in average size in the late 1980's, this trend has recently reversed, although the size distribution is not expected to change much in the next few years.

3.    Specialisation in tankers has also developed in the last twenty years, with more dedicated specialised vessels appearing in the product trades.

4.    Politics has played a special role in this sector, because of the strategic nature of the cargo, and because of the huge macroeconomic effects that the dramatic oil price changes have had upon the world economy. A study of the tanker trade is incomplete unless some discussion of this fact is undertaken.

5.    Because of its extreme political sensitivity, tanker freight rates have exhibited marked sudden increases from time to time, usually associated with wars. Whilst it is true that most commodity prices are sensitive to acts of aggression, oil prices and tanker freight rates appear to be especially affected.

In this Chapter, the reasons for the volatility of tanker rates will be explored. The essential explanation lies in the recognition of the fact that the tanker market, despite some appearances to the contrary, is a very competitive one; indeed, some sectors of it are more competitive now than they were 30 years ago. The competitive nature of the market, when coupled with its sensitivity to strategic and political issues, has made it an extremely volatile market in the past.[1]

## 6.2    SEABORNE TRADE AND THE DISTINCTION BETWEEN CRUDE AND OIL PRODUCTS

The oil market is traditionally split between the analysis of unrefined, or crude oil and the markets for refined oil, or oil products. Each barrel of oil when refined, yields different quantities of various products, ranging from petrol and kerosene (lighter fractions) to bitumen, and road surfacing

---

[1] For further detailed discussion see J. McConville (1999) The Economics of Maritime Transport, Theory and Practice, Witherby, London Chapter 10

material (heavier fractions). These different products are generated at the oil refinery, which can vary the proportions generated, but only very slightly. Some of the refined products (the lighter fractions) are more volatile than the original crude oil, whilst the heavier ones (e.g. bitumen) may have to be kept warm in order to prevent them from becoming almost solid.

The oil trades therefore consists of moving either the crude material from its place of extraction (the oil well) to the refinery, and the movement of refined products from the refineries to the final consumer. It should be clear that the location of the refinery is crucial in determining the relative balance of these two trades. In the 1950's, many refineries were built near final consumer markets, in both North America, and West Europe. This was a mixture of political and economic reasons. The political reason was to keep refinery capacity in countries that were economically stable; the economic factor is that transporting products involves small, relatively expensive vessels, whereas crude can be moved in larger, cheaper vessels. Moving the bulk of the cargo in crude form minimised the overall transportation cost to the consumer. Thus the crude trades evolved more rapidly, dominating cargo movements by volume.

This pattern has changed slightly with the construction of refineries in the Middle East, and the growth of Asian consumption, but it is still a pretty accurate description of the main forces shaping the movement of crude and products, which is now explored in more detail.

### 6.2.1    The development of Seaborne Oil Trades

Just before the First World War tankers constituted some 3% of the world fleet. By 1938 they had increased to 19% and by the late 1970s, just under 50% of the world tonnage (See Table 6.1 for the data). In deadweight tonnage terms, the world tanker fleet grew from 17mn dwt in 1938 to 332mn dwt in 1977, a spectacular increase. World oil production, which, of course, is a key driving force in the growth of the oil trades, rose from 258mn tons in 1938 to over 10 times that in 1977. It has continued to increase, albeit at a greatly reduced rate, in the 1990s.

The increase in world oil production has not however, been even. It increased fourfold between 1938 and 1957, 3.5 fold between 1957 and 1977. Growth has slowed abruptly since – between 1977 and 1988 production hardly increased at all (2915mn tons to 3050mn tons). Since 1988 production has increased gradually, reaching a historical high of 3,533mn tons in 1998.

Oil consumption growth is the key to the behaviour of production, since the two will be very close over the longer term, differences being accounted for by changes in oil stocks. Table 6.2 shows the annual growth rates of consumption over five year intervals from 1960-65 to 1990-95. It reveals significant differences in the growth pattern over this period.

In the period 1960-70, oil consumption grew at 7 or 8% per annum compound, a tremendous rate of growth. It slowed down in the 1970's, and *actually declined* in the period 1980-85, when consumption *fell* by 1.3% per annum. The nadir of the period was reached in the mid-eighties. Since then, consumption growth has become positive, although the rate for the past five years is still very small.

Whilst trends in oil production and consumption are reasonable indicators of the likely growth in demand for shipping oil and oil products, a much more accurate measure is that provided in Row 2 of Table 6.1, which shows the volume of oil shipped on an annual basis. Between 1967 and 1977 this volume doubled; 59% of all oil produced in the world was moved by sea in that year. Note the change in the *share*; the increase in the share taken by seaborne oil movements over the previous decade means that the demand for *shipping oil rose faster in this period than the growth in the demand for oil itself*. Conversely, between 1977 and 1987, although oil production remained roughly static, the share of oil shipped by sea declined to 44%. A static level of production and consumption, combined with a falling share, means falling demand for shipping services in this sector – a classic example of *derived demand* at work. Indeed, oil movements declined from 1724mn tons in 1977 to 1279mn tons in 1987, before beginning to recover. Indeed, it is only in 1994 that the total cargoes moved by sea exceeds the 1977 level, and continued to do so in the late 1990s, when measured in tons of cargo moved.

## Table 6.1 – Development of the International Oil Trade

| | 1938 | 1957 | 1967 | 1977 | 1987 | 1988 | 1989 | 1990 | 1991 | 1992 | 1993 | 1994 | 1995 | 1996 | 1997 | 1998 | 1999 | 2000 | 2001 | 2002 | 2003 |
|---|---|---|---|---|---|---|---|---|---|---|---|---|---|---|---|---|---|---|---|---|---|
| World Production Million Tons | 258 | 853 | 1,758 | 2,915 | 2,925 | 3,050 | 3,116 | 3,179 | 3,156 | 3,182 | 3,179 | 3,213 | 3,252 | 3,372 | 3,473 | 3,540 | 3,468 | 3,604 | 3,586 | 3,562 | 3,697 |
| Seaborne Trade (Mn Tonnes)[1] | — | — | 865 (49%) | 1,724 (59%) | 1,279 (44%) | 1,370 (45%) | 1,460 (47%) | 1,526 (48%) | 1,573 (50%) | 1,648 (52%) | 1,714 (54%) | 1,771 (55%) | 1,808 (56%) | 2,127 | 2,172 | 2,181 | 2,159 | 2,027 | 2,017 | 1,987 | — |
| Billion Tonne Miles | 4,130 | 11,467 | 6,016 | 6,510 | 7,276 | 7,821 | 8,281 | 8,597 | 9,166 | 9,329 | 9,320 | 9,403 | 9,880 | 9,763 | 9,510 | 9,859 | 10,035 | 10,265 | 10,179 | 9,950 | — |
| Average Haul | 4,775 | 6,65 | 4,704 | 4,752 | 4,984 | 5,125 | 5,264 | 5,217 | 5,347 | 5,268 | 5,155 | — | — | — | — | — | — | — | — | — | — |
| World Tanker Fleet Mn DWT | 16.6 | 49.6 | 103.5 | 332.3 | 245.5 | 245.0 | 248.4 | 257.4 | 264.2 | 270.6 | 270.2 | 269.4 | 263.0 | 271.5 | 272.0 | 279.5 | 284.5 | 313.9 | 327.4 | 330.07 | 333.2 |
| Tanker Productivity[2] | | | 8.4 | 5.2 | 5.2 | 5.6 | 6.1 | 6.2 | 6.2 | 6.3 | 6.4 | 6.7 | 6.8 | — | — | — | — | — | — | — | — |
| % of World Fleet | 19 | 28 | 36 | 46 | 38 | 38 | 40 | 40 | 39.8 | 40 | 40.4 | 40.6 | 39.7 | 35.8 | 35.1 | 35.4 | 35.4 | 41.8 | 42.2 | 42.0 | 40.8 |

Sources: Tutorship Manual 1989; BP Statistical Review of World Energy 1996; OECD Maritime Transport Review 1994; Drewry Statistics 1996, ISL Market Reports 1996. Average Haul defined as billion tonne miles/million tons cargo. Figures for tanker tonnage may not be exactly comparable. Those from 1987 are for tankers greater than 10,000dwt, as in the Platou Reports.

*Note:*

[1] This is the % of total production in Seaborne Trade

[2] Defined as Tons Cargo moved per dwt of fleet per year

## Table 6.2 – Oil Consumption Annual Growth Rates % per annum

| 1960-1965 | 7.2 | 1980–1985 | -1.3 |
|-----------|-----|-----------|------|
| 1965-1970 | 8.2 | 1985-1990 | 2.25 |
| 1970-1975 | 3.1 | 1990-1995 | 0.28 |
| 1975-1979 | 4.0 | 1993-2003 | 1.6 |

Source: BP Statistical Review of World Energy 1995 and 2003

### 6.2.2 Change in Tonne Miles and Journey Length

The growth and decline of oil tonnage movements tells only part of the story of demand change. As has been discussed in earlier lessons, demand can be measured in terms of tonne miles, as well as in tonnage terms. Rows 5 and 6 of Table 6.1 are well worth studying for a few minutes. Between 1967 and 1977, while oil cargo shipments doubled, the tonne miles performed nearly trebled (4130 to 11467). The difference is the two arises from the fact that the average length of haul rose from 4775 nautical miles in 1967 to 6651 in 1977. A large part of the increase can be related to the closure of the Suez Canal in 1967, which didn't then reopen until 1975. As a consequence, the haulage distance between the major exporting centre (the Middle East) and two major importing centres, North America and West Europe, increased dramatically, being routed around the Cape of Good Hope.

The increase in haul length gave a dramatic impetus to the development of large tankers, as 100,000, 250,000 and even 500,000dwt vessels were designed and built in the period 1967-1975.

Between 1977 and 1987 the average haul declined by nearly 50%. Note that this coincides with a decline in the volume of tonnage moved as well. Essentially demand for tanker services collapses dramatically during this period, creating very severe problems for tanker owners and operators. The market response to this will be considered later in this lesson.

### 6.2.3 Changes in the Regional Balance of Oil Consumption and Production

Everyone is well aware that the Middle East is the major source of oil exports. However, what is less well known is that the *share* of oil production has fluctuated quite dramatically during the period. The relevant data for production and consumption shares are shown in Tables 6.3 and 6.4 below.

## Table 6.3 – Regional Shares of World Oil Consumption

|            | 1965 | 1970 | 1975 | 1980 | 1985 | 1990 | 1994 | 1995 | 1996 |
|------------|------|------|------|------|------|------|------|------|------|
| N. America | 39   | 34   | 31   | 31   | 28   | 28   | 30.4 | 28.2 | 28.2 |
| W. Europe  | 25   | 28   | 24   | 23   | 20   | 19   | 20.5 | 19.8 | 19.7 |
| M. East    | 2    | 2    | 2    | 2    | 4.5  | 4.5  | 5.7  | 5.8  | 5.8  |
| Africa     | 2    | 2    | 2    | 2    | 2.9  | 2.8  | 3.2  | 3.1  | 3.2  |
| Asia       | 8    | 12   | 12   | 13   | 16.5 | 18.7 | 25.2 | 25.6 | 28.1 |
| USSR/EE    | 12   | 9    | 14   | 14   | 18.7 | 16.9 | 9.2  | 6.8  | 6.0  |
| Other      | 12   | 12   | 15   | 15   | 9    | 9.4  | 5.8  | 10.7 | 9.0  |

Sources: Glen (1987), BP Review of World Energy 1995, International Energy Agency 1997

North America accounted for 39% of the world's oil consumption in 1965, and 30% of production. It therefore needed to meet its full consumption needs by importing. West Europe accounted for 25% of world oil consumption in 1965, and had no oil production. It was even more dependent on oil imports than North America.

### Table 6.4 Regional Shares of World Oil Production

|            | 1965 | 1970 | 1975 | 1980 | 1985 | 1990 | 1994 | 1995 | 1996 |
|------------|------|------|------|------|------|------|------|------|------|
| N. America | 30   | 26   | 20   | 18   | 26.2 | 20.7 | 20.3 | 15.7 | 15.3 |
| W. Europe  | —    | —    | n.s. | n.s. | 6.8  | 6.3  | 9.0  | 13.9 | 9.2  |
| M. East    | 27   | 29   | 36   | 33   | 18.5 | 27.2 | 29.8 | 27.1 | 26.5 |
| Africa     | 7    | 13   | 9    | 10   | 9.4  | 10.1 | 10.3 | 9.6  | 9.8  |
| Asia       | —    | —    | —    | —    | 10.2 | 10.1 | 10.6 | 8.2  | 10.0 |
| USSR/EE    | 17   | 16   | 19   | 19   | 22.1 | 18.4 | 11.7 | 10.2 | 9.8  |
| Other      | 19   | 16   | 16   | 20   | 6.8  | 7.2  | 8.3  | 15.3 | 19.4 |
| Mn Tonnes  | 1565 | 2331 | 2733 | 3222 | 2796 | 3179 | 3213 | 3266 | 3362 |

Sources: Glen (1987), BP Review of World Energy 1995, International Energy Agency 1997

The Middle East, on the other hand, accounted for 2% of the world's oil consumption and produced 27% of the world's oil (note it was a smaller share than North America's!).

By 1980, several changes can be observed. North America's share of world consumption falls to 31% (but note that the total consumption doubled from 1565 to 3222mn tonnes), and its share of world production has fallen to 18% – it had become increasingly dependent on imports. Although North Sea Oil had been discovered, it did not come on stream until the 1980's; so Western Europe's consumption share of 23% is still dominated by imports. The Middle East's share of production now stood at 33%.

In the 1990's, the decline of output and prosperity in the former Soviet Block countries shows up clearly, with their share of consumption falling to 6% in 1996, from 17% in 1990. North America, Europe and the Middle East itself have seen their shares rise over this period, with North America accounting for 28% of the market in 1996.

During the 1980's, Middle East production was seriously reduced due to the Iran-Iraq war. This shows up clearly in the data in Table 6.4, with the Middle East's share of world production falling to 18.5% in 1985. Note the corresponding increase in shares of North America and the rise in Asian and North Sea production.

Production shares have altered in the 1990's, with the Soviet Block's share decline being mirrored by increases in the regional production shares of the Middle East (rising sharply to 29%, with small increases in West Europe's share, from 6 to 9%.) Other regions have remained broadly unchanged, with North America accounting for 20% of the world's oil consumption.

The trading pattern of the first half of 1995 is represented by Figure 6.1, using data provided by E A Gibsons (Shipbrokers). As the analysis of the share data suggested, the major exporter of crude oil is the Middle East countries, dominated by Saudi Arabia. The OECD European countries have now sourced approximately one third of their import requirements from the North Sea, the Middle East and East Europe/Russia. In Asia, 80% of oil imports are from the Middle East. Figure 6.1 also identifies the USA as a major importer, running at 6.5 million barrels per day in this period.

Table 6.5 shows similar data as Figure 6.1, except the flows are expressed in shares, and represent 1989, 1994, 1995 and 2000. West Europe and the USA accounted around 50% of all imports, followed by Japan (16%). On the export side, the Middle East dominates with 45%,

## Table 6.5 Major Oil Trade Movements (% shares)

| | | 1989 | 1994 | 1995 | 2000 |
|---|---|---|---|---|---|
| Imports | USA | 26.5 | 27.3 | 24.4 | 26.0 |
| | W. Europe | 31.0 | 27.7 | 26.4 | 23.6 |
| | Japan | 15.0 | 15.8 | 15.4 | 12.5 |
| | Rest of the World | 27.5 | 29.2 | 33.8 | 37.9 |
| Exports | N. America | 5.8 | 6.3 | 10.4 | 10.3 |
| | Latin America | 11.6 | 7.5 | 7.7 | 7.2 |
| | M. East | 44.0 | 46.7 | 46.0 | 44.6 |
| | N. Africa | 8.0 | 7.5 | 7.4 | 6.4 |
| | W. Africa | 7.7 | 7.6 | 7.5 | 7.8 |
| | USSR/E. Eur./China | 11.5 | 7.3 | 6.4 | 10.8 |
| | Rest of the World | 5.4 | 17.1 | 14.6 | 12.9 |

Sources: Glen (1987), BP Review of World Energy 1995, International Energy Agency 1997

Note: Both Products and Crude Oil are included in the above.

with North and West Africa and Latin America accounting for about 7% each. It is noteworthy that Japan, a major oil importer, has no natural raw materials at all.

## Figure 6.1 – Schematic Crude Oil Movements, 1995

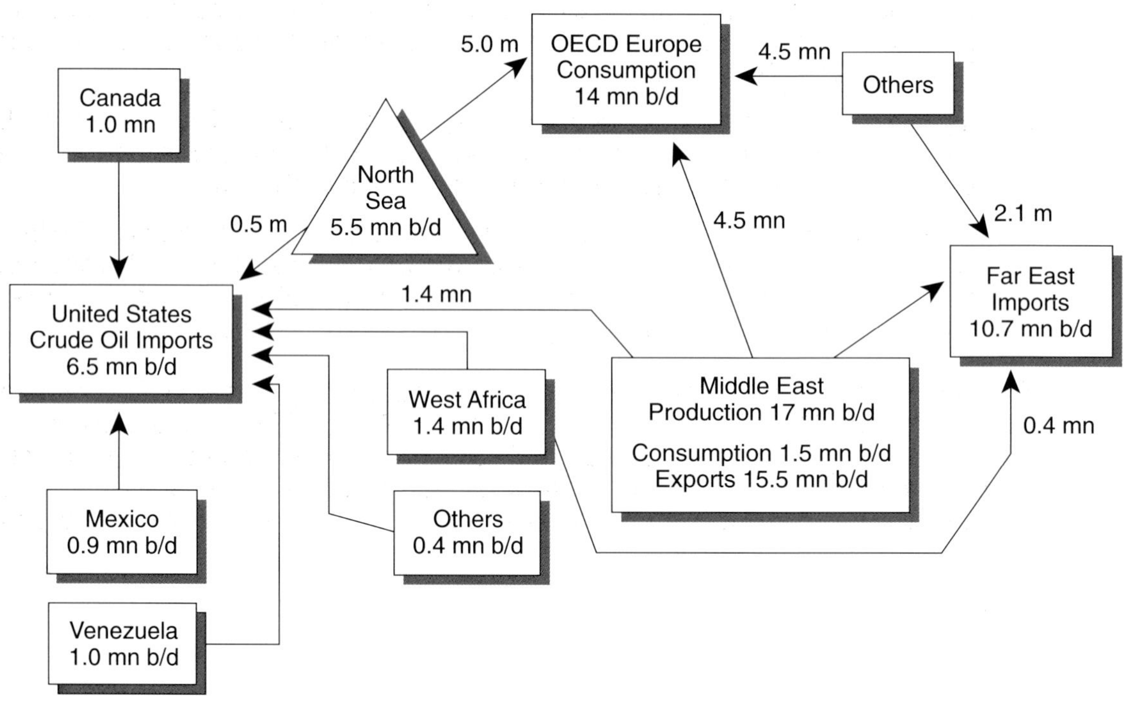

Copyright © TutorShip 2002                    Source: E A Gibson Ltd

To sum up:

1.   The USA accounts for 28% of world oil imports, and 20% of world oil production.

2.   Japan, has no indigenous raw materials, and imports 16% of the world's oil.

3.   The Middle East is responsible for 47% of all seaborne oil movements – but its dominance has changed, falling with rising oil production elsewhere (North Sea, Alaska, Mexico). It

accounted for 80% of all exports in 1975. It is forecast that the reintegration of Iran and Iraq's oil production would raise the share to 50% by the year 2000.

4.    Western Europe is still a large importer of oil, despite the exploitation of the North Sea.

5.    Latin America and the Asian NICs are potential growth areas for oil consumption in the future.

## 6.2.4    The Behaviour of the Price of Crude Oil

Much of the events that drive the tanker market are bound up with both changes in the volume of oil moved, and with its value. The decline in oil consumption and the fall in oil sea transportation that occurred in the period 1975-85 was itself triggered by the dramatic changes that occurred in the world price of crude oil.

Figure 6.2 illustrates the behaviour of oil prices for over half a century (1950-2003). It shows the price and is based on two levels.

First, the actual dollar price at the time – money on the day, or nominal price, secondly, this is based on 2003 dollar prices, the lower line. There is also an indication of some of the major historical events having an impact on the oil price during the period. To consider the money on the day situation (the lower line). For the two decades 1950 to the late 1960s the average price was between $1.80 and $2.00. It rose to $4.00 in the early 1970s. In October 1973, following on the Arab-Israeli six day war, OPEC raised the price until it reached $9.00 by the end of that year, as well as threatening oil embargoes on countries that were viewed as Israel's allies. This fourfold increase in the price of a major strategic commodity generated three immediate effects:

a)    it triggered off a huge economic recession in many Western economies, leading to permanently lower rates of economic growth (in some countries, such as the UK, real incomes fell in 1975, as a result).

b)    it generated an international banking crisis, as many oil exporting countries suddenly found themselves with large current account surpluses on their balance of payments, whilst many oil importing countries grappled with large deficit problems.

c)    it generated a sudden and dramatic stop to the euphoric progress of the tanker market, which had experienced two booms in rates, in 1970 and in 1973. These booms were generated by the huge growth in demand volumes that were going on at the time, which had also created a very rapid expansion in the tanker fleet.

The rest of the 70's were characterised by a steadily rising nominal price of oil, to about $12 a barrel. In the wake of the Iranian revolution of 1979, the OPEC price peaked at around $40 a barrel. This was the result of OPEC trying to maintain the price of oil in real terms – this in effect meant that whenever the dollar devalued against other currencies, the $ price of oil was increased to compensate OPEC members for the loss of the dollar's earning power.[2]

---

[2]    Glen, D. (1987) The emergence of differentiation in the Tanker Market 1970-78. PhD Thesis London Business School, London University. Data updated from E. A. Gibsons.

## Figure 6.2 – The development of nominal oil prices 1950-2003

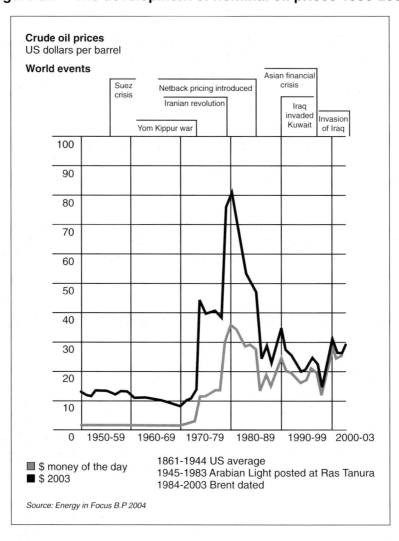

This policy was ludicrous, since it helped create a cycle of low growth; the USA tried to offset its deficit, and restore the dollar, by recessionary policies, leading to low growth, leading to falling demand for oil, leading to stagnation of oil exports. In the mid-1980's, Saudi-Arabia and other OPEC members altered their pricing policy, to match that set by Mexico, which had become a significant oil producer but who was not a member of OPEC (nor are the USA, Norway, the UK). This change in policy, coupled with rising output from Non-OPEC producers, has forced the decline in the oil price. Saudi-Arabia, for example, introduced Netback pricing for its crude, which was determined by the selling prices of the refined products at the point of final consumption less the transport and refining costs. This policy emphasises the fact that the crude oil price is driven by consumer demand for the products and the price obtained in the retail market.

As can be seen from the diagram, the major rise was in 1990, triggered by the Iraqi invasion of Kuwait and the first Iraqi war. But Middle East oil production was no longer so dominant as it had been, and the increase was short lived.

The Asian financial crisis is the background to the contraction in price in the late 1990s, in the early 2000 the boom in world economy, particularly China, created another increase in price. By 2003 oil prices were the highest nominal price for two decades with the average over the years of $29.00. This includes peaks of over $30.00 to $35.00. Both Venezuela and particularly Iraq suffered distribution in supply in the period. But this was largely overcome by increased production in Saudi Arabia. The upper line, 2003 dollar prices. First to illustration the massive price movements of what has been termed the oil crises of the 1970s, as compared to recent movement in prices. These price changes had an enormous impact on the world economy and on the maritime industry.

Indeed, in real terms (allowing for the decline in the purchasing power of the dollar over time), the present price of crude oil is about the same as it was prior to the October 1973 price increase. This appears to be a relatively little noticed fact – one which may well be related to the low levels of inflation enjoyed in the West in the past few years!

### 6.2.5 OPEC as a cartel

The principal economic reason for the dramatic rise in the price of crude oil in the early 1970's was the ability of OPEC[3] to regulate the world supply of crude oil, with all members agreeing to set common prices, and just as importantly, set production quotas to limit supply and raise price.

The ability to restrict prices depends heavily upon the quotas being kept to. In the 1980's, several countries began to break ranks, undermining this power. Nigeria, for one regularly exceeded her quota. In addition, rising production from non-OPEC countries helped to undermine their monopoly position.

After this somewhat lengthy discussion of the oil market, and changes in demand, attention is now turned to the behaviour of the tanker sector of the industry.

## 6.3 CHANGES IN THE TANKER FLEET

At its peak, the world tanker fleet accounted for 45% of all world shipping tonnage in 1977, having climbed steadily in the previous decade. Following on the events described above, this trend was reversed, with the share declining steadily, reaching 30% in 1994 (OECD Maritime Transport Review 1994, using Lloyds Register data). In fact, the decline was most marked in the period 1981-1985, with tonnage actually declining. (This can be seen in the data in Table 6.1 above).

The stock of tanker tonnage has therefore broadly followed the pattern of demand, rising rapidly until the early 1970's, stalling, and then declining in size until 1988, since when it has begun to grow again. This long run adjustment of supply to the level of demand has often been a painful process in particular periods.

An indication of the uneven development of the tanker stock can be seen in Table 6.6 below.

**Table 6.6 – Annual Average Percentage Changes of the Tanker Stock and changes in demand**

| Period | GRT | DWT | Tons Demand | Ton mile demand |
|--------|-----|-----|-------------|-----------------|
| 1963-68 | 8.0 | n.a. | n.a. | n.a. |
| 1968-73 | 10.8 | n.a. | 13.6 | 21.4 |
| 1973-78 | 8.7 | 12.3 | 0.0 | 0.0 |
| 1978-83 | -2.2 | -1.9 | -5.6 | -9.0 |
| 1983-88 | -4.1 | -4.0 | 3.5 | 3.4 |
| 1988-93 | 2.4 | 1.8 | 5.0 | 8.2 |
| 1990-94 | 1.8 | 2.3 | 3.6 | 3.8 |
| 1973-94 | 1.2 | 1.4 | -0.4 | 0.0 |

Source: Tutorship Manual 1990, Maritime Transport 1994, Fearnleys Reviews

---

[3] OPEC consists of Saudi-Arabia, Iran, Iraq, UAE, Kuwait, Qatar, Nigeria, Libya, Algeria, Venezuela and Indonesia (in 1997).

It is well worth your while studying Table 6.6 carefully. It is very clear, that even with five year averages, demand growth leads supply response. In the early 1970's demand growth outstripped supply; but then demand growth collapsed to zero, whilst supply expanded by 8-10% per year! This created a huge problem of adjustment in the tanker market, which was only really resolved by the late 1980's.

### Figure 6.3 – Fleet development by ship type as of January 1st, 1994-2004

| Ship type/ Year | Number of Ships | % share of world total | 1000 gt | % share of world total | 1000 dwt | % share of world total | 1000 TEU | % share of world total | dwt % change over previous year |
|---|---|---|---|---|---|---|---|---|---|
| 1994 | 6309 | 17.9 | 145667 | 34.6 | 273668 | 40.6 | 1 | 0.0 | 2.3 |
| 1995 | 6496 | 17.9 | 146276 | 33.4 | 270921 | 39.7 | – | – | 1.0 |
| 1996 | 6611 | 17.9 | 148951 | 32.6 | 274024 | 39.0 | – | – | 1.1 |
| 1997 | 6758 | 17.8 | 152320 | 32.2 | 279631 | 38.7 | – | – | 2.0 |
| 1998 | 6885 | 17.9 | 155455 | 31.9 | 284782 | 38.3 | – | – | 1.8 |
| 1999 | 7030 | 18.2 | 158483 | 31.9 | 289066 | 38.5 | – | – | 1.5 |
| 2000 | 7195 | 18.5 | 163160 | 32.2 | 296081 | 38.9 | – | – | 2.4 |
| 2001 | 7225 | 18.5 | 165950 | 31.9 | 300352 | 38.6 | 1 | 0.0 | 1.4 |
| 2002 | 7311 | 18.7 | 168156 | 31.3 | 303234 | 37.9 | 1 | 0.0 | 1.0 |
| 2003 | 7397 | 18.8 | 169969 | 30.8 | 305248 | 37.4 | 1 | 0.0 | 0.7 |
| 2004 | 7565 | 19.1 | 177682 | 31.2 | 317827 | 37.8 | 6 | 0.1 | 4.1 |
| Average growth rate | 1.8 | | 2.0 | | 1.5 | | – | | |

Source: ISL 2004

Figure 6.3 examines in detail the experience of oil tankers over the decade 1994 to 2004. Over this period there had been a substantial growth from the long run point of view hardly interrupted. This must be tempered by the annual experience, 1991 for example is the single year where there is a contraction in dead weight tonnage, and 2004 shows a substantial increase. This will be discussed further below when demand and freight rates are considered. Against this is a number of vessels increased steadily as does surprisingly GRT. But in relation to percentage of the total world fleet there is a small comparatively contraction.

---

[4] WorldScale and its successor, New WorldScale are tanker industry conventions designed to generate a uniform scale, or index, for tanker rates. Each route is calibrated for an assumed vessel size and cost structure. The calculated rate is set at WS100 for that route. All fixtures are then quoted relative to this rate. Large vessels will generate a WS rate of say. WS50, small vessels WS120, say, because their operating costs are so different from the assumed size (75,000dwt at present).

**Figure 6.4 – Development of Spot Market Dirty Fixtures 1992-2004**

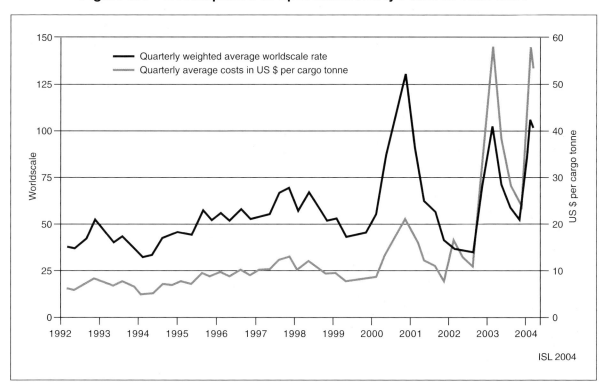

Development of spot market dirty fixtures 1992 to 2004. This figure shows the spot market freight rate from 1992 to 2004, from a long term point of view what is highlighted is a substantial movement in the rates in the recent period. The 1990s appear against this to have been comparatively stable. The high level of activity in the latter period 2002-2004 are demand reaction to the unrest in the Middle East and the increased imports of China and other OECD Asian economies. With the activities in 2003 and 2004 being driven by a number of factors, not least as stated on the supply side, disruptions in Venezuelan oil exports, combined with the Iraqi war. On the demand size, Japanese imports due to the ageing power plants and the increased Chinese requirements. Both have risen the tonne mileage required of the tanker fleet, in particular Suez max and VLCCs.

### Table 6.7 – Growth of Tanker and Combination Carrier Stock 1984-95

| | 1984 | 1985 | 1986 | 1987 | 1988 | 1989 | 1990 | 1991 | 1992 | 1993 | 1994 | 1995 |
|---|---|---|---|---|---|---|---|---|---|---|---|---|
| Tanker Stock (mn tonnes) | 265 | 242 | 234 | 231 | 234 | 241 | 247 | 255 | 262 | 267 | 265 | 263 |
| Lay-Ups (mn tonnes) | 49 | 38 | 15 | 10 | 3 | 2 | 2 | 2 | 6 | 5 | 4 | 3 |
| (% of Stock) | 18% | 16% | 6% | 4% | 1% | 1% | 1% | 1% | 2% | 2% | 2% | 1% |
| Storage (mn tonnes) | 10 | 12 | 17 | 12 | 14 | 9 | 15 | 12 | 9 | 11 | 10 | 11 |
| % of stock | 4% | 5% | 7% | 5% | 6% | 4% | 6% | 5% | 3% | 4% | 4% | 4% |
| Operating Stock (mn tonnes) | 206 | 192 | 202 | 209 | 217 | 230 | 230 | 241 | 247 | 251 | 251 | 249 |
| Combined Carriers (m tonnes) | 44 | 40 | 37 | 38 | 33 | 33 | 32 | 31 | 31 | 29 | 26 | 24 |
| In Oil Trade (mn tonnes) | 12 | 13 | 20 | 13 | 12 | 10 | 13 | 11 | 10 | 12 | 11 | 9 |
| (% in Oil Trade) | 27% | 33% | 54% | 34% | 36% | 30% | 41% | 35% | 32% | 41% | 42% | 38% |
| Operating Oil Fleet (m tonnes) | 218 | 205 | 222 | 222 | 229 | 240 | 243 | 252 | 257 | 263 | 262 | 258 |

Source: Platou Market Report 1996

## 6.5    THE STRUCTURE OF THE TANKER MARKET

In the past, the oil industry was dominated by the major multi-national oil companies. Indeed, in the 1960's, they became known as 'The Seven Sisters', seven large companies, including in the number Exxon, Shell, BP, and Mobil. These companies appeared to dominate many of the national domestic markets for oil and oil products, giving the impression of a highly concentrated market, driven by a few large players.

It appeared that such a structure must dominate all markets in which it participated, including the tanker market. Similar structures are observed in the tanker market; in the 1960's, the 'oil majors' owned one third of the world's tanker tonnage, and chartered in another third on long term (5-10 years) charters. This left only one third of the world's tonnage to trade in the rest of the market. If the big oil companies controlled up to 2/3rds of the tonnage, surely it follows that the tanker market must be an oligopoly, rather than a perfectly competitive one?

Appearances can be deceptive however. The general consensus amongst scholars of the tanker market is that it is an extremely competitive one. Moreover, the trends over the past twenty years have made the market more competitive than it was, especially in the crude oil sector. On the other hand, the continuing development of specialist vessels, such as LNG and chemicals tankers, has meant that some of the segments may be potentially less competitive than when the market was less fragmented.

The two major contributors to the academic study of the tanker market are Koopmans[5] and Zannetos[6]. A number of other studies have come since, but they have tended to accept the views put forward in the above texts. Basically, both authors have argued that the tanker market is perfectly competitive.

---

[5]  T J Koopmans (1939) Tanker Freight Rates and Tankship Building. Haarlem.
[6]  Z Zannetos (1966) The Theory of Ocean Tankship Rates. MIT Press MIT.

In Lesson 5 the basic properties of a competitive market were reviewed, so they are only outlined here. The key points to note are:

1.   all owners seek to maximise profits

2.   there are a large number of buyers of the service

3.   there are a large number of sellers, none big enough to influence price

4.   the product is homogeneous

5.   there is complete freedom of entry to, and exit from, the market

6.   full information on market conditions and rates is available to all participants.

Taking 1) as given, the other assumptions will now be related to the tanker market.

### 6.5.1   Large numbers of buyers and sellers

Large numbers of buyers. Even in the 1960's, when the Seven Sisters were at their peak, and large oil companies controlled significant proportions of the world's tanker tonnage, there were still many independent oil companies who needed to ship cargoes of oil. Since the 1970's, the economic share of the oil majors has declined significantly, for a number of reasons. Firstly, there is the rise of State owned oil companies in the Middle East and elsewhere, reducing the share of the big 7. Secondly, the development of a large 'Spot Market' in oil cargoes at Rotterdam from the early 1970's has meant that the ship's cargo may go through many owners before it reaches its destination. The rise of the 'oil trader' has led to an increase in the number of independent charterers of ships.

The rise of the Rotterdam Spot Market coincided with the loss of market power by the oil majors during the 1970's and 1980's, as independents opened up new distribution channels in many countries. The ramifications spread to the tanker market, as the oil majors reduced the amount of tonnage held on long term charter (In response to the oversupply situation of the mid-seventies) and then began to reduce their direct ownership of tonnage, partly in response to the introduction of OPA90, which makes the owner of any vessel polluting the US seaboard liable for unlimited damages.

These changes in ownership have led to a reduction in the relative importance of the oil companies, as can be seen in the data displayed in Figures 6.8 and 6.9 below. The first shows the percentage share of the 40mn dwt tons of tankers owned by the ten largest Oil Majors (ranked by tanker tonnage ownership). The data (kindly supplied by E.A. Gibsons Ltd.) shows that the top ten companies owned 14% of the world fleet (23% if State Oil companies are included). In 1966, the top 5 oil majors owned 23% of the fleet. This is a clear decline in the relative importance of these companies.

The independent owners' share of total tonnage has risen to 70% in 1996. The top ten independents account for 44.9mn dwt tons or 16% of the fleet. This implies that thousands of other independent companies control the other 86% of the 70%, or 60% of the world fleet. The largest independent tanker owner in 1996 was World Wide shipping with 5.9mn dwt, or 2.1% of the world fleet. The largest oil company fleet is VELA, the Saudi-Arabian oil company. This represents 2.5% of the world tanker fleet. Thus, the largest tanker operator is responsible for only 2.5% of the tanker tonnage.

It is very clear from these figures, that even the twenty largest tanker operators account for only 28% of world tanker tonnage. This is a very low figure for 'industrial concentration', and means that Assumptions 2 and 3 are appropriate in the context of the tanker market.

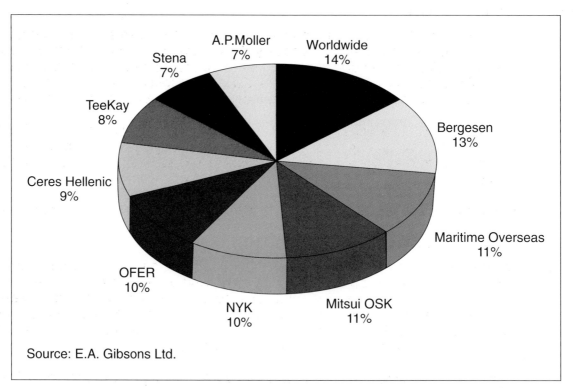

**Figure 6.7 – Top Ten Independent Tanker Owners 1996**
**Top Ten Independent Tonnage 44.9mn dwt**
**Total Fleet 276mn dwt**

Source: E.A. Gibsons Ltd.

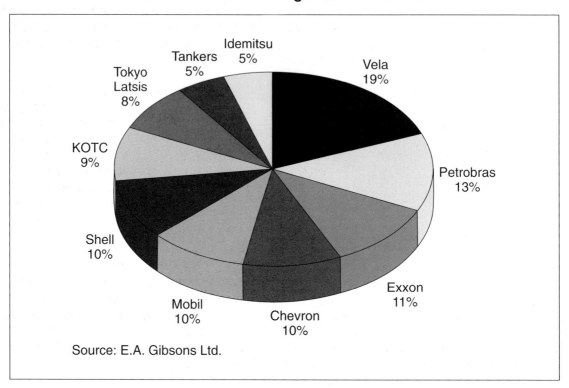

**Figure 6.8 – % Shares of Top Ten Oil Companies 1996**
**Top Ten Tonnage 39.7mn dwt**
**Total Fleet Tonnage 276mn dwt**

Source: E.A. Gibsons Ltd.

There is also a great deal of trading between the oil companies, because oil is not as totally homogeneous as might at first be thought, with different regions producing different oils, which are often blended at refineries. Demand fluctuations generated by seasonal changes also lead to a need to trade between each other.

### 6.5.2 Identical Service

Although oil itself appears to be homogeneous (i.e. all the same quality), it does in fact vary in terms of its sulphur content and viscosity. Some of the trade involves the movement of different qualities of oil to be blended at the various refineries, as different blends generate different proportions of output once the oil is refined. However, these differences are accounted for in the pricing of crude oil, and do not make any material difference to the analysis so far.

In fact, the key feature lies in the nature of the transportation of oil, not oil itself. It is clear that the transportation of oil is very homogeneous, since the service provided by one crude oil tanker is identical to that provided by another, assuming that delivery times, vessel reliability, etc. are similar.

The economic assumption that the product is homogeneous can therefore be maintained.

### 6.5.3 Freedom of Entry and Exit

The main factor determining ease of entry is access to capital to pay for a new or second-hand vessel (note the purchase of a second-hand vessel may mean the entry of a new company, but it is at the expense of an existing operator: supply has not increased overall). In relation to other industries, the purchase of an oil tanker at $100mn, say, (see Lesson 4 for some recent prices) is not a particularly large investment. The setting up of Nissan's car plant in Tees-Side, UK cost the Japanese car company £500mn.

Furthermore, many new ships are purchased with a mortgage, usually for 70% of the initial price, 30% being paid for the shipping company. So the net cost of the new double-hull tanker is $30mn, plus the repayment and interest on the loan. Many countries provide tax relief for investing in shipping, so this is an overestimate. Many of these investments are made at the top of the shipping business cycle, when freight rates and time charter fixtures are relatively attractive. This encourages shipowners to invest in more ships, and banks to lend more money in the expectation that rates will be high in the future. On the other hand, when spot and timecharter rates are low, banks are less willing to supply finance, but of course there are less owners willing to risk the purchase of a new vessel.

Exit may be by scrapping the vessel, or for an individual company, selling to another operator, although, again, the latter does not reduce supply overall. In some industries, exiting is very difficult – for example, £8bn has been committed to the Channel Tunnel, yet if the owners of the tunnel Eurotunnel, wanted to leave, they could not convert their capital into cash – the assets would have to be purchased at their expected market value – which at the time of writing, is well below the initial cost of building the tunnel. In this case, the company would find it very difficult to leave the industry, in the sense of getting out with its capital intact. In the tanker industry, this means of exit is much more likely, since there are so many buyers and sellers – only in exceptionally bad market conditions might there be a problem with 'exiting' the market, as in the early 1980's.

The physical mobility of the vessels themselves means that the large proportion of capital invested in this sector is literally mobile. This means that any regional demand imbalances can be quickly rectified by a shift in relative supply. This statement must be qualified by the fact that the development of very large crude carriers means that some segments of the market are less flexible than others – VLCCs are excluded from some trading routes by either port or draught restrictions. For example, the very largest vessels cannot trade into the US East Coast ports because of the shallow waters there. In fact, there are only two ports that take VLCC's on this seaboard – LOOP, the Louisiana Offshore Oil Port, and New York.

Furthermore, the largest vessels cannot use the Suez Canal when laden, (draught), and some cannot when in ballast (beam). These characteristics mean that the Suezmax tankers are more flexible than the bigger vessels.

Despite this qualification, the substitutability for one tanker for another on most routes or trades means that all sectors tend to move together. Supply can be very flexible in the short run, as Table 6.7 reveals. The existence of a stock of laid up tankers meant that the increase in demand between 1984-87 was easily met by a sharp fall in lay-ups. Once lay-ups had fallen to 1%, such a response would not have been available, and only new entry would increase supply in this situation.

### 6.5.4 Full Information

The market is extremely well served by the specialised shipbroking companies who keep in constant contact with both owners and charterers on a 24 hour basis all round the world. Many shipbroking companies have offices in strategic points all round the world to offer this service. London plays a crucial role, because it is located in a time zone which can trade with the Far East on the same day (early morning, London time) and then still trade with New York in the same trading day (late afternoon, London time). This unique position makes London the ideal base for such companies. In addition, there are many specialist companies offering consultancy services to companies.

All this activity means that charterers and owners are continuously informed of recent events and prices. Many shipping fixtures are publicly reported, with all salient details available. This makes the provision of market information relatively cheap and very efficient.

Overall then it would appear that all of the fundamental assumptions of perfect competition are fulfilled when one examines the tanker market. This means that modelling its behaviour using demand and supply analysis can thus be justified.

## 6.6 SEGMENTED SUPPLY

The above analysis has taken for granted that the market for all tankers is the same: the market for 50,000dwt crude is identical to the market for 350,000dwt crude vessels. But one or two authors have suggested that the changes that occurred in the 1970's have made that assumption incorrect.

The growth in tanker sizes has already been touched upon. Svendsen, in a study in 1981, showed that different tanker sizes had different own-price and cross-price elasticities of demand with respect to freight rates. This implies some degree of differentiation in the market. D Glen[7], in a study of tanker profitability in the 1970's, showed that the gross profit margins varied widely between sizes, and that large tankers had significantly greater variability in those margins. If the tankers were all in the same market, the variability should have been the same.

The question arises, does this mean that the tanker market has become less competitive? Glen argues that the answer to this is a resounding no, because although the segments within the tanker market may have become more distinct, allowing them to behave differently in the short run, it does not follow that they are unrelated in the long run. This is because shipowners have the choice of investing in all of these segments – none is closed to them. Thus free entry and exit exists in all parts, so that market imbalances may exist for a few years, but will be self corrected by different rates of entry and exit in the sectors. Thus, if the market for VLCC's is badly hit, this sector will have very high lay-ups, higher than average scrapping rates, and few new orders – owners will be concentrating on the sectors that are relatively more profitable – until the excess supply problem is resolved.

In the long run then, one would expect to see the same common factors driving each of these sectors, and common trends appearing.

---

[7] D R Glen (1990) The emergence of differentiation in the oil tanker market, 1970-78 *Maritime Policy and Management*, 17, No. 4, pp 289-312.

## 6.7    MODELLING DEMAND

It should be clear from the above discussions that the demand for oil transportation is likely to be extremely price inelastic. Remember it is a *derived* demand and the freight rate elasticity of derived demand depends on:

1.    the own price elasticity of demand for the final product

2.    the ease with which shipping can be substituted by other modes of oil transportation (cross price elasticity)

3.    the share of freight costs in the final delivered cost to consumers

4.    the elasticity of supply of tanker transport services.

The elasticity of oil transport demand will be *lower*, the *lower* is the value of 1), the *lower* is the value of 2), and the *higher* is the value of 3).

In normal conditions, with spare tonnage laid up, one would expect the own price elasticity of demand for tanker freight services to be very inelastic. This is because:

1.    The own price elasticity of products derived from crude oil are very low, because

a)    there is limited technical substitution (cannot put methane in a petrol engine), and

b)    there is limited substitution for oil as an energy source in the long run.

One estimate, for the UK by the author, gave a value of –0.17. This is inelastic.

2.    Ocean oil transportation is highly specialised. Oil pipelines act as substitutes for some trades (e.g. North Sea fields), but in other areas there is no practicable alternative.

3.    The share of freight costs in the retail price of petrol in the UK is about 2%, say 1p on 59p. Oil products are often highly taxed at the retail end because of the low price elasticity.

4.    Supply elasticity is usually quite high, but can fall to zero in extreme booms, as in 1973. But October 1973 was an exception, so assuming a moderate value is not unreasonable.

All the above points lead to one conclusion. The responsiveness of demand to changes in freight rates can be regarded as close to zero, i.e. extremely inelastic.

Although demand is very inelastic with respect to the current freight rate, *it is very sensitive to* the level of economic activity, as seen in earlier sections. Thus one might represent demand as more or less vertical schedule when plotting the quantity demanded (in tonne miles or tonnes of cargo) against the freight rate, for a given level of economic activity. When the rate of economic activity increases, the entire schedule can shift very rapidly – it may be very volatile. It will shift to the right in booms, and to the left in recessions.

## 6.8    MODELLING SUPPLY

The supply schedule for the market as a whole is assumed to have a shape that is very similar to that developed in the lesson on the Dry Cargo Market. It will be *elastic* when there are significant amounts of tonnage laid up, as this tonnage is readily available to increase the size of the active fleet. As the laid-up proportion falls, and the share of combi's trading in oil rises, the sources of extra short run supply become more limited, so that the elasticity declines. This shape is shown in Figure 6.10 below.

The 80:20 split is based on the analysis by Platou[8] of tanker rate volatility – they argue that practically all of the variations that are observed in the tanker market are observed when the utilisation of the fleet was in the last 20% – this is consistent with the shape of the supply curve below – elastic over the 80% range, but becoming less and less elastic until full capacity utilisation was achieved.

It is important to remember that this is a model for the short run supply of shipping. The assumption is being made that the stock of tankers is unchanged; variations in tonne miles produced are generated by variations in lay-ups, storage, and speed.

**Figure 6.9 – Tanker Supply Curve**

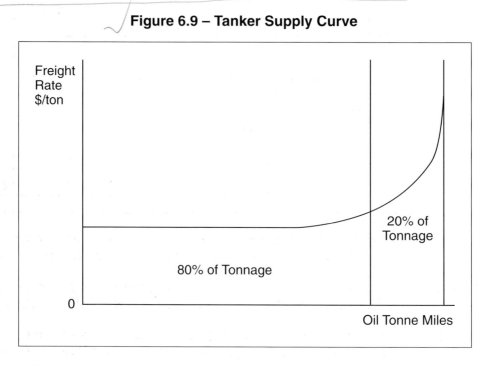

### 6.8.1   The Market Model

Putting the very inelastic demand schedule together with the varying elasticity supply schedule generates a model of the equilibrium spot freight rate for tanker services, as shown below in Figure 6.11.

---

[8]  R S Platou 1995 Platou Market Report Oslo Norway

## Figure 6.10 – Modelling Demand and Supply in the Short Run

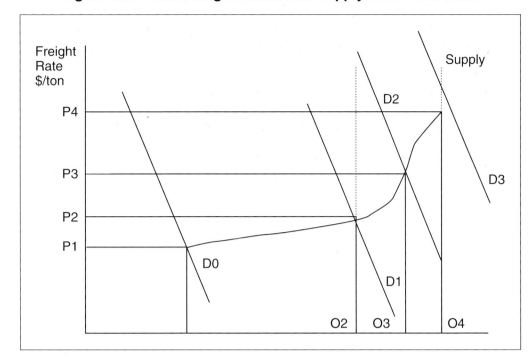

| D0 – D1 | Large *shift* in demand, but little effect on rate; lots of spare capacity. (Freight rate moves from P1 to P2, whilst tonne miles increases from Q1 to Q2). |
|---|---|
| D1 – D2 | Smaller *shift* in demand, capacity is less readily available; larger increase in rate. (Freight rate rises from P2 to P3, and tonne miles increase from Q2 to Q3). |
| D2 – D3 | Supply nearly perfectly inelastic; small shifts in demand can generate large increases in rates. (Freight rate rises rapidly from P3 to P4; tonne miles performed rise slightly from Q3 to Q4). |

The above model is consistent with

a)   great rate volatility

b)   the possibility that rate increases do not increase the short run supply at all – once full utilisation of the existing fleet is achieved. The model is very similar to the one developed for the dry cargo sector, because both are very competitive sectors.

## 6.9   TANKER AND DRY CARGO RATE VOLATILITY COMPARED

If the models are so similar, why then, is it observed that tanker rates appear to be more volatile than those for dry cargo? The answer to this question appears to be found in the following points:

1.   *The dry cargo market is in fact, not a single market at all.* It consists of several major bulk trades, plus large numbers of other commodities being transported on a tramp basis. This means that, if one sector of demand grows whilst another declines, tonnage can be shifted from the declining sector to the growth sector – but this process keeps rate volatility in check in the individual markets.

2.   *The average size of dry cargo vessels, even the bulk ones, is very much smaller than that for tankers.* There is a direct link between rate volatility and vessel size – which can be explained in common sense terms. Recall that large vessels generate economies of scale, so that the average rate is lower than those for smaller vessels. The same size increase in rate for both sectors will generate a larger proportional increase for the lower initial rate

– i.e. for the larger vessel. Thus rate volatility might be higher because of the differences in average vessel size between the two sectors.

3. *The oil industry has a special place in Western economies.* As well as being indispensable to the transport sector, oil is an important energy source for factory power, and a feedstock for the chemicals industry. The plastics industry is based on oil-derived feedstocks. As has been shown, the principal export region, is the Middle East. The West's strategic grip on this region declined sharply in the 1960's, with the rise of Arab Nationalism and the Arab-Israel conflict. Practically every significant 'spike' in tanker rates has been associated with an event which has highlighted this strategic aspect. The 1956 closure of Suez/invasion of Egypt by France/UK; the 1967 six-day war; the 1973 Yom Kippur war; the 1979-84 Iran-Iraq war; the 1990 Iraq-Kuwait war can all be observed in the tanker rate data.

The reason for the early spikes is easy to see – the large multinational oil companies ordered as much oil as possible to be lifted from the Middle East as soon as tensions flared up – but this was associated with no extra supply – so up go the rates. It is also important to note that recent rate increases, such as occurred in 1990, appear to be much more short-lived. The Middle East is no longer quite so dominant in export shares as it was; oil companies are not so vertically integrated. In 1990, Saudi-Arabia's reaction was also quite different. Fearing invasion from Iraq, they co-operated with the western military forces, and also deliberately increased their own oil production to compensate for the loss of Kuwaiti output. The price of crude oil fell, and until the last quarter of 1996, traded around \$20-25 a barrel. No stockbuilding surge was experienced, so freight rates also declined after the initial scare.

4. *The role of expectations.* Zannetos[9] suggested that tanker rates were affected by what he called 'price elastic' expectations. That is, the higher the rate, the more sensitive the market became to rates themselves, and the market raised its expectations about future rates by more than was warranted – but this new level of expectations would cause a shift in the current demand curve, which would raise prices, until 'ridiculous' levels where reached.

It is very like a 'speculative bubble' occurring, where all traders know the price is not related to the 'economic fundamentals', but everyone is making so much money out of the perpetual rise in prices that no-one really asks whether the process can continue indefinitely. The answer is that it cannot!

A modern version of Zannetos' idea is called **rational expectations** – market behaviour, the movement of tanker prices say, is driven as much by what we expect to happen to future tanker rates (and future profitability), as it is by anything else – indeed, if the market is efficient, then all the known information about such a market is argued to be captured in its present market price – freight rates or second hand tanker prices, in this case. Changes in expectations about the future will then automatically alter current prices – a war in the Gulf will send both oil prices, freight rates and second hand tanker prices up immediately because of the likelihood of greater profitability as a consequence.

---

[9] See Z Zannetos op. cit.

## 6.10 FLUCTUATIONS IN MARKET FREIGHT RATES

The actual behaviour of spot tanker freight rates was illustrated for annual average data, in Figures 6.4-6.6 above. They illustrate peaks in 1967, 1970, 1973 and 1979, all years associated with wars in the Middle East. Examination of rates over quarterly, monthly, or even weekly time periods would generate even more variation, as tanker rates reflect, for example, the seasonal increases in demand generated in the West for oil in the winter months. The interested reader would have to collect data, as provided in *Lloyd's List*, for example, to construct their own series.

## 6.11 CONCLUSION

This has been a rather long lesson. After reviewing the driving force of tanker demand, changes in regional production and consumption patterns, the principal factors affecting the growth of oil tonne mile demand was outlined. The price of oil played a key role, not directly, but because of its macroeconomic effects on world economic growth rates over the period 1970-1990. The structure of the tanker market was examined, and it was shown that it has become more open and competitive than in the 1960's – when it was considered by many to be competitive. The possibility of market segmentation was briefly discussed, and a model of freight rate determination was introduced. Factors that made tanker rates more volatile were examined in the penultimate sections.

## 6.12 SELF-ASSESSMENT AND TEST QUESTIONS

Study Figures 6.11, 6.12 and 6.13 and write short notes on the following:

1. The relation between tanker orders, demand growth, and spot rates.

2. The relation between scrapping and spot rates.

3. The relation between world tanker fleets 1966-2004 and the earlier discussion.

4. The problems you experience with the materials that is table figures etc. in writing these short notes.

**Figure 6.11 – Quarterly Tanker Order Book Development 1998-2004**

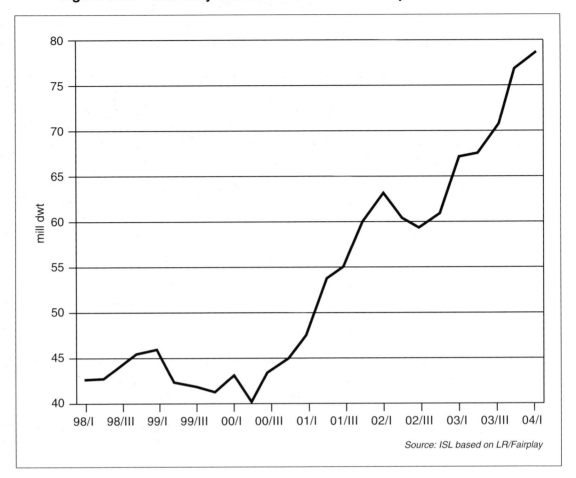

Source: ISL based on LR/Fairplay

**Figure 6.12 – Tankers Broken-up 1994-2004**

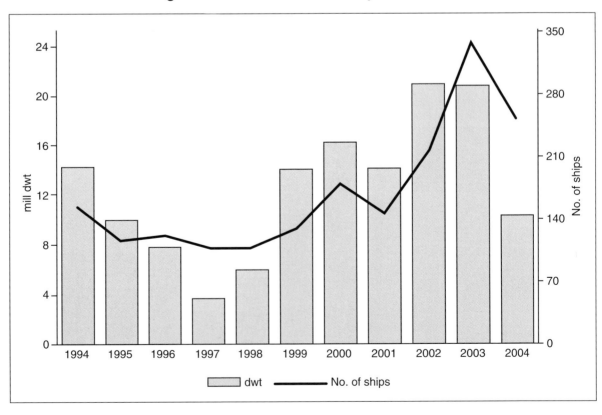

**Figure 6.13 – World Tanker Fleet – Age Structure by Year of Build as of 1st January 2004 (a)**

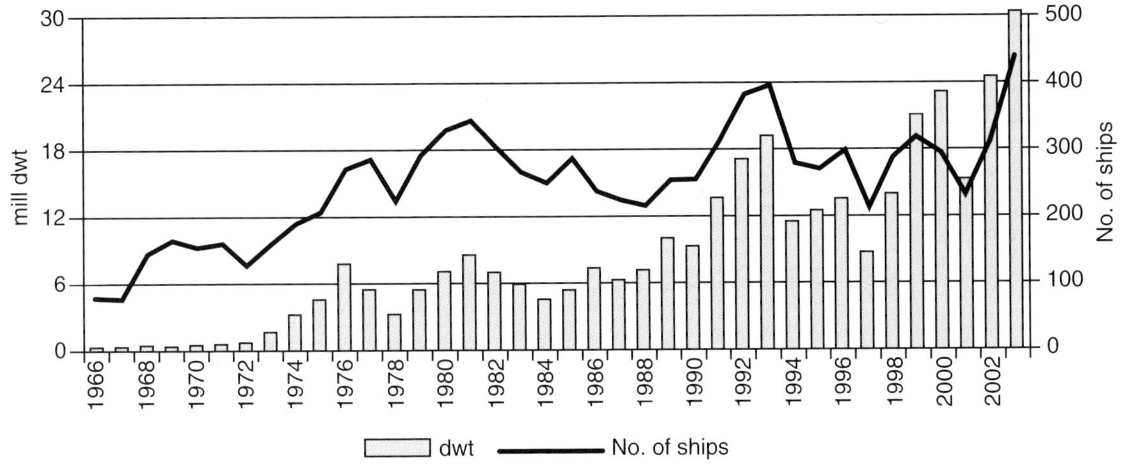

dwt ——— No. of ships

(a) Tankers built before 1966 comprise 471 ships with a tonnage of 2.2 mill dwt

ISL2003

Having completed Chapter Six, attempt the following and submit your essay to your Tutor.

Why have tanker rates appeared to be more volatile than dry cargo rates? Explain your answer with reference to developments in the tanker market in the past 25 years, and use a model of rate determination to illustrate the effect of booms and slumps on market rates.

What factors help to explain the slow adjustment of the tanker stock to the excess supply problem of the 1980's? Do you think such a situation can ever repeat itself? Explain your answer.

# Chapter 7

# THE LINER TRADES – AN EXAMPLE OF AN OLIGOPOLISTICALLY COMPETITIVE MARKET

## 7.1   INTRODUCTION

In this lesson the development of another important sector of the shipping markets, the liner trades, is reviewed. In contrast to the bulk trades considered in previous lessons, there are many significant differences, both in terms of the nature of the service being offered and the consumers of that service, and in the way the service is provided by liner shipping companies. Essentially, the liner trades may be viewed, in economic terms, as being an *oligopolistic* market structure, in contrast to the perfectly competitive markets so far considered. It must be emphasised right at the outset, however, that this *does not mean* an absence of competition in this market – it means that the *forms of competition* that are present are not simply observable in the market price. Perfect competition implies that operators compete solely on a price basis – but once market structures alter, many other types of competitive behaviour between companies can be observed – and this is true of the liner trades.

The second point to note is that the liner trades have been revolutionised by the widespread introduction of containerisation. Some of the early classic analyses of the liner trades, widely referred to in the literature, are now very dated in terms of the technology that they describe. Nevertheless, the economic organisation of these trades cannot really be understood without some knowledge of the historical development of both the trades and an important institutional arrangement which still exists today, the *liner conference*. Knowing the history, and the effects of containerisation on this sector, helps to explain the current developments in this rapidly growing sector of shipping.

## 7.2   DEFINITION OF A LINER SHIPPING SERVICE

"Liners differ radically from other sectors of the industry. Accordingly, it cannot be defined on the basis of the individual specialised technology of the vessel, as, for example, tankers. Liners, rather, consists of a group of widely differing vessel types. It is, therefore, more appropriate to seek a definition in terms of their operational characteristics, rather than technology used. The cardinal feature distinguishing liners from other sectors is that they are engaged in the provision of scheduled services between specific ports. Secluded services are those operating at a regular frequency on a particular trade route, according to a published timetable."[1]

According to Bennathan and Walters[2],

> "The main operating distinction between tramp and liner is that the latter runs on regularly scheduled services advertised in advance, whereas the former has no schedule and picks up traffic where and when it can profitably compete....
>
> A liner service is in quite a different class from a tramp carrier. The value of the service may be reflected in the fact that it is *available* at regular intervals, whether it is used or not. The shipper, therefore, may regard the availability of a regular service as being of considerable value to him..."
>
> Bennathan and Walters, *op. cit.* pages 2, 3.

---

[1]  J. McConville (1999) The Economics of Maritime Transport, Theory and Practice, Witherby, London, page 323
[2]  E. Bennathan and A.A. Walters (1969) The Economics of Ocean Freight Rates Praeger: New York

Two points arise from the quotation given above, which are still relevant today. Firstly, the service being provided has to be *regular*, and *scheduled*. Users of the service know that sailings to a certain region/set of ports will take place on a certain day at a certain time, week in, week out. Shippers can thus rely on their goods being delivered to their destinations within a very narrow time frame.

Secondly, B&W emphasise availability of cargo space. Hamburg has claimed to be able to load a containerised cargo onto a vessel with just 20 minutes notice. While this claim may be exaggerated, it emphasises the fact that there must be capacity on the vessel to accept such cargo at such a short notice – there must be available carrying capacity on the vessel or vessels.

C. E. Fayle[3], in an earlier work, provides another definition which is still relevant today.

> "Strictly speaking, a liner service implies today a fleet of ships, under common ownership or management, which provides a fixed service, at regular intervals, between named ports, and offer themselves as common carriers of any goods or passengers requiring shipment between those ports and ready for transit by their sailing dates. A fixed itinerary, inclusive in a regular service, and an obligation to accept cargo from all comers and to sail, whether full or not, on the date fixed by the public schedule. These, and not the size and the speed of the ship nor the number of vessels in the fleet are what distinguishes the liner from the 'tramp seeker' or general trader – the ship which can be hired as a whole by the voyage or by the month, to load such cargo and carry it between such ports as the charterer may require."
>
> C E Fayle *op. cit.*

This definition is worth reading several times. The following points are worth emphasising.

1. fleet of ships under common ownership or management
2. fixed service at regular intervals
3. between named ports
4. common carrier obligations
5. vessels sail whether full or not.

## 7.2.1 Fleet of Ships under Common Ownership or Management

The typical liner service requires the use of several vessels if it is to provide regular frequent services. Normally most liner services are defined on a minimum frequency of 14 days, as for example, in the USA's Federal Maritime Commission (FMC) determination of a liner operator for the purposes of the 1984 US Shipping Act. Table 7.1 below shows a representative sample of two modern liner companies providing a service between North Europe and the Far East, with Ports of call, and number of vessels. At least eight largish container vessels are used to provide a fortnightly service calling at each port.

The examples in Table 7.1 indicate that this type of service is operated by 'alliances' of liner companies – they have pooled their shipping resources to provide a jointly operated liner service from North Europe to the Far East and back again. Although the vessels are not under a single owner, they are in effect, being managed by one, the alliance itself. Note also that the two services quoted overlap in several ports, but provide a specific access to others. This is a common feature in liner services.

## 7.2.2 Fixed Services at Regular Intervals

Another key feature of the definition is that the service is guaranteed to shippers. The vessels will sail according to the timetable. This means that shippers can rely on a steady flow of cargo to their warehouses or customers, which is increasingly important now that manufacturers use Just –in-Time production methods to minimise inventory holdings. JIT depends upon reliable and regular delivery services at all stages of the supply chain.

---

[3] C. E. Fayle (1933) A Short History of the World's Shipping Industry

**Table 7.1**

| Operator | Ports Called | Vessel Nos. | Vessel Capacity TEUs |
|---|---|---|---|
| Maersk/Sea-Land | Gothenburg, Rotterdam, Southampton, *Algeciras*, Singapore, Hong Kong, Kaohsiung, Kobe, Nagrya, Yokohama, Kaohsiung, Hong Kong, Singapore, Rotterdam, Hamburg, Gottenburg | 9 | 3,500-6,000 |
| YangMing/K-Line | Hamburg, Felixstowe, Le Havre, Hong Kong, Kaohsiung, Kobe, Nagrya, Tokyo, Kaohsiung, Hong Kong, Singapore, Rotterdam, Hamburg | 8 | 3,456-3,502 |

Source: 'Europe/Far East Trades under pressure', Lloyds Shipping Economist, October 1996, p13.

*Note:* Ports shown in italics are wayports, which means the operator has loading/discharge rights.

### 7.2.3 Vessels Sail, Full or Not

The liner vessel is obliged to sail according to the published timetable. Shippers expect their cargoes to be delivered to the correct port at the correct time, so reliability and running-to-time are paramount. The obligation to maintain the schedule means that vessels may often sail with less than a full cargo load. This is especially likely to occur if trade volumes are unbalanced between outbound and inbound legs of a route, since the capacity required will be determined by the volume on the busiest leg. This means that the 'thin' leg will operate with vessels trading at low levels of space utilisation. It follows that one of the prime concerns of the liner operators is to ensure that cargo carrying capacity is utilised to the maximum. Many of the distinctive features of liner tariff structures flow from this concern.

One final point to be noted from Fayle's quote is the mention of passenger traffic. The decline of passenger liners coincided with the rise in international air travel, which became a cheaper and much quicker alternative. Passenger traffic is still important in two sectors – the short sea ferry trades, and the cruise market. Whilst there are still vessels designed to carry some passengers and freight, their numbers are greatly diminished, and they are not a significant part of the market. (See Table 7.2 for numbers).

In general, the market has shown signs of increased specialisation, as vessels are designed to meet the specific requirements of market niches. Figure 7.1 below highlights this, by indicating the way that the Passenger and Cargo Liner trades have evolved into a number of segments, reflecting changing market conditions over time. The specialist vessels indicated in the Figure are not comprehensive, but the diagram clearly indicates the way in which the traditional all-purpose vessel of sixty years ago has evolved into specialised sectors.

**Figure 7.1 – Development of the General Liner**

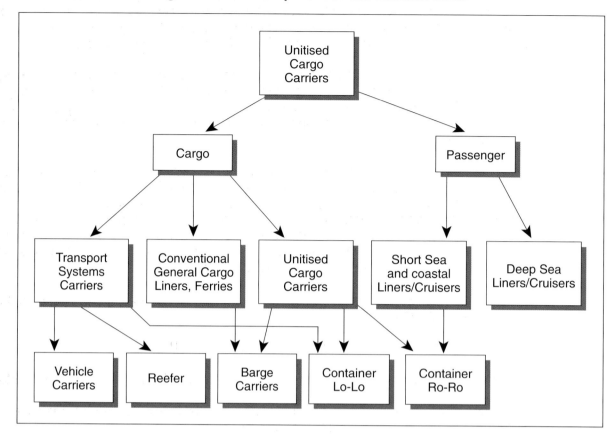

## 7.3  SHIP TYPES SERVING IN THE LINER TRADES

Figure 7.1 revealed the evolution of vessel types meeting a variety of needs gathered under the term 'General Cargo'. Table 7.2 shows how the major components of these ship types have evolved from 1980. The table provides data on gross registered tonnage, numbers, and average ages of the vessels in that sector. A number of points are worthy of note.

1.  The number of Container vessels (Lo-Lo) has trebled in the past 16 years, rising from 575 to 1635. This represents a compound growth rate of 6.5% per year in numbers, and 7.4% in grt. It appears that the average container vessel of 6000grt or more has become slightly larger over the period, rising from 22,181 grt to 25,686grt. Average age has also risen slightly, but it is well below the corresponding figure for general cargo and passenger (cruise) vessels.

2.  General cargo vessel numbers and grt has moved in the opposite direction, declining from 4857 in 1980 to 3025 vessels in 1996. The average size has however increased, from 9,815grt to 11,467. Note the steady increase in average age. Declining numbers and rising age implies a fall in the relative importance of the sector. It is clear that as containerisation extends its reach to trades not previously large or important enough to be unitised, the market share of these vessels will continue to decline. It must be noted that this does not *necessarily* imply their complete disappearance, since growing total trade volumes combined with falling market shares may still mean that demand volumes can increase.

3.  The number of specialist vessels have increased. Reefer numbers have increased from 336 in 1980 to 529 in 1996. However, their average size has declined, from 11,207 grt to 9,310 grt. The compound growth rate was 3% per year, markedly lower than that for containers.

4.  Another specialist sector which shows considerable expansion is the Cruise Liner business, which grew at 4.8% compound over the period, in grt terms, or by 1.8% per year in number terms. It is interesting to note the high average age of these vessels, ranging from a youthful 22 years in 1980, to 25 in 1987, to its present 24 years.

5.  The only sector that appears to be in significant decline in the Table is the Passenger Cargo/Container sector, with numbers falling from 74 in 1980 to 27 in 1996, and grt falling as well. This sector is clearly the one that may well have only a limited long term future: the twin pressures of unitisation and specialisation may eliminate this ship type altogether in the future.

6.  Roll-On/Roll-Off/ Container vessels appear to be stagnant in terms of numbers over the period. After 1985, the stock of vessels stays constant. It is noteworthy that the average age of the stock rises by one year, every year, after 1986, which is of course what must logically follow if no new vessels are delivered nor old ones scrapped. Note that this section of the Table may be a little misleading, as many vessels of this type may be smaller than 6000grt, since they are employed in the short sea ferry business. The Table has focussed on deep-sea vessels, using 6000 grt as a cut-off point.

7.  Overall, the average compound growth rate for all vessels was 2% per year, when measured by vessel grt.

Three clear trends can thus be identified from Table 7.2. They are:

1.  The rise of the container ship as the most common form of liner cargo transportation.

2.  The separation of passengers from cargo, as vessels specialise in one or the other of these now distinct market sectors of deep-sea shipping.

3.  The decline in the importance of the general cargo vessel, which is clearly being 'substituted' out by other ship types.

## Table 7.2 – Development of Ship Types in the Liner Trades

| | | 1980 | 1981 | 1982 | 1983 | 1984 | 1985 | 1986 | 1987 | 1988 | 1989 | 1990 | 1991 | 1992 | 1993 | 1994 | 1995 | 1996 |
|---|---|---|---|---|---|---|---|---|---|---|---|---|---|---|---|---|---|---|
| General Cargo | No. | 4857 | 4755 | 4751 | 4632 | 4431 | 4123 | 3854 | 3588 | 3433 | 3351 | 3323 | 3303 | 3256 | 3166 | 3104 | 3050 | 3025 |
| | GRT. | 47676 | 47105 | 47386 | 46773 | 45468 | 43373 | 41419 | 39090 | 37724 | 37080 | 36862 | 36780 | 36524 | 35705 | 35192 | 34763 | 34688 |
| | Age | 13 | 13 | 14 | 14 | 14 | 14 | 13 | 14 | 14 | 14 | 15 | 16 | 16 | 17 | 17 | 18 | 18 |
| Passenger/ General Cargo | No. | 74 | 62 | 61 | 54 | 51 | 41 | 39 | 38 | 36 | 29 | 28 | 28 | 28 | 28 | 28 | 26 | 27 |
| | GRT. | 787 | 632 | 622 | 540 | 497 | 399 | 368 | 350 | 336 | 273 | 261 | 268 | 273 | 273 | 273 | 263 | 275 |
| | Age | 25 | 26 | 25 | 25 | 24 | 24 | 25 | 24 | 24 | 24 | 24 | 24 | 24 | 25 | 26 | 25 | 25 |
| Container | No. | 575 | 602 | 645 | 712 | 770 | 935 | 882 | 891 | 909 | 939 | 998 | 1066 | 1142 | 1225 | 1348 | 1478 | 1635 |
| | GRT. | 12754 | 13399 | 14287 | 15758 | 17416 | 19021 | 20603 | 21270 | 22378 | 23455 | 24941 | 26906 | 28964 | 31131 | 34154 | 37718 | 41996 |
| | Age | 8 | 8 | 9 | 9 | 9 | 8 | 9 | 9 | 9 | 9 | 9 | 10 | 10 | 10 | 10 | 10 | 10 |
| Refrigerated Cargo | No. | 336 | 337 | 349 | 379 | 408 | 407 | 410 | 414 | 429 | 447 | 473 | 490 | 522 | 560 | 554 | 536 | 529 |
| | GRT. | 2998 | 3028 | 3125 | 3366 | 3687 | 3720 | 3767 | 3807 | 3937 | 4100 | 4345 | 4512 | 4817 | 5168 | 5135 | 4989 | 4925 |
| | Age | 9 | 9 | 10 | 10 | 9 | 10 | 10 | 10 | 11 | 11 | 11 | 12 | 12 | 12 | 13 | 13 | 13 |
| Ro-Ro Cargo/ Container | No. | — | — | — | — | 3 | 7 | 7 | 7 | 7 | 7 | 7 | 7 | 7 | 7 | 7 | 7 | 7 |
| | GRT. | — | — | — | — | 171 | 348 | 348 | 348 | 348 | 348 | 348 | 348 | 348 | 348 | 348 | 348 | 348 |
| | Age | — | — | — | — | 0 | 0 | 1 | 2 | 3 | 4 | 5 | 6 | 7 | 8 | 9 | 10 | 11 |
| Passenger (Cruise) | No. | 232 | 231 | 232 | 232 | 236 | 237 | 239 | 242 | 247 | 254 | 264 | 277 | 284 | 291 | 293 | 298 | 307 |
| | GRT. | 2557 | 2620 | 2718 | 2741 | 2855 | 2877 | 2973 | 3073 | 3164 | 3288 | 3622 | 3946 | 4192 | 4469 | 4608 | 4985 | 5551 |
| | Age | 22 | 23 | 23 | 23 | 24 | 24 | 24 | 25 | 24 | 24 | 24 | 23 | 23 | 23 | 24 | 24 | 24 |

Source: Lloyds Register of Shipping

Notes: Age measured in years. GRT is in 000's.

## 7.4　THE NATURE OF DEMAND FOR DEEP-SEA LINER SERVICES

Thousands of different cargo types are moved by liner services, with many different products being carried in the same vessel. This makes discussing the demand for liner services qualitatively different from the dry bulk and wet trades, where cargoes are of one type and carried for one charterer in a privately chartered vessel.

The huge variety of products are carried under the liner's 'common carrier' commitment: this means that the carrier is obliged to carry anything legally offered by the shipper, subject to the usual health and safety regulations.

Cargoes carried range from personal computers, electronic components, hi-fi, textiles, tea, coffee, cement, plastics, cooled cargoes, fresh and processed fruit, wool, hides, agricultural and industrial machinery, cars (flat packed and assembled), broken glass, and many others. Note that the majority of these products are relatively durable, especially when stored under controlled conditions, so that shippers are interested in the regular delivery of their shipments, to match anticipated consumption in the destination country.

As a result of dealing with so many cargoes, liner companies have evolved a highly complex structure of pricing (tariffs) for classes of commodities. Essentially, every potentially transportable commodity is allocated a product 'group' or class, and charged accordingly. The structure of these prices will be explored in a later section of this lesson.

Although little can be said about the precise type of cargo carried, because of the huge diversity, there are some essential characteristics common to all cargoes moved by the liner trades. These are to be found in the nature of the service offered to shippers by the liner companies. Alderton[4] quotes the results of a survey of a number of American shippers, who were asked to rank the relative importance of a number of features of the liner service. The results are displayed in Table 7.3.

The table highlights the importance placed upon timeliness and delivery, with price coming third. Note that Ford, as a shipper of cars, puts safety record above price, and also emphasises the financial stability of the supplier – it does not want to commit itself to suppliers who may go out of business, and disrupt their logistics supply chain in the process.

This emphasis on reliability has become more and more important over the past twenty years, as shipping companies become more intermodal in their operations. Many large liner companies now offer integrated door-to-door freight services to shippers, having diversified into land based transport operations. This level of integration requires:

1.　land transport from factory to terminal

2.　movement from terminal to port (If cargo consolidation takes place off port limits)

3.　port Terminal operations, transfer to vessel

4.　vessel movement to destination port

5.　movement from destination port to shippers final destination.

---

[4]　PA Alderton (1995) Sea Transport: Economics and Operations.

### Table 7.3 – Ranking of Service Characteristics by Shippers

|   | What Shippers Want |   |   | What Fords Want |
|---|---|---|---|---|
| 1 | On-Time Delivery | | 1 | Safety Record |
| 2 | Overall Responsiveness | | 2 | Price |
| 3 | Price | | 3 | Financial Stability |
| 4 | On-Time Pick-Up | | 4 | Transit Performance |
| 5 | Transit Time | | 5 | Handling of Damage Claims |
| 6 | Service Territory | | 6 | Equipment avail/suit |
| 7 | Billing Accuracy | | 7 | Equipment Condition |
| 8 | Correct Equipment | | 8 | EDI Capability |
| 9 | Degree of Control | | 9 | Ease of doing business |
| 10 | Claims Processing | | 10 | Innovative initiative |
| 11 | Tracing Capability | | | |

Source: Alderton 1995, quoted from American Shipper Survey, 1990

Efficient use of these elements has led to the processes being increasingly integrated. One significant innovation, which has materially helped in this process, is the use of containerised cargo for freight. This is briefly discussed in the next section.

## 7.5  THE "CONTAINER REVOLUTION"

In 1966, the first deep-sea container service was started by Sea-Land, a company set up by Malcolm Maclean, based on his innovative development of containerised truck freight in the USA. The system used 20'x8'x8' metal boxes, or containers, which were transported to and from the port using trucks and chassis. The containers were stored on the chassis, and then loaded into a dedicated vessel for sea transport. The vessel was fitted with cell guides to locate and secure the containers, which were lifted onto and from the ship using large gantry cranes.

This system of cargo handling revolutionised the liner trades. Traditionally, general cargo vessels spent a large proportion of their time in port, being loaded and unloaded by gangs of stevedores. Cargo handling was slow, prone to high rates of pilferage, and in a way, an art, since cargo had to be packed and secured safely, but in the right location for retrieval at its correct destination. The development of a standard unit has transformed all this. The large dock labour component has been swept away, replaced by large capital investments in sophisticated ships, strengthened quaysides (for container storage), container storing, stacking and retrieval systems, and container stuffing services, which are now often in the secure arena of the shipper's own premises. Very little container filling is carried out at the port or terminal.

The huge capital investment required was repaid with a dramatic increase in productivity. Container ships now spend little time in port – they can be loaded and discharged in a matter of hours, rather than weeks. A 1970 study by Lambert Brothers showed that one new container vessel was likely to displace up to 5 conventional cargo vessels in terms of cargo moved per year. Container movements per hour are such that the tons of cargo moved per hour has grown tremendously.

The investment effort required to develop the system has also created fundamental changes in the structure and organisation of liner trades themselves. In the 1970's, a new form of shipping organisation emerged, the consortia. A number of UK shipping lines (which included The Ocean Steamship Company, P&O, Shaw Savill & Albion, the Clan Group[5]) merged to form Ocean

---

[5]  See Deakin, B. and T. Seward 1973 Shipping Conferences CUP Cambridge UK p134

Containers Limited, or OCL. They needed to do this to become large enough to finance investment in the new technology, as well as to create enough trade volume to make the investment worthwhile. This organisation became P&OCL, P&O's container operation, which itself has recently merged with NedLloyd (in 1996) to form a new joint company, P&O/NedLloyd. The process of change and concentration into larger shipping companies still continues. Recent developments in the nature and structure of liner organisations are discussed in section 9 below.

## 7.6 PRICING BEHAVIOUR IN THE LINER AND TRAMP TRADES

The dynamic behaviour of freight rates in the bulk dry cargo trades has been covered in Lesson 5. A characteristic feature is the high level of volatility of the rates on a monthly or daily basis. This was explained by the competitive nature of the sector, creating a situation where the market rate was determined by the interplay of demand and supply. Consider the data shown in Figure 7.2 below. The Lloyd's Shipping Economist data shows the behaviour of freight rates in the dry bulk trades for the year of 1995-6. The other information on the graph shows the rates charged on a number of unitised conference routes, that is, the average rates charged for the shipment of a standard 20' container (i.e. per TEU). The data has been converted into index number form for easy comparison.

The striking feature of the rates charged on the unitised routes is their constancy over the period. There is no variation whatever in the rates quoted by the LSE on the conference routes over the period, in contrast to the single voyage dry bulk rate.

**Figure 7.2**
**Relative behaviour of Liner and Tramp Freight Rates 1995**

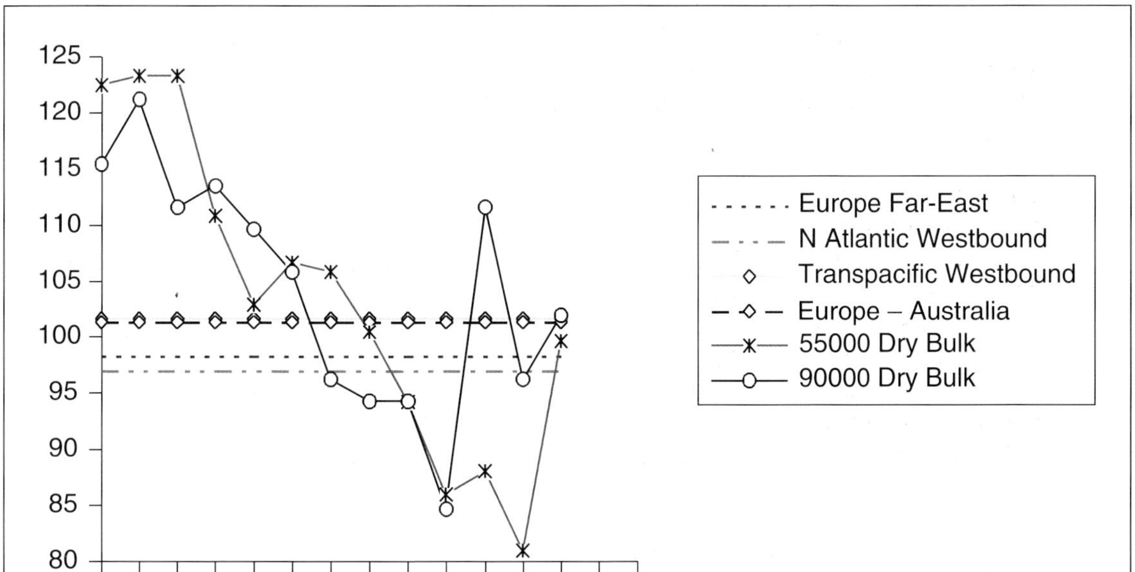

Source: Rates and Prices Data, *Lloyds Shipping Economist*, February 1997

*Note:* Data converted to index form. 1993 average is used for each of the rates as the base value.

The interesting question which arises is: *Why are there no variations in the rates for containerised cargo over the year?*

It is very clear that there is a trend decline in the dry cargo bulk rates, with quite large variations on a monthly basis. If demand and supply works in the bulk trades, why are there no corresponding variations in the market rate for unitised cargoes?

There are two answers to this. The first is to use the economist's concept of *administered prices*. This term captures the idea that in certain market situations the *market price does not reflect the daily fluctuations in demand relative to supply*. Administered prices are common in markets where supply is controlled by the main company or group of companies providing the product, which is a feature of oligopolistic market structures ("competition amongst the few"). Many industrial markets have this characteristic. For example, car prices in many European countries remain the same for a year, and are adjusted annually, to reflect changes in costs, not changes in demand conditions. Competition is fierce in the car market, but it is fought mainly on non-price terms, via styling, accessories, location of dealerships, and quality differentiation. Price competition, in the sense of a weekly variation in the price to reflect present demand conditions, is notably absent.

Administered prices may exist either if it is expensive to alter them on a frequent basis, or if the supply companies co-operate to regulate tariffs charged by all companies operating similar services on a particular route. There is an element of truth on both of these explanations.

The liner trade carries thousands of cargo types. The prices 'book' runs to several volumes. Imagine, in a pre-computer era, the labour required both to update these prices on a weekly basis, and keep the shippers informed. The transactions costs imposed on the firm would be huge. A far cheaper alternative is to regulate the tariff structure, altering rates less frequently (three monthly or six monthly intervals). This also has the merit of providing shippers with some degree of certainty as to the level of freight charges that they face over the next few months. One explanation of rate stability may lie in the fact that the transactions costs, or "menu costs" of altering prices were too large for anything other than intermittent price changes.

Stability of one liner organisation's rates may save administration costs, but these can be negated if rival liner services try to compete by price. This in fact, was a problem of the early liner services, in which there were marked cycles of boom and bust for shipowners in the 1860's and 1870's. But if liner companies go bust, they fail in their obligation to provide a common carrier service to shippers. Shipping companies importing Tea on the UK Calcutta route agreed to set up a "Conference" of shipping lines, who would agree to offer a regular service in co-operation with other conference members, and who agreed to charge a set of common tariffs to all shippers. The "conference system" was born, and despite rumours of its death, there are several hundred still active today. This is the second element of the explanation: many liner routes are still characterised by the presence of a "conference" organisation, which organises and co-ordinates the economic activities of its members. In economic terms, such collusion usually means less competition, more profits for the shipping lines, less innovation and dynamism than in a competitive industry. The conference system is explored in the following section.

## 7.7 THE CONFERENCE SYSTEM: KEY INSTITUTIONAL ELEMENT OR HISTORIC THROWBACK?

After the inauguration of the UK-Calcutta Conference in 1875, many other conferences came into being. Deakin and Seward, in their 1973 study, claimed that there were 360 active deep-sea conferences, with memberships ranging between 2 and 40 lines. This figure appears to repeat itself like a mantra over the next 25 years: many comparatively recent texts still quote this 25-year-old figure. Inquiries made by the present author suggest that there are still two to three hundred active conferences, but it is probably true to say that their economic impact on the market is less significant than it was 25 years ago, as their control of industry market share has declined markedly in certain key trades.

In essence, a conference, if it is able to enrol all liner companies serving a particular trade between named ports, becomes a monopoly supplier of the shipping capacity on that route. It is important to note that this monopoly is *only over the liner service* component of the trade. Liner conference members still face competition from tramp operators, and from air transport, for certain types of cargoes to be moved between the two ports. But the key element in the conference is that its *members limit the degree of internal competition between themselves*.

This limitation of competition is achieved by entering into various legal agreements. The main areas covered are:

1. Agreements on Common Tariffs to be charged to shippers

2. Cargo allocation arrangements

3. Revenue pooling arrangements

These arrangements can become very sophisticated, and require monitoring by the conference organisation itself. A simple model of a profit maximising cartel, developed in Appendix 1 of this chapter, shows why such arrangements might be needed. It is often insufficient to regulate prices alone, because competition is then diverted into other forms, such as over expansion of capacity (too many ships) or by individual lines 'cheating' or 'chiselling' on their partners by offering secret discounts on the official tariff rates to key shippers.

Deakin and Seward (op. cit. p64) point out that many conferences do organise sophisticated cargo allocation schemes, under which certain lines may be allowed to load and discharge at certain specified ports, their sailing frequency may be regulated, or there may be limits on the amount of cargo that they can lift.

Conferences spread rapidly after their 1875 inauguration. Deakin and Seward estimated that 360 were active in the late 1960's, with individual membership ranging from 2 to 40 shipping lines. Jansson and Shneerson[6] state that

> "There is no accurate figure available for the total number of conferences in operation". (J&S, op. cit. p.35)

They go on to state

> "Anyway, conferences exist in most liner trades and in practically all intercontinental trades" (J&S, op. cit. p.35)

Two very important trading routes for the liner shipping are the Europe/Far East and Transpacific trades. In 1996, Conference lines held 67% of the Eastbound slot capacity, 65% Westbound, with non-conference lines accounting for the remainder. Conference members held a much smaller proportion, 56%.[7] These shares are still large enough for the sectors to be classified as an oligopoly or monopoly under present UK competition law.

## 7.7.1 Activities of the Conference Organisation

Conferences essentially provide a means for member lines to **co-ordinate** and run joint services, and **co-operate** with each other. These functions may appear to be inconsistent with normal competitive behaviour, where rivals act independently in all key decisions. They also agree with other conferences where their geographic range starts and ends, in effect dividing the total market into distinct sectors.

The degree of co-operation starts with setting agreed common tariffs for shippers, and then progresses into more sophisticated arrangements covering tonnage provided, cargo lifting/discharge rights, and ultimately, revenue pooling.

## 7.7.2 Types of Conferences

Two principal types can be observed: **Open** and **Closed**.

A **Closed** conference was the original type. Essentially the liner companies would provide a monopoly service between two ports, with entry by other lines being permitted only by the unanimous agreement of its members. Since the existing lines would lose market share to any

---

[6] J. Jansson and D Shneerson (1987) Liner *Shipping Economics* Chapman and Hall: London

[7] *Europe/Far East liner trades under pressure* LSE October 1996; *Lines regroup to regain competitive edge* LSE February 1996

new entrant, this inhibits competition. Such conference structures became the subject of a number of government studies in the early 1900's, in the UK and USA. As a consequence of the 1916 US Shipping Act, later updated in the 1984 Act, US Congress agreed that conferences would be exempt from the Anti-Trust legislation, provided that such Conference arrangements which involved trading into and out of US ports must be such as to permit the free entry of any company wishing to operate a liner service, and be bound by the rules of the conference.

### Open Conferences

As might be inferred from the above paragraph, an Open conference tries to regulate tariffs and capacity on a particular route, but new members are free to join in the service provided that they satisfy the rules and obligations of membership. The 1984 US Shipping Act states that such a commitment means the liner company being willing to operate a scheduled service with a *minimum* frequency of 14 days. Providing that condition is met, existing members cannot prevent entry to any trade operating to or from a US Port.

The 1984 Act also has another important clause, highlighted by Janssen and Shneerson.

The clause states that "Each conference agreement must provide that any member of the conference may take *independent* action on any rate" [8] This gives the right to any member of a US related conference the right to compete by cutting rates, which of course defeats their principal object.

One other point which applies to all conferences operating under the jurisdiction of the US legal code, is that the 1984 Act expressly requires that freight rates must never be less than the *marginal cost* of moving that cargo. One way of seeing the importance of this clause is to relate it to the ability of members to vary the rate. The US government has tried to limit the potential damage to liner operators that might be triggered by a rate war, by laying down a lower limit for the rate itself.

### 7.7.3 The UNCTAD Liner Code

The emergence of a new national shipping line from the developing countries in the 1970's led to an international debate concerning the difficulties they faced in entering the conferences that often dominated their trades. The code tried to regulate these trades by insisting on a 40-40-20 rule for cargo allocation, 40% each for the companies at the origination and destination areas, 20% for cross-traders. At the time the agreement was negotiated, an important agreement, known as the 'Brussels package', was introduced. In effect, the Brussels package made the new code inapplicable to trades to and from Europe. The USA has never signed the Code. These two events prevented the code from being enforced on many major trades, and it is now more or less completely ineffective.

### 7.7.4 Conference Pricing of Cargoes

There are essentially two distinct issues to consider when exploring the structure of tariffs in the liner trades, and inside conferences in particular. Firstly, no discussion is complete without a discussion of the way that conferences set their tariffs. Secondly, conferences have developed certain methods that are designed to limit competitive pressures on the market. These two aspects will be considered in turn.

### Basis for charging

Delegates at the 1941 Inter-American Maritime Conference identified 27 different factors which were felt to influence the structure of freight rates charged in the liner trades. In a study by the Economic Commission for Latin America (ECLA)[9] tested these factors against real world data using regression analysis. They found that they could reduce these factors to two key determinants of the rate structure, namely the *unit value of the commodity*, and the *cargo*

---

[8] Jansson and Shneerson (op. cit.) pp.44-45

[9] ECLA 1970 Special Studies on Latin America, Part 3. Recent trends in Latin American Maritime Transport. Economic Commission for Latin America E/CN 12/851. Ch. 3.

*stowage factor.*[10] Deakin and Seward's econometric model of the freight rates set for companies operating on UK related conferences found similar results, with 'demand based' (i.e. unit value) accounting for 2/3rds of the explained variation in rates, and 'cost related' factors (primarily the stowage factor) the other third.

Table 7.4 clearly shows the large variation in the rate charged for moving containers of different commodities between Germany and Israel in 1985. Note the highest rate is for alloyed metals, followed by Pharmaceuticals. These are both high unit value items. Wood and paper and Machinery are priced much lower.

It should be noted that such pricing structures are continually evolving, as new products are invented and old ones die away. The conferences used to regard the 'rate books', which were often massive volumes, as highly confidential documents, to be kept in a very secure environment. Whilst rate structures have been simplified, the essential characteristic still remains, which is to charge different prices for different commodity types, even though they now mainly all go by container.

**Table 7. 4**
**Tariffs per TEU by Commodity Type**
**Germany to Israel (Closed Conference)**
**1985**

| Commodity Type | Price $ |
|---|---|
| Food | 4225 |
| Chemicals | 4400 |
| Pharmaceuticals | 4665 |
| Alloyed Metals | 7480 |
| Wood and Paper | 3860 |
| Machinery and Tools | 3620 |

Recently, a number of commentators have suggested that since it costs the same to move a box, irrespective of what it contains, rates should be set at the same standard value, irrespective of content. This is known as FAK, or freight all kinds. Although there appears to be some merit in the argument, from an economics viewpoint, it is fallacious. Companies are quite right in charging by unit value as long as differences in unit value reflect differences in the underlying price elasticity of demand for the commodity. This point is explored in more detail below.

**Limiting competitive pressures**
There are two sources of competitive pressure, one external, one internal.

*External Pressure*

External pressure is brought to bear from

1.  air freight competition

2.  tramp shipping.

Air freight puts a limit on the rates that can be charged for high unit value, low weight cargo types. Air freight has grown steadily in the past decade, and its major advantage is in moving

---

[10] The cargo stowage factor shows the ratio of volume of space required to the weight of the cargo.

items very quickly. Perishable high value items such as cut flowers, tomatoes, mange-touts are often moved this way. The high transport cost is still a small proportion of the retail price of the cargo, and it is essential that its freshness be preserved. Air freight still carries a small proportion of the total, because in many cases speed is not critical. Nevertheless, the existence of a substitute means of transport implies that certain commodities will be more price sensitive as a result.

Large volume, low value, high weight cargoes can always be moved by tramp operators. Tramps have no common carrier obligation, nor do they need to keep to a published timetable. As a result, their operating costs may be lower than a liner's for certain volumes of cargo. In order to prevent tramps from gaining business, conferences have set low prices for the bulk commodities in which tramps have a potential advantage. These rates may indeed not cover the long run average cost of providing the service, but, in line with the 1984 US shipping Act, they do cover the average incremental cost, or marginal cost, of lifting and moving that cargo.

Thus competition from air freight and tramps helps to determine the nature of the tariff structure set in the liner trades. It also implies that demand might be price sensitive at the top end, price insensitive in the middle, and price sensitive again at the low unit value end of the market, given the competition from air freight and tramps.

In addition to the tariff structure, conferences often provide one of two types of tariff rebate scheme, which have the effect of increasing shipper loyalty. These are known as the *deferred rebate* scheme and the *exclusive contract* scheme. The deferred rebate operates by the conferences offering a refund on the published tariff rate to a shipper, if they can show that over the previous six months they have not used a non-conference member's services to move their cargoes. Once the shipper has entered such a contract, this sum is in effect a 'fine' to be imposed, should that shipper renege.

Under an exclusive contract scheme, the shipper agrees to send all their cargoes on conference member vessels, in exchange for a lower tariff. In this case, the tariff applies immediately.

Both of these schemes try to tie in shippers to conference members, and thus reduce the potential loss of trade that might be caused by tramp and air freight competition.

*Internal Pressure*
Internal pressure arises when individual liner companies try to cheat or chisel on the agreement. This is usually dealt with in the conference by the setting up of more complex agreements between members, permitting the central organisation to monitor the activities of individual lines, to ensure that cargo lifting and capacity agreements are honoured. Appendix 1 shows how the incentive to cheat is created.

## 7.8    PRICE DISCRIMINATION IN THE LINER TRADES

The discussion about the competitive pressures on the liner trades, generated by air freight and tramp operations, suggests that different commodities being carried by the liner trades have different freight rate elasticities of demand. Very high value commodities with low weight can use air freight as a substitute. The commodities in the middle, too heavy to be moved by air, but too complex and valuable to be moved easily in bulk, are the commodities with the lowest own price elasticities of derived demand. Tramp competition for bulk cargoes again raises the price elasticity, since they become good substitutes for liner services. The liner trades, and conferences, have taken advantage of this fact by setting *discriminatory prices* [11] by different cargo types. Shippers are not in themselves interested in the rates charged by the conferences

---

[11] Price discrimination exists when the conference sets different rates to move cargoes, which cost it the same amount of money; i.e. different rates for cargoes even when the marginal cost of moving those cargoes is identical.

for goods which are quite distinct from their own – this allows the conference members to practice price discrimination.

One might expect to observe a demand curve that looks like the one drawn in Figure 7.3 below. At high rates per ton, demand is more elastic (flatter) than in the midrange, which is where there is the least external competition. Low value commodities also face increased competition, generating a rather odd shaped demand, or average revenue curve. The principles of price discrimination are laid out in Appendix 2.

Essentially, profit maximising behaviour by a conference, or indeed, any oligopoly supplier (one facing an inelastic demand curve), yields the proposition that the market should be segmented and different prices set in each segment, if possible. This always leads to the generation of greater total revenues, and hence greater profit for a given level of total costs.

**Figure 7.3**

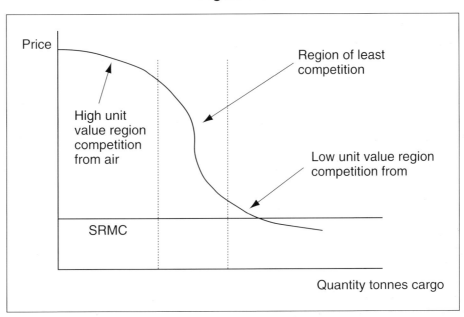

## 7.9 THE CONFERENCE PARADOX

On the face of it, the conference system has all the classic features of a joint-profit maximising cartel. The lines gang together to reduce capacity and raise rates, thus raising profits. Entry is prevented by the closed conference, and the threat of 'cheating' or 'chiselling' between members may be dealt with by the use of trade share agreements.

If the conference system is a powerful monopoly, one would expect it to generate large and sustained profits. Yet the empirical evidence is precisely the opposite. The Rochdale Commission of Enquiry into British Shipping (1970), and Deakin and Seward's study (1973) provided evidence that profits, if anything, were lower than in other shipping sectors.

The fact that a cartel seems to make low profits has become known as *The Conference Paradox.* Economists have evolved a number of different explanations for this anomaly. They are:

1.  The Short Run Profit Maximisation Hypothesis (also known as the *utilisation maximisation* hypothesis)

2.  The *Contestable Markets* thesis

3.  The *Empty Core* thesis

### 7.9.1    The Short Run Profit Maximisation Hypothesis

Most textbook models assume that companies maximise profits; but which ones, short run or long run? In the conference system, it is argued that there is a strong incentive to maximise short run profits rather than long run profit. This will actually reduce long run profit!

Since costs are very largely fixed, this is more or less identical to maximising revenues. (If all costs were fixed, it would be exactly the same). Because there are very low marginal costs in the short run (Stopford[12] provides an estimate that only 15% of total costs are variable (Stopford, Table 5.1 p182), and there is over-capacity, the best thing to do is to generate as much revenue as possible. This is achieved by taking every extra unit of business in which the extra revenue is greater than or equal to the extra cost. But since the extra cost is very low, this means that you take business whose **average cost is greater than the extra revenue**, although the extra revenue is larger than extra cost.

This implies that low value cargo will be taken, as long as the above condition is satisfied, at a price which is less than its long run costs – i.e. there will be some **cross-subsidisation** of high price, profitable cargo (in long run terms) by low price, unprofitable cargo.

The diagram below illustrates the idea.

**Figure 7.4**

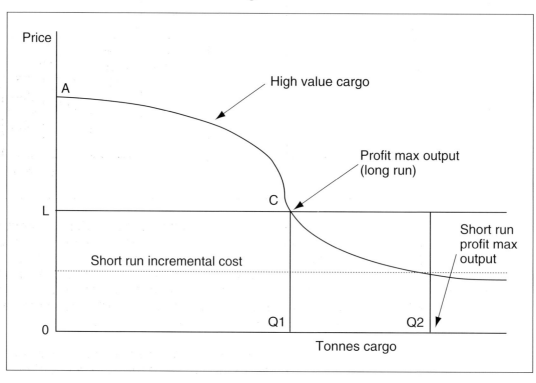

The implication of the existence of cross subsidisation is that profits are lower than they would otherwise be – hence this feature of the conference system generates lower long run profits than might otherwise be expected.

The above figure implies that maximising long run profits will lead to taking cargo quantities OQ1, and accepting only high value cargo. But if short run incremental costs are very low, and there is spare capacity (e.g. ships sailing half full), there is an incentive to forego long run profits and take extra cargo, as long as the extra revenue derived from that cargo exceeds the associated additional costs. This generates an output level of OQ2, which implies greater vessel utilisation. It also implies that some cargo is carried at unit prices which

---

[12] M. Stopford 1988 *Maritime Economics* Routledge. London

are lower than the long run unit cost of providing the service – that is, they are being 'cross subsidised' by the 'high value, profitable cargo'.

### 7.9.2 Evidence

Figure 7.5 below, taken from J A Zerby and R M Conlon (1978), provides some support for the model.

**Figure 7.5 – Behaviour of Average Rates on Australia-Europe Conference 1973**

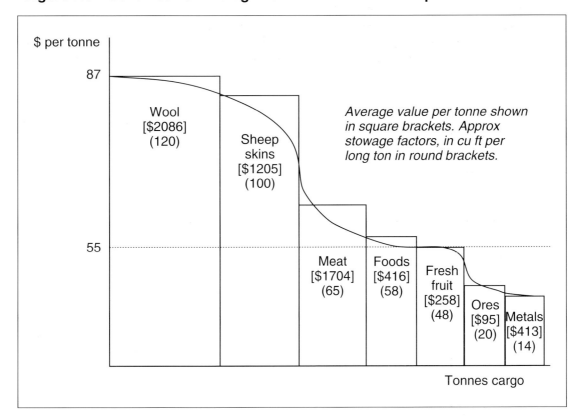

The bold curve reflects the estimated average revenue curve derived from data for the Australia-to-Europe conference for the years 1973-4. It shows very clearly the large difference in rates charged for the principal cargoes on that trade. The high value cargoes are carried at high freight rates. The rates taper off because of competition from air transport. The prices for metals and ores do not seem to cover average costs of $55 per tonne, but do cover the short run incremental costs, which have been estimated at 20% of long run average costs, as noted above. The estimate for AIC is $11 a tonne in this case.

The authors also estimate that the long run costs were $55 per tonne, and 36% of all Australian exports fell into categories which were charged close to that rate (Meat, Foods, fresh fruit).

The evidence quoted above does seem to provide tentative support for the persistence of the utilisation maximisation hypothesis, and the average revenue schedule derived in their study is very similar to that which can be hypothesised from the basic principle of price discrimination. It is a plausible explanation of the presence of cross subsidisation and low profits.

### 7.9.3 The Contestable Markets Hypothesis

In 1981, the new President of the American Economics Association, William Baumol[13], gave his inaugural address. In it he summarised what has become known as the theory of Contestable Markets. It was meant to be 'an uprising' in economic theory, as it claimed to

---

[13] Baumol, W. (1981) Contestable Markets: An Uprising in Industrial Economics *American Economic Review, vol 71.*

develop techniques for modelling multi-product companies operating in several markets, and developed new criteria for determining how competitive an industry or firm will be.

The new approach was centred on the idea of *potential* competition. It was argued that even a single supplier of a product might be forced to behave in a very competitive way if the conditions were right. The condition that ensured that a single supplier (a monopolist) would behave competitively turned out to be the condition that new firms could enter and exit the market with no cost disadvantage to them.

This translates into the fact that a new entrant, if they chose to enter, would be able to offer the same quality of service as the present supplier (assume it's a monopoly seller) at the same level of unit costs; it would therefore not be possible for the existing firm to drive the entrant out again by the simple device of cutting prices.

On the other hand, the new entrant, once in, would have no difficulty in leaving; it could find another company willing to purchase the assets it needed to enter the market at the same price it paid for them.

Under these rather special conditions, it can be shown that the monopoly seller must behave exactly like a competitive firm. The firm may *appear* to have monopoly power, but potential competition is sufficient to prevent it from exploiting that power. If it were to raise prices above the competitive norm, potential entrants would become real entrants, and the incumbent firm would be forced to reduce prices again.

This is the essence of contestable markets. It points up the fact that industries that appear to be monopolies or oligopolies, may in fact be forced to act very competitively, provided the special conditions outlined above are satisfied.

Some economists have argued that the low profits of conference members can be explained in this way. They point to the fact that in many cases, non-conference lines can compete for business. They can also enter and leave trade routes quickly and easily, at little or no extra cost compared to the incumbent lines. For these reasons, they argue that liner conferences make no profit because they are forced to be competitive.

Other authors have not accepted this position. Prof. Emeritus S. Gilman[14] has argued that there are substantial exit costs in the liner trades. If a liner company goes bankrupt, the sale of its ships seldom realises the book value that they were recorded at. Entry thus involves a risk of substantial loss if it is not successful.

### 7.9.4 The Empty Core Thesis

The final alternative to be put forward is a recent and novel argument, first developed by William Sjostrom. He has argued that the Conference system developed in order to create the very market in which it has evolved. In essence, the 'market' for regular scheduled sailings between fixed ports is only sustainable if the conference system acts to regulate competition for this type of business. In other words, the *market would fail* without the institutional structure given to it by the conference system itself.

The argument put forward to justify this position is a technical one, but its essence can be outlined. The cost structure of companies operating in the liner trades is such that the bulk of their costs are *fixed*. If companies have a high proportion of fixed costs, then ruinous price wars are more likely, because short run variable costs, the costs determining the 'floor' for prices, will be very low. There is good reason to expect that there will be marked price instability. But liner companies will be driven out of the market at low prices – and it is argued that there will now be *insufficient* supply. In other words, the market will never converge to a stable market

---

[14] Gilman, S. (1994) Contestability and Public Policy in Liner and Short Sea Shipping, in Molenaar, H. and E. Van de Voorde (1994) *Competition Policy in Liner Shipping*, University of Antwerp/IAME, Antwerp, Belgium pp45-64.

equilibrium. The definition of a liner service is the provision of regular guaranteed services – and this will not be possible under the above conditions. It follows that the conference structure provides the necessary stability, as a replacement for the chaos that would occur if the market were left to its own devices.

## 7.10 RECENT DEVELOPMENTS IN THE LINER TRADES

### The Rise of 'Global Alliances'

In the last twenty years, liner companies have got bigger, operating larger fleets, and using larger capacity vessels. The capital needed to support such expansion has led to the emergence of container consortia providing such services jointly. One notable feature of the trade is the fact that these consortia can be found both inside and outside the conference system; there appears to be an increasing level of fluidity, as large individual companies switch in and out of conference membership, and in and out of strategic alliances with other liner operators. The European Commission, prompted by complaints from large European shippers, has investigated a number of practices employed in these trades. In addition, the US government has examined some of the capacity management agreements[15] that have evolved on trades into and out of its ports.

### 7.10.1 Strategic Alliances

The liner trades have continually evolved new routes and new services as a means of competing with each other, and to meet evolving shipper needs. One innovation, started in the mid 1980's, was the introduction of one way round the world (RTW) services, a concept pioneered by Evergreen, the Taiwanese based container operator. A number of other companies followed suit, such as American President Lines, but they ran into difficulties and abandoned their service. At present, Evergreen is the only operator of such a service.

Other lines have combined to run highly competitive services in strategic alliances, offering shippers fast, regular, and reliable sailings. An example of joint services is to be seen in Table 7.1, at the beginning of this chapter.

It has been argued that "The advent of such agreements, dubbed as global strategic alliances, can be considered as a substantial breakthrough in the industry's co-operative practice since, unlike previous partnerships, they are not limited to a single trade lane, but aim to cover every major route as well as a number of relevant north-south trades and regional/feeder links. At the same time, these strategic alliances extend their area of influence well beyond vessel operations towards the shared use of terminals, joint equipment management, inland transport and logistics, joint purchasing and procurement.[16] The article goes on to suggest that "firms can achieve a satisfactory level of stability and efficiency by focusing on one or more of the three following measures, reduction in the number of partners, differentiation in their roles and contributions, and co-ordination of sales and marketing activities".

Existing links between alliance members will need to be modified by the merger of P&O Containers and NedLloyd, as these companies have been in rival alliances in the past. The industry has claimed that such alliances are essential if the operators are to provide the necessary frequency of service at competitive rates – the pooling of resources permits the lowering of overhead, increased utilisation and better sailing schedules.

It should be pointed out that many of these arrangements exist outside the conference system. Indeed, as was noted earlier in this lesson, the market share of conference members

---

[15] These are agreements whereby members agree to limit the slot capacity of the service. In other words, they regulate the output of the alliance.

[16] Midoro, R & Pitto A, A critical evaluation of strategic alliances in liner shipping, Martime Policy & Management 2000, Vol. 27, No.1

on some routes has declined to 50 or 60% in recent years. Does this mean that conferences are no longer effective?

The answer to this appears to be no. Where conference shares have declined, a relatively new phenomenon, *Capacity Management Agreements*, have arrived to take their place. On the TransPacific routes, a Tonnage Stabilisation Agreement was introduced in 1989. At present, it covers 90% of the companies offering liner services on this route, although Conference Membership covers only 55% of the trade.[17]

## 7.11   THE EUROPEAN COMMISSION AND THE LINER TRADES

Articles 85 of the Treaty of Rome prohibits anti-competitive agreements which significantly affect trade between its Member States. Article 86 prohibits abuse of dominant market positions. Director General IV has powers to grant block exemptions from these articles. The block exemption must be applied for, and companies participating in such agreements have to notify DGIV of the agreement, which will be approved if one of four criteria are met. The criteria are a) the notified agreement promotes technical and/or economic progress; confers on customers a fair share of the benefit of the agreement; and b) that the restrictions on competition contained in the agreement are the indispensable minimum to achieve a) or b) above; and that substantial competition is not eliminated in the market in which the agreement operates.[18]

In 1987 the Council of the Commission approved a regulation, Regulation 4056/86, which granted block exemption to liner conference agreements, "provided that they have as their objective the fixing of rates and conditions of carriage". It also permitted the other principal functions, namely, the co-ordination of timetables, frequency of sailings, and regulation of cargo capacity. The exemption is subject to the proviso that equivalently placed shippers will not be discriminated against without objective justification, and that certain obligations are observed, such as the maintenance of price transparency (seeing how prices are determined) through publicly available tariffs.

In 1994, the EC prohibited the Transatlantic Trade Agreement (TAA). In January 1995, it took proceedings against the similar Europe-Australia Trade Agreement (EATA), which is a capacity management agreement for these trades. It objected to such agreements, regarding them as a restraint of trade, which inevitably leads to higher prices. It is much more sympathetic to scrapping or mothballing programmes.

The EC has also taken action over multimodal pricing. Liner conference tariffs have been extended to cover the land based legs of 'door-to-door' shipment, with the result that some European shippers have accused them of extending their market power, enabling them to discriminate between shippers who use their door-to-door services and those that just use the sea-leg part, arranging the land based legs through other carriers. The argument is that land-based carriers are subject to anti-trust rules, but the conference players are not, as they have been exempted from Articles 85 and 86 under the block exemption for conferences.

According to Ruttley[19] the EC found in favour of the shippers, in effect outlawing multimodal tariffing by conferences. It pointed to the fact that independent Asian lines appeared to be able to operate in complete independence of the conference system, and inferred from this that a conference is no more than a simple profit maximising cartel.

The Far East Freight Conference was in litigation with the EC for several years over this issue. It argued that multimodal pricing was the norm. The EC did not accept this position.

---

[17] See LSE Feb 1996 p 7
[18] Ruttley, P. (1995) EC *Competition Law and shipping*. LSE January, pp6-8.
[19] *Ibid.* p9

Similar action occurred in the US, with the FMC acting to ensure that the TSA, Transpacific Stabilisation Agreement, first put in place in 1989, became ineffective in limiting capacity.

It is clear from these events that the regulation of competition in the liner trades is still a very live issue.

## 7.12   CONCLUSION

This section has tried to cover a very large amount of material. The liner trades have been transformed over the past 25 years, as the containerisation revolution disseminates throughout the globe. Despite this transformation, certain key features still exist, namely the application of price discrimination, and the Conference System. Economic models of the conference system were explored, in an attempt to explain what has become known as the 'Conference Paradox'. Lastly, the development of global alliances, and the relationship between the European Community and Shipping Conferences was discussed.

### APPENDIX 1 – The determination of market equilibrium in a two liner conference

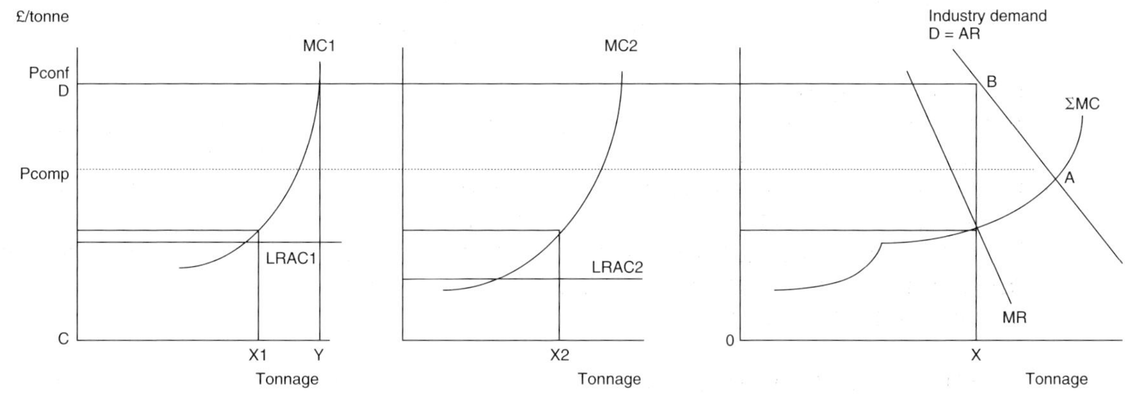

**Figure A1a**     **Figure A1b**     **Figure A1c**

If two liner companies collude in the transportation of a particular commodity between two named ports, they are able to raise both prices and profits, according to the standard model of cartel behaviour. Figure A1 above illustrates the idea. Figure A1a shows the short run marginal cost of moving extra cargo tonnage faced by liner company 1. Its long run costs are given by LRAC1, which is drawn as a horizontal line to reflect the assumption that there are constant returns to scale in the industry. A similar set of curves are drawn to represent the cost structure of liner company 2. Note that by assumption, this company has lower average costs than company 1.

In order to construct the industry supply curve, the two marginal cost curves are added up in a special way. The result is shown in Figure A1c. The 'kink' arises because at very low prices, only liner company 2 can still set marginal cost equal to price; company 1 has left the market. The combined MC curve must have a flatter slope than any single MC curve, because when output is expanded by one unit from company 2 say, company 1's output and therefore MC is unchanged. When the next increment in output is being considered, company 2's MC has increased, but MC1 has not. Successive additions made in this way imply that the overall MC rises more slowly than any individual MC – in other words, it is flatter.

### Competitive Equilibrium

If the market were competitive, price would be determined at the point where supply equals demand, i.e. at point A in Figure A1c. Each firm would be profit maximising, and in the model above, both companies would be profitable.

## Conference Equilibrium

If the companies organise themselves into a closed conference, they behave as a single monopoly supplier. A monopoly supplier maximises profits by setting its marginal costs to its marginal revenue schedule, in this case the MR derived from industry demand shown in Figure A1c.

As can be seen, the new position involves setting a higher common price, and restricting output. Both companies limit supply; each produces X1 and X2 respectively, with the combined output equalling OX in Figure A1c.

## Cheating and Chiselling

Why should conferences wish to regulate tonnage as well as price? The answer can be seen in the diagram. From company 1's point of view, the regulated market price is now CD, but its output is only CX1. If it took the market price as given (behaving as if it was a in perfectly competitive environment), its own profit maximising output level would be OY, where its MC = Pconf. But this involves cheating on the conference, by offering shippers secret rates just below CD in order to attract extra business. Conference organisations can limit this process by setting tonnage share limits for each of the conference members. This would be defined in terms of the tonnes of cargo, or market share of the trade, that the company was permitted to carry. Nowadays, slots on container vessels are used to measure capacity; a new entrant to a conference is often described as taking up the slot capacity of a line which it has replaced.

## APPENDIX 2 – The Principles of Price Discrimination

In many sectors of the economy, companies use price discrimination to increase the total revenues they generate from the sale of their goods or services. It is important to realise that discrimination *does not necessarily* require that a monopoly exists. A good example to illustrate this point is the Film and Video industry. When a new film is released in a country, it is first shown in the cinema. Hopefully, all the development costs of the film will be recovered during this phase, but it is not always the case. When the film's popularity declines, the rights to show it are sold, firstly to satellite television companies, who pay larger royalties than the terrestrial based ones, at least in the UK. When these markets are exhausted, the film is released on video, on a rental basis. Even here, video companies charge a premium rate for products that are recently released in that format.

The company is using price discrimination *over time* to maximise the revenue potential of its product. Each film can be said to be unique, but it faces strong competition from the hundreds of other films available, newly released or on video. By limiting its release to each segment over different time periods, and charging different prices, the company maximises its revenues, and hence profits.

The ability to carry out this kind of discrimination depends on three factors.

1.   There must be different market segments, with differing own price elasticities of demand.

2.   The company must be able to prevent resale, that is prevent one client from reselling the product or service to another client.

Different elasticities have to exist to make price discrimination worthwhile. If each sector had the same elasticity, they respond in the same way to a price change, and, from the economic point of view, can be treated as the same sector.

If the company cannot prevent customers trading with each other, it is clear that if customer A is charged £30, and B £10, A can persuade B to buy two units at £10 and then resell one on, say at £12. A saves £18 and B gains £2. The loser is the company.

## Pure Price Discrimination

Suppose that the product supplied by a company could be sold, unit by unit, onto a market. An auction would be a good example. The supplier would offer the first unit at the auction, and receive the highest bid for it. Then the second, the third, and so on. The first item would sell at the highest price, as it would be unique. The second would fetch slightly less. This situation is shown in Figure A2.1 below.

### Figure A2.1 – Pure Price Discrimination

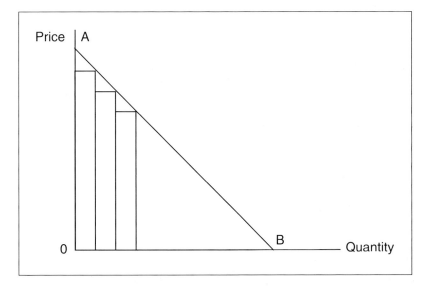

If one calculates the Total Revenue generated by selling every possible unit in this way, it will equal the area OAB. Furthermore, the extra revenue generated from the sale of one more unit must be equal to the price that the unit sells at, since it is being sold by auction. It follows that under these special circumstances, price, or average revenue, is identical to marginal revenue.

## Price Discrimination and Profit Maximisation

The traditional rule for maximising profits is to set marginal revenue equal to marginal cost. In the traditional model, this leads to a single price charged for all units sold, as shown in Figure A2.2 below. In contrast, Figure A2.3 shows the effect of applying pure price discrimination to the market. It is clear that output, total revenues, and by implication, profits, are higher than in the usual case.

**Figure A2.2**                    **Figure A2.3**

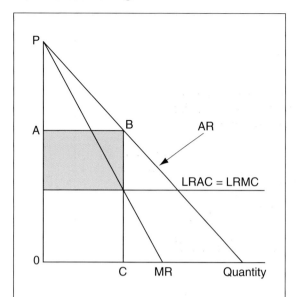
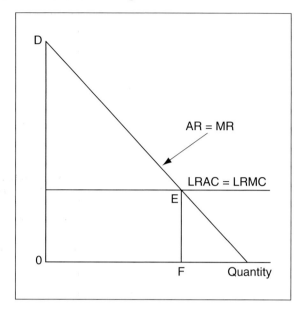

Figure A2.2 shows the long run profit maximising equilibrium for a seller with some ability to differentiate their service from rivals. Output will be set at OC units, and a standard price of OA is set. The shaded area represents total profits. By comparison, the profit maximising firm does better if they can sell each unit at a specific price. Then the Average and Marginal Revenue curves are the same, and profit maximising output is OF in Figure A2.3. There is no such thing as an average price here, because each unit is sold at the maximum it could fetch on the market. Total Revenue is then area ODEF, much larger than OABC, assuming identical demand conditions. It is clear that profits are larger in the second case, as Total Costs would be given by the height of the average cost curve multiplied by the number of units sold.

## Cross Subsidisation and Price Discrimination

In the particular conditions of the Liner trades, it was noted that average incremental cost, or short run marginal cost, was very low, much lower than long run average cost. Figure A2.4 shows the *short run* profit maximising equilibrium achieved under these conditions. Note that certain units are being sold at less than their long run average (and marginal) cost of production, even if they still cover their short run attributable or direct costs. This is called *cross subsidisation*, as it implies that certain services (units Q1Q2) are being sold to the public at less than the long run opportunity cost of its production. This is regarded as inefficient, since it implies a misallocation of resources; those resources would generate better returns if they were applied elsewhere in the economy.

**Figure A2.4 – Short Run Profit Maximisation and Cross Subsidisation**

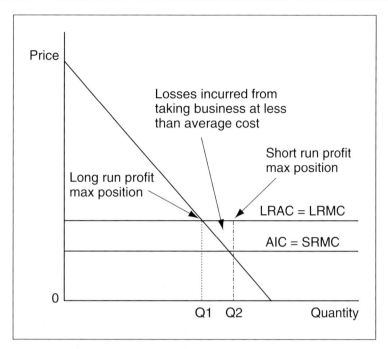

## 7.13    SELF-ASSESSMENT AND TEST QUESTIONS

Attempt the following and check your answers from the text:

1.    Redraw Figure 7.1, but adding in the following segments – high-speed ferries, products tankers, dry bulk tankers.

2.    The model in Appendix 1 has been drawn with 'traditional' shaped marginal cost curves. What would happen if these were replaced with simple horizontal lines, running below the companies' respective average cost curves? This might represent the measure of the short run marginal cost, or incremental costs. The answer is that the model generates the same conclusions, but profits will be lower. See if you can work it out for yourself. (Hint: the supply curve will have a kink in it at the point when the second company starts to supply output).

Having completed Chapter Seven, attempt the following question and submit your answer to your Tutor.

'Freight conferences may still have a role to play'. Assess the validity of this statement, making reference to recent developments in the liner trade.
(ICS Exam 2000)

# Chapter 8

# PORTS, SEA CANALS, AND WATERWAYS

## 8.1 INTRODUCTION

Ocean and coastal shipping, unlike other modes of transport have no need for an infrastructure of tracks, signalling, bridges, etc. Ships do however need elaborate and usually extremely expensive terminal facilities in the shape of harbours and ports. This is probably one of the most difficult tasks of maritime economics, the allocation of resources in an optimum way to create an economically efficient port. A problem highlighted in two ways; firstly where a massive and very expensive port investment has been undertaken to construct a port few vessels visit. Secondly where a port lacks necessary investment long and costly delays are imposed on vessels awaiting a berth. Some of the basic elements of the problem will be examined in this Lesson. Ideally ports and the facilities they provide should be designed as part of an integrated transport system. Account should be taken of the ships that will use them, the port facilities at the other end of the major routes, the role of ship canals and waterways where applicable as well as the interaction with land transport.

## 8.2 DEFINITION OF PORTS AND HARBOURS

These can be defined simply as:

**A harbour** can be classified as a haven for the protection of ships, a place where vessels can shelter from inclement weather and if required, undergo repairs and/or re-victualling. Harbours are of two distinct types, either natural or artificial. Natural harbours are those sufficiently protected by their situation not to require any artificial aid. They are physically protected or enclosed by the coastline. Prime examples of this type are Sydney Harbour, the bay at Rio de Janeiro and Milford Haven.

Artificial harbours are harbours which require the natural configuration of the coast to be supplemented to a greater or lesser extent by breakwaters and the like. A harbour is formed by the natural structure but requires man-made breakwaters, piers or jetties to complete the task.

Prime examples of this are Dover Harbour in the United Kingdom, which is almost purely artificial, possessing a length of breakwater of over 3km and Tema in Ghana is another example.

The majority of harbours are a combination of the two types. The latter, artificial harbour, is the most important from an economic cost point of view as it will generally be the most expensive form of harbour, using a large amount of factors of production particularly capital in its construction and maintenance.

**A port** is sometimes referred to as a commercial harbour since ports are primarily designed and organised for commercial use. They are often called gateways between land and sea or water as 'ports' can refer to seaports, river ports or ports on canals or waterways.

The central function of a port is to be a point of transfer of commodities and people from land to water and vice versa. It is a place where land and water transport modes come into contact and the services are provided for the purpose of the interchange of cargoes and passengers as an essential feature of the whole national and international transport network.

## 8.3    THE FUNCTION OF PORTS

There are three general methods of examining a port's function at a rather simple and obvious level. These functions are:

a)    Traditional functions.

b)    Transport or transit functions.

c)    Industrial functions.

d)    Network functions

It is necessary in any analysis to make clear the close inter-relationship between these functions.

a)    **Traditional Functions of Ports.** These can be looked at from a broad perspective as, firstly, the seaport performs an important link in the total chain of transport. Secondly seaports usually provide areas or facilities for the storage of goods until transported to their destination. The storage function can range from a simple parking area for road haulage vehicles to massive tanks holding millions of barrels of crude oil. Thirdly seaports are often alternative locations for industry, particularly heavy industry and those associated with shipping.

b)    **Transport Functions of Ports.** Not only do ports provide the essential link between the transport network, a further distinction has to be made in the area of trans-shipment of goods. Trans-shipments can be from seagoing vessel to barges using canals and waterways, railway trucks, road haulage, aircraft, or any other modes of transport. Increasingly it is between seagoing vessels and another seagoing vessel. The transport function is characterised essentially by the transport mode used which in turn is a function of the type of goods carried and the length of journey to be made as well as the geographic and other conditions. The storage function of a seaport is directly related to its transport function. Seagoing vessels are several times larger than units of inland transport so for transport overland the total cargo carried in one trip by a seagoing vessel has to be split up into smaller consignments. These are consignments which are going to be conveyed along a route determined by factors other than those that influence the need to dispose of a ship's total cargo as quickly as possible. The provision of storage space provides an obvious answer for perishable and non-perishable goods which do not depend on onward shipping by sea transport.

c)    **The Industrial Function of a Port.** This is the logical offspring of its two other functions. The consideration that trans-shipment always involves handling costs as well as onward shipping in smaller, generally more expensive, transport has induced many industries, notably those of processing raw materials to locate in seaports. For a port to fulfil these various functions facilities are needed for ships, waterways, harbour bases, berths for inland transport, canals, roads, railways and storage and industrial land and buildings as well as the services they require. All these facilities call for a large investment with a very long life-time which will determine largely the physical and economic continuance of the region.

d)    **Network functions: Hub and Spoke Ports, or the Load Centre Concept.** The increased use of containerisation methods in shipping has led to a change in the way that ports are viewed. Because of the need to exploit scale economies, which require large cargo volumes, ports serving the liner trades have become increasingly specialised into one of two types, hub ports and feeder ports. A hub port, or load centre, as it is sometimes called, acts as an important focus of container trading activities. It is served by many ships calling to load and discharge cargo on many different routes. It has become a centre of cargo distribution which is often of great regional geographic importance, rather than merely a national or local one. Singapore and Hong Kong both serve this function in the Far East. Rotterdam does the same in Europe. A feeder port, as its name implies, is of lesser significance, as cargo volumes are smaller. Economies of scale are not so easily exploited, so the routes it serves will be less busy, with smaller vessels engaged on them. A hub port will be at the centre of a local network of these smaller ports, a system which has been called 'hub and spoke operations', because of the fact that cargo is first moved to a hub port, and then radiated out along the spokes. This arrangement is also to be observed in the world of air transport, where it is used for the same reason; to exploit scale economies by using large aircraft to serve the hubs, and smaller ones on the feeder routes.

The development of the hub port concept means that ports in the future may not necessarily need to have large industrial hinterlands close to them. An example is the important container port of Algeciras, which has little or no industrial development close by. But it is ideally located to act as a transhipment terminal, where containers can be shifted from one vessel to another in order to minimise the liner companies' overall costs of providing their shipping services. According to this viewpoint, port development will be closely tied in with its location, since this will determine its strategic importance the liner companies' route networks.

## 8.4  PORT COSTS AND SHIPS' TIME

### 8.4.1  Port infrastructure and Investment

One of the basic elements of which all students of transport or shipping economics must be aware is the functional difference between mobile plant and fixed plant from an economic point of view, for it has a major impact on the industry. The economic characteristics of the mobile plant or equipment, for example, motor vehicles, planes or ships, are that they are cheap relative to the investment expenditure involved in setting up a large infrastructure item, such as a port or an airport. Aircraft or ships also have a short economic life relative to ports and airports (Eurotunnel has an assumed economic life of 50 years), have alternative uses and in most cases only limited economies of scale. J.M. Thomson points out in 'Modern Transport Economics (1974)' that fixed plant or infrastructure has a number of important characteristics. Firstly it is an extremely costly investment. Secondly once constructed it is exceptionally long lasting; ancient ports and roads are still in commercial use. Thirdly they have little or no alternative uses. They are unwanted in other than their original function. Fourthly they often possess considerable potential for economies of scale (see Chapter Four).

To summarise, transport infrastructure like ports, canals and waterways is typically expensive, single purpose and offers economies of scale if it can be designed and built from the start for a high volume of traffic or cargo.

### Criteria for investment appraisal

A number of methods have been developed to enable the systematic evaluation of investment in large capital items, such as port facilities. They can be split into two broad categories: – those that do not involve discounted cash flow techniques, and those that do. A brief outline of these techniques is given here. Excellent treatments can be found in books on Investment Appraisal, and occasional articles in Lloyds Shipping Economist also discuss these issues.

### a)  Non-discounting methods

The simplest form of this is the Payback method. Essentially, an investment project is evaluated by estimating the cash outflows associated with the project over the initial period of its construction, the expected cash outflows generated by operating the facility once it is in use, and the cash inflows arising from the charges levied on users of the facility. This is to be done for every year of the asset's economic life, which may be a considerable period, lasting many years, in the case of port investments. Finally, estimates are made of any inflow arising from the sale of the asset at the end of its life, or additional costs involved with its disposal.

This method thus builds up a cashflow profile of revenues and costs associated with the asset. In fact, all systematic appraisal techniques use this as their base.

The payback method simply finds the answer to the following questions:

1. How much has been expended on setting up the asset i.e. what is the value of the investment?

2. How many years will it take before the surplus from revenues less the operating costs of the asset accumulates to a sum equal to the value of the investment?

The answer to question 2 is the payback period. Companies repeat this exercise for all projects they are evaluating, and then rank them by their payback period. They then select a criteria – e.g. Shell UK may require all investments to have a payback of 3 years. If the proposed project meets this criterion, it will be approved for funding. If the funds are available, the project can be undertaken.

The United Nations UNCTAD Secretariat in its handbook entitled 'Port Development' examines a number of evaluations of the nature and magnitude of port investment. In particular it looks at the payback period method which is illustrated in the following figure.

The payback method must be taken literally for it means that there is a considerable time gap, a period of years, required to recover or pay back the initial investment. Section 1 is the installation period, the time it takes to construct the facility. During this period there are only costs and no revenue or income. Income begins in section 2 when the facilities are beginning to operate and therefore gaining revenue from tariffs. Section 3 shows a period where income is in excess of operating costs. The payback period in this example, is clearly a long time, as the accumulation of capital from section 1 and the losses incurred in the start up period in section 2, will have to be recouped from the surpluses of revenue over operating costs expected in section 3.

## Figure 8.1 – Accumulated Costs and Revenues and Payback

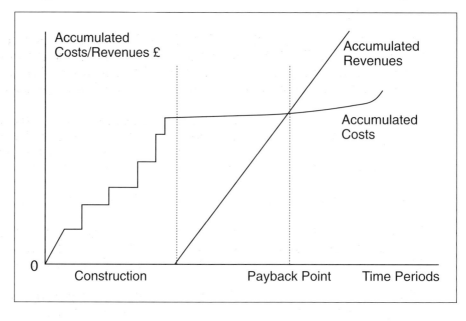

The payback period has many advantages. It is simple to understand and is easy to apply, once the cash flow projections have been made. Unfortunately, it is logically wrong and deeply flawed as a technique.

One reason for its logical failure is simple to see. In the introductory section, it was suggested that certain projects might require expense at the end of their lives. For example, Shell ran into great difficulty over the disposal of an old oil rig, which it planned to sink at sea. This would cost it very little. But public pressure forced them to abandon the idea after Greenpeace occupied it. They are now spending millions of pounds on the safe disposal of the rig. This additional expenditure appears at the end of the asset's life, and is not included in a Payback calculation.

A second, and much more fundamental flaw, is also more difficult for students to grasp. The fact is, cash earned by a company this year is not worth the same as cash generated in one year's time, which itself is not worth the same as cash in two year's time, and so on. In fact, the further forward one goes, the less is the current, or present value of that cash. The implication of this is simple. Without adjustment, one cannot add up this year's cash and next year's cash, because they are not the same things.

**b)  Discounted Cash Flow Methods**

Discounted cash flow analysis has been developed to deal with this problem. There are two principal investment appraisal techniques which use discounted cash flow analysis – they are known as Net Present Value, and Internal Rate of Return.

*Net Present Value*

The computation of the net present value of a project would start in the same fashion as the payback procedure. The first step would be to set out the cash flow profile that the project is expected to generate. The second step is to multiply net cash inflows or outflows by the appropriate discount factor for the year of the project. The third step is to add up the discounted cash flows, taking due account of the sign of the cash flow itself; positive for inflow, negative for outflow. Finally, the net present value rule is applied. This states that it is worthwhile for a company to invest in any capital project, at the assumed discount rate, if the net present value is positive, i.e. if the result of adding up the discounted negative and positive cash flows, over the entire life of the project, yields a number greater than zero.

This approach is clearly much more complicated than payback, but it has the merit that it incorporates all the cash flow information into the final result, and correctly adjusts for differences in the value of money over time.

*Internal Rate of Return*

This technique is very similar to that of the NPV. Indeed, it can be shown to rely on the same basic equation linking the value of the investment to the cash flows it generates. However, it asks a slightly different question. The question is: What rate of interest, or yield, generates a net present value of zero for the cash flow projections of a given project?

In other words, what rate of interest makes the present value of the capital investment going into the project exactly match the present value of the excess of revenues over operating costs which are generated by the project? Since these are negative and positive respectively, their sum will equal zero when this condition is met.

The rate of interest which achieves this is called the internal rate of return, or IRR.

The IRR rule stated simply, is: – invest in any project in which the IRR exceeds the opportunity cost of capital to the firm. The latter may be measured by the borrowing rate, if the firm finances the project by 100% loans, or the firm's own required rate of return.

NPV and IRR are general investment techniques, and can be applied equally well to ships as to port investment. Indeed, NPV and IRR are standard procedures in marine banks, when evaluating any proposal for a loan for ship finance.

A detailed explanation of these techniques is beyond the scope of this course.

**8.4.2  Ships and Port Time**

Turning to the consumer or customer of ports it must be emphasised that the size of the ship in terms of deadweight tons will be very closely related to the time it spends in port. The following rules hold in virtually all cases. The less time the ship stays or lies in port the larger will be the size of the vessel. Staying in port means that the ship is not earning income – it has an opportunity cost in terms of income foregone. Large ships forego more lost income than small ships – hence decreasing port time means that larger ships can be employed, as the higher foregone income per day is offset by the fewer days spent in port. If port time or port turn-round in certain trades is slow then the smaller the size of the ship will be. If the cargo a ship will carry in a certain trade is difficult and time consuming to handle in port, say for example loose dressed timber, the optimum size of the ship will be less than for carrying other easily handled cargoes. If on the other hand the cargo is easily loaded or unloaded for example oil or ore, the vessel's size will be considerably greater. (This is an opportunity to review Chapter Four). Obviously steaming distance will be of importance. Short sea or coastal vessels will be in port very often therefore port time must be seen in its wider sense. Thus preferred vessel sizes tend to be inversely related to the proportion of time that it has to spend in port.

**Figure 8.2 – The correlation between Port Time and Ship Size**

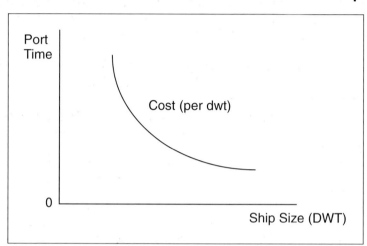

All other things being equal, one sees that as port time increases ship size dimension in economic terms also decreases. As port time contracts ships size increases therefore larger vessels become more economic. Transfer this to the empirical example, Table 8:1.

This table illustrates the fact that vessel size will relate very closely to port time. Tankers (and for that matter Bulk Carriers not included in the table) become massive in size for a number of reasons, as discussed in Chapter 4. One factor which encourages their growth in size has been the fact that load and discharge times have not been increased, thus reducing the proportion of time spent in port. General Cargo liners on the other hand as the table shows spend 60% of their time in port. One of the principal gains arising from containerisation has been a dramatic reduction in the proportion of time spent in port by container vessels compared to General Cargo liners. This has permitted them to become significantly larger.

### 8.4.3  Port Efficiency or Inefficiency with Regard to Ship Turn Round time

Port time is time required for any ship to carry out the essential functions in port. Any waiting time at anchor may be divided for the purposes of analysis into three parts:

a)  Time spent at anchor. This is perhaps the greatest variable due largely to congestion. It is the first point about which management must be particularly concerned as it can be the time consuming proportion which is subject to the greatest variable and hence the greatest opportunity for reduction in port time. A vital consideration in shippers', freighters' and ship's costs is the aim to remove congestion.

b)  Time spent in internal manoeuvres. Some of the time spent in motion in the channel waiting for tugs and pilots shipping towards berths and time lost before and after cargo handling. This can be subject to improvement only within strict limits for example moving a ship too quickly within a port might cause damage or accident.

c)  Cargo handling time. The truly productive time at a berth is from the commencement of cargo handling until its completion. This encompasses a large number of sub-systems, each of which will have different handling times which may, of course, include periods of storage.

## 8.5   PORT COST STRUCTURE

The purpose of a port is, as has been said, to make a smooth transfer of freight between sea and land transport. This is a productive process for port management and other management. In what follows there is an analysis of the production and particularly the all important cost functions.

### 8.5.1   Port Costs (i.e. strictly shore costs) are made up of two parts:

a)   The fixed cost component (FC) that is independent of the tonnage throughput which involves the capital costs of quays, sheds, cranes, etc. As the tonnage handled at the berth increases, such fixed costs or fixed components, expressed as costs per ton, decrease (curve A). Curve A shows the average fixed cost declining with traffic volume, as the same total fixed cost is divided by larger and larger units.

### Table 8.1 – Average % of Ship Time at Sea and in Port
### (early 1980s)

|                   | Passenger | Cargo | Deep Sea | Container | Tankers |
|-------------------|-----------|-------|----------|-----------|---------|
| **% Time at Sea** | 63        | 40    | 57       | 72        | 81      |
| **% Time in Port**| 37        | 60    | 43       | 28        | 19      |

Source: Drewrys Shipping Statistics and Economics

### Figure 8.3 – Average Port Costs and Traffic Volume

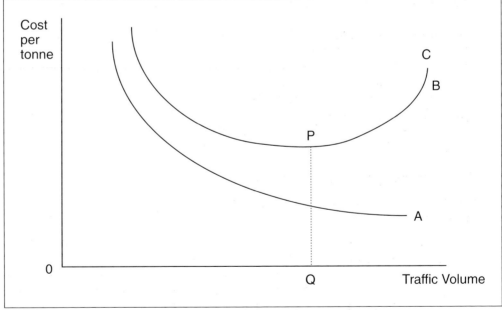

b)   The variable component or variable cost which depends on throughput includes labour, staff costs, fuel, container costs, etc. This variable cost when expressed as an average cost per ton will remain fairly stable until the port berth becomes under pressure to achieve higher tonnage throughput. The average variable cost per ton will tend to rise at this point, owing to the need to use more costly methods of handling cargo (curve B). The model illustrates the relationship between port costs *per tonne* and throughput or traffic volume. The average total cost curve (C) is the sum of the average fixed (A) and variable cost (B) components, reaching a minimum at point P. Traffic volume at this point is OQ. This is the most efficient level of Traffic Volume, because average total costs which are incurred by the port are now minimised. In other words, the lowest cost per ton possible is achieved with a cargo throughput of OQ. It would therefore be in the port management's interest to try to ensure that cargoes actually handled were close to this target figure.

### 8.5.2    Ships' Costs

The above model would be appropriate from a purely commercial, or private perspective. The port authorities would be primarily concerned with their own costs, their own revenues. But economists sometimes take a broader view, examining the total resource costs involved in the operation of a large entity like a port, which is often publicly owned and controlled. The efficient working of a port affects the way that ships can be used, so the value of their time can also be included as a port related cost from this broad perspective. If both shipowner and port are from the same nation, the analysis is being conducted in terms of the social costs and benefits that efficient port operation may bring, rather than focussing on the ports own direct commercial interests

Ship's time spent in port is made up of two parts, firstly the time the ship spends at the berth, that is berth utilisation when the ships are actually loading or unloading; and secondly the time the ship spends waiting for a berth to become vacant. As traffic increases the time spent waiting to get alongside or onto a berth increases at high berth occupation.

**Figure 8.4 – Ship's Time Costs in Port and Traffic Volume**

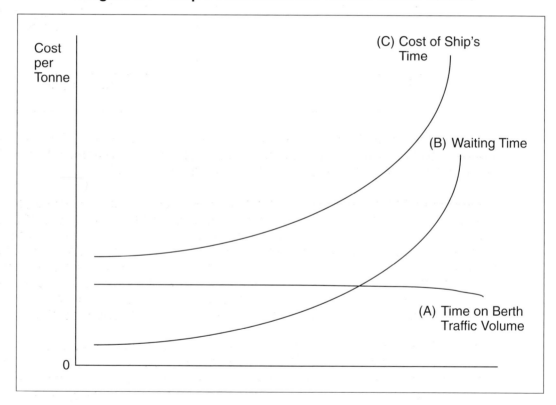

In the above model curve A represents the time on berth, curve B shows the extent to which the costs will increase quite rapidly with waiting time. This rapid increase occurs when the port is operating close to full capacity. The World Bank report of 1996 has highlighted the growing threat to further economic development in the Far East created by a failure to expand port capacities and related transport infrastructure in line with their recent strong economic growth. The result is that many ports in the region are operating inefficiently, imposing congestion costs on ship operators in the region.

The cost of ship's time in port is shown as curve C, a summation of curve A, ship's time and curve B, berth and waiting time, equal to curve C. Note that all of these curves are measured on an average cost, or per tonne basis.

### 8.5.3  Total Port Costs

The average total costs incurred by both ships when in port, and the port operations themselves, are found by adding together actual port costs and the costs of the ship i.e. model 8.3 and model 8.4 will equal model 8.5.

**Figure 8.5 – Combined average costs of Port Operations and Ship's Time**

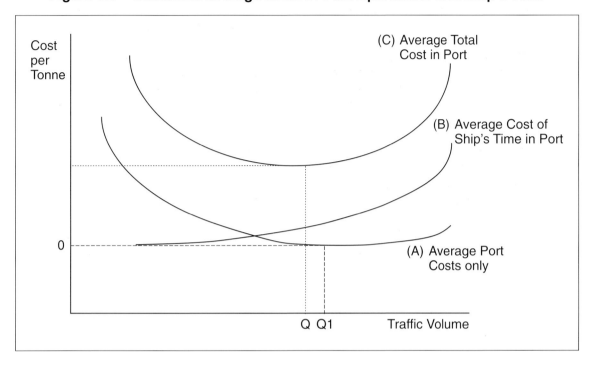

The average total cost per ton curve is at minimum point at point B. This means that from the broader point of view, i.e. taking into account both ships time and port operating costs, the lowest level of average total cost occurs at Traffic Volume OQ.

It is important to note that this is not the volume that minimises the average total cost of the port itself though. The minimising of the average total cost of the port (CQ1) occurs at traffic volume OQ1, which is greater than OQ. In other words, port managers have a cost incentive to run a port at a greater traffic volume level than might be deemed efficient from a broader viewpoint. Indeed, the consumer may well be very concerned, as minimising port costs on their own will generally result in an unsatisfactory level of service for the consumer, in this case the shipowner or operator, whose costs of ship time in port increase rapidly beyond FQ. This can lead to conflict, and is commercially and economically unacceptable.

Indeed, this model may well explain why so many large ship operators either lease or build their own dedicated terminal facilities. Large oil companies build private terminals linked directly to their refineries; ferry companies own or lease facilities to speed up their own ferry turn-round times; liner companies lease or jointly own large container terminals, as part of an investment in through transport. In every case, the shipowner has 'vertically integrated' the ship operation and port operation sides of the business in order to minimize the overall costs of delivering the product. By this means, they are in effect, including the cost of ships time as well as the costs of ports themselves.

## 8.6  THE AIMS OR PRINCIPLES OF PORT TARIFFS

Port tariffs will be the main instrument by which port authorities cover their costs or earn some surplus or profit. But such tariffs for port services are not merely instruments to ensure the accounts are balanced. The port tariffs have an important effect in encouraging or discouraging the use of port services. However, because of the importance of ports to national and particularly international trade and industry, it can be argued that general port policy is motivated by the desire to promote the national interest. This concept has not been thoroughly worked out because it is often difficult to identify specifically "national interest" in the way particular port policies or tariffs are created. All ports will claim that one of their main concerns is to promote the national interest.

In order to understand the extent to which this idea underlies management pricing and investment in ports it is necessary to examine the two main principles or doctrines on which port development tends generally to be based. These are known as:

i) Anglo Saxon or Peninsular doctrine.

ii) The European doctrine.

The Anglo Saxon view states notwithstanding the benefits to the hinterland the port should stand on its own feet, not incur losses and aim to make a reasonable profit. This is a principle on which many ports in the United Kingdom operate. This view has been sharpened by the privatisation of Associated British Ports, which runs many of the UK's ports and terminals. Now in the private sector, ports are driven by the profit motive and commercial considerations, to a greater extent than they were before.

The European doctrine views the port as part of the social structure of the whole region. The value of the port should be assessed not in the account of the port but in terms of the progress of the industry, transport and trade of the port in the port region or hinterland. As the name suggests, this view lies behind the development of many European ports and is often the basis on which subsidies for port development are justified.

While implicit in both these principles there is the requirement to cover costs and be efficient, the extent to which this will be the main aim will depend on the context within which pricing and investment decisions have to be made.

For management, therefore, the aim will either be:

a) to run an efficient port whose assets assist regional development

or

b) have a policy for tariffs and investment geared to making money.


## 8.7    PORT PRIVATISATION: OWNERSHIP AND EFFICIENCY

Port management structures have been radically transformed in the last 15 years in the UK, with the floating of the Nationally owned trust ports, and their privatisation. Associated British Ports is now a private company, running many of the UK's well-known ports on a commercial basis. Port privatisation is a policy that may well spread to other countries, where state ownership is the norm.

There are many conflicting arguments about the benefits and costs of such an approach. In the UK, privatisation has been accompanied by the abolition of the National Dockworkers scheme, thus making labour relations much less inflexible than they were. Ports can seek capital from private sources, and have to operate in a commercial fashion. The Anglo-Saxon doctrine is sharply reinforced with these developments. UK ports have shed significant numbers of labour following these developments, and, it is claimed, have become more efficient and more flexible.

The rising popularity of privatisation has led many observers to raise the question of the link between ownership and economic efficiency. There are those that argue that ports should be run as part of a nationally integrated plan, and the best way of achieving this is through state ownership. There are others who argue that privately owned and run ports are more efficient, because they respond more flexibly to market needs.

The evidence on this question is mixed. It is best summed up by Professor Goss's analysis of the relative merits of the Ports of Singapore and Hong Kong. They are both regarded as being very efficient; but Singapore's is state owned, whilst Hong Kong's is private. Goss concluded that ownership was not the key issue; management competence, investment, and cultural factors were of far greater significance.

## 8.8 PORT COMPETITION

Ports are often in an uneasy relationship with one another. If they share the same hinterland, they may indeed, try to compete, by offering better facilities for cargo handling, storage and distribution, or through simple price competition. For example, there is considerable rivalry between Antwerp and Rotterdam. Both of these ports are subsidised by their respective local and national governments, as both believe that they have a major impact on their domestic economies. By contrast, the well known decline of London as a major port was not accompanied by any subsidisation by the UK government.

From an economic viewpoint, it can be argued that competitive subsidies offered by Antwerp and Rotterdam are inefficient. Both ports serve the larger European market. Both should therefore compete on equal terms. The fact that many ports are still in national hands will always create a risk that political considerations will lead to 'interference' in the way the port sets its tariffs, and runs its affairs.

## 8.9 SEA CANALS AND INLAND WATERWAYS

The economic importance and effect of sea canals and waterways can be summarised as reducing nautical distance, due charges, economics of ship size and hinterland and port development.

There are a number of reasons for constructing major waterways, economic, political and strategic or military. There are two important categories of waterways. Firstly sea canals like Suez, Panama, Kiel and the Corinth which join two seas or oceans and, secondly, those providing internal access, for example the St. Lawrence Seaway, Manchester Ship Canal and North Sea Canal.

At its simplest, these waterways reduce nautical mileage as the following table illustrates.

### Table 8.2 – Different Nautical Distances

| From the Port of Rotterdam to | Via Suez | Via Cape of Good Hope | Via Panama |
|---|---|---|---|
| Kuwait | 6,500 | 11,300 | — |
| Auckland | 12,670 | 13,480 | 11,380 |
| Melbourne | 11,060 | 11,900 | 12,950 |
| Yokohama | 11,150 | 14,470 | 12,520 |

Such shortening of distance appears to present shipowners or operators with extremely simple choices, but these choices are far more complicated than at first sight. This is best seen by constructing a number of simple voyage estimates[1]. Although the rate data are very out of date, the principles are unchanged to this day.

---

[1] The example is from A S Svendson (1958) Sea Transport and Shipping Economics, p77-78.

The model assumes:

i) A cargo of grain conveyed from Sydney Australia to Liverpool.

ii) There are three routes which can be used.

iii) The decisive factor will be in the choice of bunker and canal costs.

iv) Daily revenue or earnings are given as $700.

v) The vessel is able to find employment all the time. Extra days taken to make the same journey therefore create an opportunity cost, of foregone earnings, which in this case is taken to be $700 per day.

**Nautical Distances are:**

| Routes<br>Sydney to Liverpool | N Miles | Knots | Days |
|---|---|---|---|
| 1. Via Cape of Good Hope | 12,300 | 11 | 46 |
| 2. Via Suez | 11,500 | 11 | 43 |
| 3. Via Panama | 12,500 | 11 | 47 |

Approximate calculation would be:

| | | $ |
|---|---|---|
| 1. Via The Cape of Good Hope: | | |
| Operating Cost 46 Days average $350 | | 16,100 |
| Oil: 46 Days average 12 tons average 14$ | | 7,728 |
| | Total | 23,828 |
| 2. Via The Suez Canal: | | |
| Operating Cost 43 Days average $350 | | 15,050 |
| Oil: 43 Days average 12 tons average $14 | | 7,224 |
| Canal Charges | | 6,300 |
| | Total | 28,574 |
| 3. Via The Panama Canal: | | |
| Operating Cost 47 Days average $350 | | 16,450 |
| Oil: 47 Days average 12 tons average $14 | | 7,896 |
| Canal Charges | | 2,800 |
| | Total | 27,146 |

To these figures must be added the opportunity cost of lost earnings if the journey time is longer than the minimum (43 days).

| Loss of Earnings: ($700 a day) | |
|---|---|
| Via Cape Debit Three Days | 2,100 |
| Via Panama Canal Debit Four Days | 2,800 |

The total costs (direct expenses plus opportunity cost) would be:

| | | $ |
|---|---|---|
| Via | Cape | 25,928 |
| | Suez | 28,524 |
| | Panama | 29,996 |

Other factors could also be added to the analysis, for example:

1. Bunkers were cheaper at Panama.
2. Via Suez the ship can carry an additional 200 tons of cargo.
3. Via Cape in winter, bad weather causes delays of up to 5 days.

In all this discussion the level of freights will be of major importance, for example high freight rates will make time saving important.

Another model, on a slightly different basis is presented below. Here the voyage is between Newcastle, Australia and Rotterdam, with a cargo of coal.

**Nautical Distance**

| Via | Miles | Knots | Distance per Day |
|---|---|---|---|
| Cape of Good Hope | 12,765 | 14 | 336 |
| Suez | 11,464 | 14 | 336 |
| Distance Saved | 1,301 | | |

Suez Route Nautical Miles Saved:

1,301 miles 336 Distance per day = 3.87 Days

| | | $ |
|---|---|---|
| Cost Per Day | | |
| Running | | 4,500 |
| Bunkers $100 ton average 40 tons | | 4,000 |
| | Total | 8,500 |

| | | $ |
|---|---|---|
| Reduction in Expenses if Suez Canal used | | |
| 3.87 Days x 8,500 Daily cost | = | 32,887 |

Cost of using Suez

| | |
|---|---|
| Canal Dues | 120,000 |

Cost of Using Suez rather than Cape of Good Hope = Cost of Canal Dues minus the Saving that the shorter journey makes to expenses when compared to CGH

Canal Dues Minus Cost Saving = $120,000 – $32,887 = ($87, 113)

It follows from the model that under normal conditions the Suez Routes would be the more expensive, adding $87,000 to costs. Such a simple model does not take into consideration a number of factors, the most obvious being the weather condition for rounding the Cape of Good Hope, and the level of freight rates which could make time saving an important criteria.

It should also be pointed out that both the Panama and Suez Canal operating companies bear the costs of alternative routes in mind when setting their toll charges. In this case, a toll of only $30,000 would have reversed the conclusion of the example. The Canal authorities will monitor rates and bunker costs when setting their charges; they will not be determined just by costs.

It has been argued here that the basic aim of any canal system is to cut distance, increase speed of transit and lower cost. While the models used examples of sea canals, they served to highlight that these basic aims, for example of shortening nautical distance, do not in all circumstances satisfy the economic efficiency criteria of minimising costs.

## 8.10    CONCLUSION

The aim of this lesson has been to analyse port sea canals and waterways and their interaction with the shipping industry. These combine to make up what is referred to as the Maritime Industry or Maritime Transport. The lesson defined not by description but rather by their central function ports as an essential link in the transport network and sea canals and waterways as shorteners of the transport gap. Much of the discussion was around their importance in relation to ships' costs and the problems this creates. Emphasis was also laid on the relationship between the mobile transport unit, the ship, which is relatively inexpensive and its infrastructure. This infrastructure it was pointed out, was exceedingly expensive, had a very long economic life and was built to perform a single function which meant it had no alternative use, factors which are of vital importance in any operational or economic analysis.

In the examination you may well be required to apply this theoretical analysis to examples of different ports throughout the world. It is important, therefore, that as part of your work on this lesson you assess the extent to which it applies to ports and trade routes with which you are familiar as well as the major ports in the world.

## 8.11    SELF-ASSESSMENT AND TEST QUESTIONS

Attempt the following and check your answers from the text.

1.    Explain what is meant by a 'hub' port. What functions do hub ports perform that are different from those of a more traditional port?

2.    Construct some simple voyage estimate models similar to those above. But change some of the assumptions, for example bunker costs or canal dues and speed, to demonstrate how this might change the ship operator's route decisions.

Having completed Chapter Eight attempt the following and submit your essay to your Tutor.

With reference to consolidation activities in the shipping sector, assess the extent to which shipping companies are shaping port development.

# Chapter 9

# SHIPPING AND INTERNATIONAL TRADE

## 9.1    INTRODUCTION

This lesson discusses the relationship between international trading activity and shipping demand. It then presents the principal explanations of those trade flows used by economists as an aid to understanding their development. The arguments for and against 'free trade' are briefly discussed, as is the role and significance of transport costs as a barrier to trade. An outline of the role of GATT, now known as the World Trade Organisation, concludes the lesson.

## 9.2    THE PATTERN OF WORLD TRADE

World trade has expanded enormously since the end of the Second World War. Between 1947 and 1991 it expanded forty fold in value terms, and twelve-fold in volume terms.[1] This growth has generated a corresponding growth of demand for transportation services, both in shipping and elsewhere. Some parts of the world have grown much more rapidly than others over this period; West Europe and the USA dominated in the 1950's and 1960's, Japan and the Far East in the 1970's and 1980's, although recent WTO[2] figures imply that the Far Eastern 'Asian Tigers' have slowed their growth rate, and it is Latin America which is now generating double digit growth rates.

Despite the rise of the Asian Tigers, an examination of the value of trade flows between the various countries reveals some interesting information. Table 9.1 shows that World Merchandise Trade, in dollar terms, doubled between 1984 and 1993, reaching $7.4 trillion. The developing economies trade rose from $1 trillion (Exports and Imports combined) to $2.1 trillion. A noticeable feature of the statistics is the stagnant growth of OPEC member exports over the period – from $170bn in 1984 to $183bn in 1993. The reason for this is that the volume growth of oil exports has been masked by the fall in the value of those exports, as the world price of oil declined from its peak level in 1979-80. The last part of the Table shows the same data, expressed in terms of percentage shares, for the major groups of countries. The proportions which these blocs account for are remarkably stable; in 1984, Developed Market Economies accounted for 67% of world merchandise trade; by 1993, 69%, a slight increase! Developing Market economies share rose from 25% to 28% in the period – the losers, in share terms, being OPEC, down very slightly, and 'Other'. Note that this Table says nothing about who these trading blocs trade with, nor about the group of countries formerly known as the Centrally Planned Economies, i.e. the former USSR, and East Europe.

The broad nature of trading relationships between the above categories is shown in Table 9.2, which provides data for merchandise *exports* for the years 1980 and 1992. The data are shown both in $mn, and by market share. The decline in the dollar value of OPEC trade is brought out even more clearly here, with exports falling in value from $304bn in 1980 to $174bn in 1992. Their market share of world exports declined from 15% to 5% in the same period. Developed Market economies have a share of exports of 72%, in line with the overall share of trade. Note the dramatic fall in the export performance of the former Soviet Union bloc, with exports falling

---

[1]  Greenaway, D. (1991) GATT and Multilateral Trade Liberalisation: Knocked Out in the Eighth Round? Economics, vol XXVII, No 115, pp100-106.
[2]  WTO stands for the World Trade Organisation, which replaced the General Agreement of Tariffs and Trade in 1995. Its remit is to provide a forum for all 142 member countries to sort out trade disputes, and its core is committed to lowering trade barriers. China is due to join this year.

in dollar value because of the break up of COMECON trading arrangements, and the painful transition to market economy status.

Table 9.2 also provides an analysis of the principal trading partners of each regional trading bloc. The major trading partners of the developed market economies are – other developed market economies! In 1980, approximately 45% of the 63% of trade was of this sort i.e. a massive 71%. By 1992, this figure had altered to – 75%! Three quarters of the developed market economies exports are to other developed economies! The next largest share of the developed market exports were to developing market economies – the share being 16% in 1992, 16% in 1980. This is only one third of the size of the premier market.

A surprising fact emerges when one examines the export pattern of the less developed market economies. The share of their exports going to the developed economies has fallen from 68% in 1980 to 56% in 1992. Again, a significant percentage of their exports go to – other developing market economies. This share has risen from 27% (7.84/29.22) to 40% (10.11/25.2). It appears that there are significant flows of trade that do not fit in with the common caricature of developing countries exporting raw materials to developed countries in exchange for imports of manufactured goods.

Indeed, much modern trade is much more complex and sophisticated then implied by the above crude model. Modern multinational car companies regularly generate trade flows that do not fit the above stereotype. For example, Ford's engine plant in Bridgend, South Wales, regularly exports large numbers of car engines to other Ford car assembly plants in Belgium, Spain, and Germany. The engines become parts of new Fiestas (Spain), Mondeos (Belgium, Germany). The newly assembled cars are then exported to – the UK! Thus what was exported by the UK (engines) becomes part of an imported finished good – and note that this trade is between developed market economies, on the UN definition.

These facts must be borne in mind when discussing economic explanations of trade flows, as some of the early, and most widely known theories, are not designed to explain examples such as that given above.

## Table 9.1 – World Merchandise Trade, selected years

| Merchandise Trade | 1984 | 1990 | 1991 | 1992 | 1993 |
|---|---|---|---|---|---|
| **Imports mn US$** | | | | | |
| Developed Market Economies | 1,352,949 | 2,589,822 | 2,591,496 | 2,710,739 | 2,535,248 |
| Developing Economies | 474,908 | 781,066 | 862,158 | 999,831 | 1,091,065 |
| — of which OPEC | 116,957 | 110,293 | 128,021 | 156,892 | 353,325 |
| Less Developed Countries | 18,810 | 24,353 | 22,815 | 25,211 | 25,267 |
| Other | 91,235 | 95,802 | 92,016 | 94804 | 90,393 |
| Total World Imports | 1,937,902 | 3,491,043 | 3,568,485 | 3,830,585 | 3,741,973 |
| **Exports mn US$** | | | | | |
| Developed Market Economies | 1,241,881 | 2,467,895 | 2,491,048 | 2,642,032 | 2,538,789 |
| Developing Economies | 505,610 | 797,052 | 840,034 | 923,883 | 998,254 |
| — of which OPEC | 170,483 | 180,036 | 169,682 | 173,439 | 182,809 |
| Less Developed Countries | 10,085 | 12,634 | 10,205 | 12,377 | 12,903 |
| Other | 187,502 | 172,453 | 90,247 | 90,230 | 95,047 |
| Total World Exports | 1,945,078 | 3,450,034 | 3,431,534 | 3,668,522 | 3,644,993 |
| **Total Merchandise Trade** | | | | | |
| Developed Market Economies | 2,594,830 | 5,057,717 | 5,082,544 | 5,352,771 | 5,074,037 |
| Developing Economies | 980,518 | 1,578,118 | 1,702,192 | 1,923,714 | 2,089,319 |
| — of which OPEC | 287,440 | 290,329 | 297,703 | 330,331 | 536,134 |
| Less Developed Countries | 28,895 | 36,987 | 33,020 | 37,588 | 38,170 |
| Other | 278,737 | 268,255 | 182,263 | 185,034 | 185,440 |
| Total World Trade | 3,882,980 | 6,941,077 | 7,000,019 | 7,499,107 | 7,386,966 |
| **Shares of World Trade** | 1984 % | 1990 % | 1991 % | 1992 % | 1993 % |
| Developed Market Economies | 66.83 | 72.87 | 72.61 | 71.38 | 68.69 |
| Developing Economies | 25.25 | 22.74 | 24.32 | 25.65 | 28.28 |
| — of which OPEC | 7.40 | 4.18 | 4.25 | 4.40 | 7.26 |
| Less Developed Countries | 0.74 | 0.53 | 0.47 | 0.50 | 0.52 |
| Other | 7.18 | 3.86 | 2.60 | 2.47 | 2.51 |
| Total World Trade | 100.00 | 100.00 | 100.00 | 100.00 | 100.00 |

Source: UN Statistical Yearbook

### Table 9.2 – Regional Trading Bloc Shares in World Trade, various years

| Trade Shares by Bloc 1980 | Developed Market | Developing Market | (OPEC) | E. Europe + USSR | World |
|---|---|---|---|---|---|
| Developed Market | 891453 | 316150 | 99886 | 42235 | 1249838 |
| Developing Market | 401228 | 155476 | 22844 | 23015 | 579719 |
| (OPEC) | 231096 | 70072 | 3966 | 3716 | 304884 |
| E. Europe + USSR | 43269 | ,32406 | 4936 | 78714 | 154389 |
| | | | | | 1983946 |

| By % Share | Developed Market | Developing Market | (OPEC) | E. Europe + USSR | World |
|---|---|---|---|---|---|
| Developed Market | 44.93 | 15.94 | 5.03 | 2.13 | 63.00 |
| Developing Market | 20.22 | 7.84 | 1.15 | 1.16 | 29.22 |
| (OPEC) | 11.65 | 3.53 | 0.20 | 0.19 | 15.37 |
| E. Europe + USSR | 2.18 | 1.63 | 0.25 | 3.97 | 7.78 |

| 1992 | Developed Market | Developing Market | (OPEC) | E. Europe + USSR | World |
|---|---|---|---|---|---|
| Developed Market | 1993439 | 589798 | 103248 | 62770 | 2646007 |
| Developing Market | 536384 | 369548 | 41725 | 14934 | 920866 |
| (OPEC) | 117543 | 53935 | 8930 | 2117 | 173595 |
| E. Europe + USSR | 52292 | 16814 | 1493 | 17954 | 87060 |
| | 43269 | 32406 | 4936 | 78714 | 3653933 |

| By % Share | Developed Market | Developing Market | (OPEC) | E. Europe + USSR | World |
|---|---|---|---|---|---|
| Developed Market | 54.56 | 16.14 | 2.83 | 1.72 | 72.42 |
| Developing Market | 14.68 | 10.11 | 1.14 | 0.41 | 25.20 |
| (OPEC) | 3.22 | 1.48 | 0.24 | 0.06 | 4.75 |
| E. Europe + USSR | 1.43 | 0.46 | 0.04 | 0.49 | 2.38 |
| | | | | | 100.00 |

Source: Derived from Direction of Trade Statistics Yearbook, UN, 1994

## 9.3 TRADE AND ECONOMIC GROWTH

The above section has highlighted the growth of world trade, and noted the broad pattern of trade that has evolved in the past 15 years or so. The World Bank has researched the link between trading performance and economic growth over many years in many countries, and has concluded that two key features appear to be vital ingredients for an efficient, dynamic economy. The two major features are a) the development of increasingly 'Open' economies, and b) the liberalisation of markets.

What is meant by an 'Open' economy? Economists define 'openness' in terms of the degree to which the national economy is affected by trade growth. One way of measuring this is to measure the value of a country's exports, and express it as a percentage of the Gross National Product of the country, the GNP. Since exports are a part of the total output generated within the economy, the higher this figure, the larger the degree of dependence of that economy world trade growth, and the more competitive that economy has to be in world markets. A number of interesting points emerge from Table 9.3, which provides some data on the relative openness of a number of economies for 1994.

Although the USA is still the largest exporting country in the world, with $7 trillion (million million) worth in 1994, it is, in fact a relatively closed economy. It only exports 10% of its GNP, in contrast to Germany, France and the UK, who all have share of 22-25%. Note too, that Japan, regarded as a great exporter, has an export share of 9%, less than the USA! The two greatest exporting nations are themselves relatively isolated from trade growth fluctuation compared to the major exporting countries of Europe. One warning – much of the UK's trade is now with Europe, within the EC. So too, will be Italy's, France and Germany – a large part of their trade will also be with other EC member countries.

### Table 9.3 – The Openness of Selected Economies

| Share of Exports in National Income 1994 | | | | |
|---|---|---|---|---|
| | GNP $mn | GNP/cap | Export Share | Exports $mn |
| USA | 6,737,367 | 25,860 | 10 | 6,737,367 |
| Japan | 4,321,136 | 21,350 | 9 | 3,889,022 |
| Germany | 2,075,452 | 19,890 | 22 | 4,565,994 |
| France | 1,355,039 | 19,820 | 23 | 3,116,590 |
| Italy | 1,101,258 | 18,610 | 23 | 2,532,893 |
| United Kingdom | 1,069,457 | 18,170 | 25 | 2,673,643 |
| Netherlands | 338,144 | 18,080 | 51 | 1,724,534 |
| Greece | 80,194 | 11,400 | 22 | 176,427 |
| Brazil | 536,309 | 5,630 | 7 | 375,416 |
| Russian Fed | 392,496 | 5,260 | 27 | 1,059,739 |
| China | 630,202 | 2,510 | 26 | 1,638,525 |
| Luxembourg | 15,673 | 31,090 | 86 | 134,788 |
| Hong Kong | 126,286 | 23,080 | 139 | 1,755,375 |

Source: World Bank Atlas 1996

## 9.4 TYPES OF TRADE FLOWS: INTRA INDUSTRY TRADE AND INTER INDUSTRY TRADE

An important distinction is now made between Inter Industry and Intra Industry trade. When Saudi Arabia exports crude oil to Japan, and imports in exchange, manufactured goods such as cars, or electrical equipment, or ships, the trade so generated is known as Inter Industry Trade. It fits in with the conception of trade discussed earlier. But nowadays, only 50% or so of world trade is of this type. The other 50% is what is known as Intra Industry trade. When Rolls-Royce and Jaguar, both British based companies, export luxury cars to Germany, and BMW and Mercedes, both Germany based companies, export luxury cars to the UK, it is not clear why such trade takes place, as both countries are capable of producing luxury cars, and only one country can have a cost advantage over another, not both at the same time. When IBM export computers to Japan, and Japan exports computers to the USA, who has the cost advantage? When Ford exports Escorts from Dagenham UK to Germany, and Mondeos from Germany to the UK, who has the cost advantage in car manufacturing? It is clear that this type of trade flow has to be explained in a different way from the oil/cars trade between Saudi Arabia and Japan.

One important factor underlying some of the trade flows mentioned above involves the rise of Multinational Corporations as important players in world trade. It has been estimated that one third of world trade is between two subsidiaries of the same MNC! Glaxo-Wellcome UK will be actively trading with Nippon Glaxo, Ford UK with Ford Germany, IBM UK with IBM France, etc. Such trade flows may be dictated by factors that have little to do with relative costs in the countries concerned, but to do with transfer pricing and differential tax regimes. Transfer pricing is the device used by large multinational corporations to maximise the value added processing of its subsidiaries in the countries of low taxation. For example, a subsidiary in a high tax country can sell its product at a low price to a country with a low tax regime – so that the greater mark up is made in the country with the lowest tax. Since the MNC owns both subsidiaries, where the accounting profit is made is largely immaterial to it. Tax minimisation becomes a factor in determining the value of trade flows, since export prices are affected by these considerations.

The above points highlight the fact that in today's global markets, it is no longer possible to explain all trade flows with just one economic model, or theory of trade.

## 9.5 TRADE GROWTH AND THE DEMAND FOR SHIPPING SERVICES

The spectacular growth in world trade has generated a corresponding growth in the demand for transportation services, particularly shipping. As was demonstrated in Chapter 2, the volume of cargoes moved, both in tonne mile and tons of cargo generated per year, has grown in line with the growth in world trade volumes. It is a good idea to review the data provided in Chapter 2, which demonstrated the growth in volume of cargo moved – there being a strong link between the growth in world trade, industrial production, and seaborne trade.

This point is worth re-emphasising. All industry analyses of the shipping markets begin with an analysis of the key elements generating the demand for those services, which are to be found in the volume and pattern of world trade. In Chapter 6, the changing demand for oil tankers was shown to be linked to changes in trade patterns for crude oil. The growth of the containerised liner trades is most marked in the Far East, which is the region with the highest rates of economic growth and industrialisation in recent years. No self-respecting shipping analyst examines the demand for any shipping sector without first examining and analysing trends in the markets that generate the demand, namely the flows of current and expected world trade.

## 9.6 ECONOMIC MODELS OF TRADE FLOWS

There are two 'traditional explanations' of trade flows, both concentrating on the supply side of the economy. They essentially argue that trade flows are driven by relative costs only. The models try to explain why one country exports certain commodities and imports other, *different* commodities in exchange. It implies that one country has a cost advantage relative to the other country, for one industry. Thus Saudi Arabia is abundant in oil, which can be extracted cheaply because its fields are on land, easily drilled and extracted, and moved to the coast for export. It has a cost advantage in oil production. On the other hand, Japan has a cost advantage in car production, so both can trade. Note that this is *Interindustry* trade, not *Intraindustry* trade.

### 9.6.1 Absolute Advantage

This is sometimes called Ricardian Trade, after David Ricardo, the first economist to develop the theory. The theory basically argues that a country will export those commodities which it produces more cheaply than any other country, and in exchange, import those products which it produces less cheaply than elsewhere. The obvious examples of 'absolute advantage' would be a country's natural endowments of raw materials and natural resources. In Saudi Arabia's case, as mentioned above, an absolute advantage exists in oil production, as it does in other Middle East economies which are similarly blessed. Brazil and Australia are endowed with iron ore, Japan has none. A natural trade is for Japan to import these essential manufacturing raw materials as it has no such materials itself.

One question that arises in this theory is this. Suppose an economy say economy A, was absolutely more efficient in production in all goods, compared to another economy B. If Ricardo's doctrine is correct, it would appear that economy A should never trade with B, since it is capable of producing both products more cheaply than B. Since, in real life, it is often argued that Japan, say, or the US, is capable of producing all goods more cheaply than the UK say, then why should these two economies trade?

It turns out that Ricardo's theory is flawed. Absolute advantage is not required to generate trading opportunities. The major traditional theory of international trade is known as the theory of comparative advantage, which is discussed in detail below.

## 9.6.2 Comparative Advantage

The doctrine of comparative advantage is the most widely known theory of trade flows. The idea behind it is best understood with the aid of an example. Suppose that you are a computer whiz, and also good at decorating and painting. In fact, you are better at these two activities than your neighbour, Fred. Fred is not too good at computing, but very good at decorating and painting, though not as good as you.

Initially, both you and Fred spend equal amounts of time in both activities. But if you trade, both can gain. This is because Fred is comparatively good at painting and decorating; if he concentrates on that activity, while you concentrate on computing, you can trade the service to each other and both be better off. This gain arises from the fact that resources have been reallocated towards their most efficient uses; as a result, more total output (computer services and paint/decorating) is produced, to be reallocated between the two people. In reality, comparative advantage is nothing more than the extension of Adam Smith's principle of the division of labour to trade between countries. Each country will tend to specialise in producing those products which it is relatively good at producing, and trade some of the increased output from the expanded sector for imports which replace the output lost from the shrinking, less productive sector.

## 9.6.3 Formal Models of Comparative Advantage

A formal model of the principle of comparative advantage is presented below

### Model 1 – Assumptions

1. There are two countries, country A and country B.
2. Both have one factor of production, labour, which is used in producing the outputs.
3. Labour productivity (average and marginal) is constant in all sectors.
4. Total personhours available are 1200 per year in A and 2000 in B.
5. Technology is identical in both countries.
6. There are two goods, cars and rice, produced in both countries.
7. There is no trade between the two countries to begin with.
8. Initially, each country allocates 50% of its resources to each product. This implies demand conditions are identical in each country.
9. Labour is always fully employed in both countries.
10. Competitive conditions prevail, leading to prices equalling opportunity costs.

Table 9.4 shows the labour input requirements in each country per unit of output.

### Table 9.4 – Labour Input Requirements per unit of Output (hrs)

|  | A | B |
|---|---|---|
| Cars | 20 | 20 |
| Rice | 30 | 10 |

The information in the assumptions above, the maximum output achievable if all the available labour is employed in that sector is given in Table 9.5.

### Table 9.5 – Maximum Output achievable in the two countries

|  | A | B |
|---|---|---|
| Cars | 60 | 100 |
| Rice | 40 | 200 |

If Country A puts all its resources into car production, it can produce 1200/20 = 60 cars per period. B, on the other hand, can produce 100 (2000/20). They have the same labour efficiency, but B has the larger resources. Country B can produce 2000/10 = 200 units of rice per period if labour solely devoted to rice production, whilst A can produce a maximum of 40 (1200/30). Given the assumption that resources are split 50:50 between cars and rice in the pre trade situation (or autarky, as it is called in economics texts), the actual output is given in Table 9.6.

**Table 9.6 – Initial Output in the two economies**

|  | A | B |
|---|---|---|
| Cars | 30 | 50 |
| Rice | 20 | 100 |
| World | 50 | 150 |

It is very important that you note the assumption being made in this model that labour productivity is constant, no matter how many units of labour are being employed in car or rice production. This assumption means that the trade-off between the two outputs is always the same. If one less car is produced in country A, it follows that 20 labour hours are released. If moved into rice production, the 20 extra hours will generate 2/3 of a unit of rice, since one unit of rice requires 30 hours. In country A, the loss of one unit of car production frees up the same 20 labour hours, by assumption, but rice production requires only 10 hours per unit, so the shift in resources generates 2 units of rice. These trade-offs are assumed to be the same, whether we are talking about the loss of the 60th unit of car production in Country A (i.e. the very last unit) or the very first unit. This assumption implies that the Opportunity Cost of output is a constant in both countries, although the value of that constant differs between them.

## 9.6.4 Opportunity Cost

How do these two countries gain from trade? Recall the earlier example. If one country is 'better' at making one good relative to the other country, then an opportunity for trade may exist. In order to measure relative efficiencies, economists use the concept of Opportunity Cost. Opportunity Cost is defined as the output foregone in consequence of producing one more unit of output. In Country A, one extra unit of car 'costs' 2/3rds of a unit of Rice, since producing one more car takes up 20 hours, so releasing 2/3rds of a unit of rice reduces 2/3(30) = 20 hours. Alternatively, the production of one more unit of rice requires 30 extra hours in A, or 1.5 cars foregone.

The Opportunity Costs for the two countries are shown in Table 9.7.

**Table 9.7 – Opportunity Costs of Extra Output**

|  | A | B |
|---|---|---|
| 1 Extra Car | 2/3 Rice | 2 Rice |
| 1 Extra Rice | 3/2 Cars | 1/2 Car |

It is clear that the two countries have differences in the pre-trade opportunity cost ratios. Country A can produce cars at the least opportunity cost (2/3 < 2), while Country B can produce rice at the least opportunity cost (1/2 < 3/2). *It is clear that there is a potential for a global increase in production and consumption if specialisation and trade is introduced.*

In the pre-trade position, both countries are limited to consuming exactly what they produce. Table 9.6 above therefore can be read as a Table of consumption levels in both countries as well as production. But once trade is permitted, consumption and production can differ by the amount of exports and imports generated. An assumption has to be made about the rate at which the two commodities exchange with each other.

The opportunity cost ratios which exist in the pre-trade position provide limits on the opportunity cost ratio that will be agreed. Assumption 10 stated that opportunity cost ratios can be viewed as price ratios. The equilibrium trade ratio must therefore lie between the two ratios that already exist.

| | | |
|---|---|---|
| Opportunity Cost Cars; | 2/3Rice(A) < x < 2Rice(B) | (1) |
| Opportunity Cost Rice; | 3/2Cars(A) > y > 1/2Cars(B) | (2) |

Note that the relationships above are highly related; relationship 2 is simply the same as 1, but inverted. Once one is satisfied, the other must be!

In order to determine the final position, an agreed rate of exchange must be determined. The rate of 1R = 1C has been selected – note that it falls between the extremes given in 1) and 2). At this rate it is more 'profitable' for country A to specialise in car production and import rice from B. Each extra unit of car 'costs' it 2/3rds of a unit of rice domestically speaking, but exchanges for **one unit** of rice when traded with B. Thus by switching more resources to car production, and trading with B, an extra 1/3rd of a unit of rice is 'created'. The creation occurs because labour is moved to the sector in which it is relatively most efficient, in both countries. If B reduces car production by one unit (thus leaving *world* car production unchanged), resources capable of producing two extra units of rice are released. So, rice production goes up by 2 in B, down by 2/3rds in A. Car production goes up by 1 in A, and is down by 1 in B. Two extra units of rice have been generated by this reallocation, which can be split between the two countries. World car production is unchanged, so it follows that world consumption and production is greater than in the no trade situation. Free trade has created larger output and greater consumption!

Because there is no change in the relative opportunity costs described in the above paragraph, the incentive to raise production of cars in A and production of rice in B exists all the time. The process must stop only when it no longer becomes possible for resources to be switched into the expanding sector, which only occurs, in this example, when all of A's labour resources are employed in car production. At this point, the production figures are shown in Table 9.8.

### Table 9.8 – Final Production Levels with Trade

| | A | B |
|---|---|---|
| Cars | 60 | 30 |
| Rice | 0 | 140 |
| World Production | 60 | 170 |

Comparing Table 9.8 with Table 9.6, it is clear that trade has increased production of both commodities. From a global viewpoint, it is clear that both countries can be materially better off, since there are more cars and more rice to go round!

The example can now be completed by assuming final consumption points for A and B. The model developed above does not explain the final consumption points, and models that do are beyond the scope of this course. The consumption points chosen are therefore somewhat arbitrary, but they illustrate the point that both countries can gain from trade. It will be assumed that Country A exchanges 30 units of cars for 30 units of rice, which is the agreed rate of exchange for trade. Using A's domestic opportunity cost ratio, A's loss of rice production is 20 units. But if B reduces its car production by 30 units, it has released 600 personhours for rice production, which generates 60 extra rice units. The re-allocation generates up to 40 extra rice units. But since rice and cars exchange at an equal rate in trade, this is equivalent to 40 extra car units, or some combination of both. Table 9.9 provides one possible equilibrium position for both countries, and the implied trade flows.

## Table 9.9

| | Production | | Consumption | | Trade | |
|---|---|---|---|---|---|---|
| | **A** | **B** | **A** | **B** | **A** | **B** |
| Cars | 60 | 30 | 40 | 50 | Exports  20 | Imports  20 |
| Rice | 0 | 140 | 40 | 120 | Imports  20 | Exports  20 |

Note that the rate of exchange of rice to cars is 1:1, and A completely specialises. B moves towards specialisation, as it now produces relatively more rice than it did in the pre-trade position. Trade is balanced, in the sense that at the going rate of exchange, each country's value of imports equals the value of their exports. In the world of comparative advantage there are never any crises generated by trade imbalances!

Both countries' consumption levels are higher than they were in the pre-trade position. Country A has 10 more units of rice and the same level of consumption of cars; Country B has 10 more units of cars and 20 more units of rice. Note that the total gain adds up to 40 units.

### 9.6.5 Gains from Trade and the Terms of Trade

The example above generated gains to both parties. This arose because the agreed rate of exchange, or the terms of trade, differed from the pre-trade price ratios that existed in both countries. When a large country trades with a small one, it is likely that the price ratio in the large country will not be affected by the trade volume itself. In this case, all the gains from trade would accrue to the small country, since the difference between the pre-trade price ratio and the agreed terms of trade determines the degree to which a country can reach a consumption point which was not open to it previously. For example, if the relative price of computers and apples is unchanged in the USA following its opening up of trade with New Zealand, but New Zealanders find that the relative price of apples to computers has increased, New Zealand will benefit from increased apple production and trade with the USA at these higher prices. The gains will go to New Zealand, since the resource reallocation that occurs in the USA is at exactly the same rate as would have occurred in the absence of trade.

The distribution of trading advantages can be affected by movements in the relative prices of imported and exported goods. When world oil prices increased by 400% in 1973, the terms of trade for oil exporters moved sharply in their favour, whilst oil importers experienced the opposite effect. An improvement in the terms of trade for oil exporters means that for a given volume of oil exports sold abroad, a larger physical quantity of imports can be financed. The oil exporting countries found themselves much better off, and the oil importing countries much worse off, as a result of this change. The decline in oil prices since 1980 has had the opposite effect, one which was noted in earlier sections, when the decline of OPEC's share of world trade was noted.

### Model 2 Comparative Advantage with variable Opportunity Cost

The above model, although complicated, is not complex enough for a complete analysis of comparative advantage. Two key assumptions have to be modified to improve this. Firstly, the assumption of constant opportunity cost has to be dropped. Secondly, production is undertaken with several factor inputs, land, labour and capital, which are combined to produce either cars or rice. If the assumption is made that rice requires a relatively large amount of land, and car production requires a relatively large amount of capital, it no longer becomes possible to assume that the opportunity cost of cars or rice remain constant as resources are reallocated.

The reason for this is not too difficult to understand. Suppose that A has a relatively large amount of capital, and B a large amount of land. Now suppose all A's resources are concentrated on car production. Then it moves some of those resources into rice production. Efficient reallocation would mean moving the inputs which are most productive in generating rice, so the wettest lands, the most suitable labour, etc. are diverted from car production to rice production. This process is repeated. But each time it is repeated, the land that is shifted, the labour that is moved, is slightly less appropriate for rice production and more appropriate for car production. This means that in terms of opportunity costs, early movements of resources do not reduce the production of cars by much, but they increase the output of rice a great deal. In economic jargon, the marginal product of factors employed in car production is low, since all resources have been pushed that way. The extra rice produced, from an initial value of zero, will be very large – the marginal product of factor inputs in rice production will be high. This relative situation will alter as resources shift into rice production. The marginal product of the last few inputs into rice production will be very low, as all the most suitable land was used for rice long ago, so that expensive methods of irrigating dry land need to be employed. The resources being switched in are in fact much better used in car production, and are less efficient in terms of output when employed in the rice sector.

### 9.6.6 The Production Possibility Frontier

In order to understand how the variation in Opportunity Cost can be modelled, the concept of the Production Possibility Frontier has to be defined. Figures 9.1 and 9.2 show two such frontiers for countries A and B respectively.

**Figure 9.1 – Country A's Production Possibility Frontier**

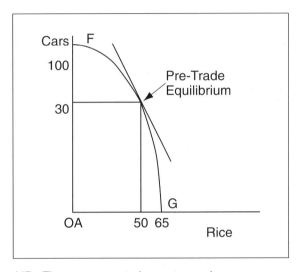

**Figure 9.2 – Country B's Production Possibility Frontier**

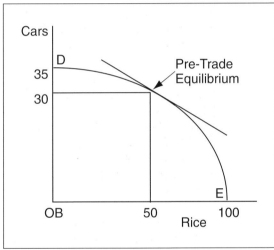

*NB.* Figures are not drawn to scale.

The PPF for A shows that if all its resources are fully employed in car production, 100 cars per year will be produced. If all of A's resources are employed in rice production, only 65 units of rice will be produced. This is consistent with the idea that A's resources are best suited to car production, as it has more capital and less suitable land than B. The curve FG shows all the possible combinations of cars and rice that can be produced with the full employment of resources in country A. Consider the process of moving from point G to point F. When there is a large level of rice output, no cars are being produced; releasing capital and labour from rice production will reduce rice output and increase car output. Under the model's assumptions, there will be a large increase in car output at the cost of a small reduction in rice production. The reason for this is that the resources being released at this stage are the ones most suited to car production, and least suited to rice production. The marginal product of factors employed in cars will be large at this stage, but the marginal product of the inputs in rice will be low. So extra car production does not 'cost' much in terms of foregone rice production. By the time resources have been shifted to point F, this is no longer true. The resources being released from rice production will now be the most productive ones, the best lands, the best farmers. They will help increase car production, but not by much. At point F, the marginal product of those few factors remaining in rice production has become very high. The opportunity cost of one extra car now becomes very much greater, i.e. much larger losses of rice production occur.

These changes are the reason for the changing slope of the line FG. In fact, the slope of FG measures the opportunity cost, the 'price' paid for an extra unit of cars as measured by the lost output of rice. This opportunity cost is very high when car production is high, and low when rice production is high. It varies as the relative mix of cars and rice is varied.

The same arguments apply to Country B. Figure 9.2 is drawn to reflect B's greater facility in producing rice relative to cars. Initial production is assumed to be as shown in the Figures. World production of cars is 30 in A, 30 in B, totalling 60. Rice production is 100, 50 in A, and 50 in B.

### 9.6.7 Trade Equilibrium

It should be clear from the visual inspection of Figures 9.1 and 9.2 that the opportunity cost ratios are quite different in Countries A and B. The slope of the straight line drawn tangent at A's pre-trade equilibrium is flatter (greater) than the equivalent line for B. This means that the opportunity cost of rice (relative to cars) in A is greater than the opportunity cost of rice (relative to cars) in B. Under the assumption of competitive conditions in all sectors this also implies that the relative price of rice (relative to cars) is greater in A than in B. Rice is therefore relatively expensive in A, relatively cheap in B.

If trade is permitted, and there are no transport costs, these two relative prices must converge to a common, equilibrium one. But this means that the relative price of rice will fall in country A, and rises in country B (the relative price of cars will fall in country B). The differences in the pre-trade relative prices and the common post-trade prices will create incentives for producers in both countries. In country A, car producers will find it attractive to make more cars and sell them to country B. Production of cars will expand, and rice production will contract. This is seen more clearly in Figure 9.3. A similar process will occur in country B, but in this case the expanding sector will be the rice sector. The changes are shown in Figures 9.3 and 9.4 respectively.

**Figure 9.3**
**Post Trade Equilibrium in A**

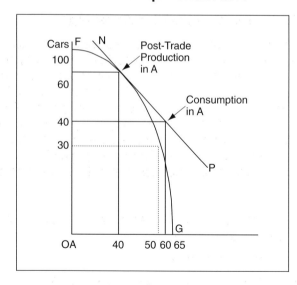

**Figure 9.4**
**Post Trade Equilibrium in B**

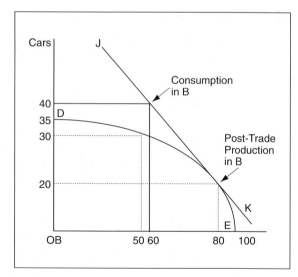

Country A will end up producing 60 cars and 40 rice units, whilst country B produces 20 cars and 80 rice units. Both countries have shifted resources into the sector in which they have a comparative advantage, but note that neither completely specialises in that sector. This is because of the fact that the relative prices alter as resources are shifted between the sectors. A second point to note is that both countries end up at consumption points which would not be possible in the absence of trade; both have gained. Country A now consumes 40 cars and 60 rice units (pre-trade it was 30C, 50R), and country B consumes 40 cars and 60 rice units (pre-trade it was 30C, 50R). Country A exports 20 cars and imports 20 units of rice; country B exports 20 units of rice and imports 20 cars. The implied post-trade rate of exchange is one car = one unit of rice, that is the relative price ratio is unity.

It is important to note that the lines NP and JK have the same slope (of unity). This must be the case, because the slopes of these lines measure the agreed common rate of exchange between cars and rice for the two trading partners. One can also see how production has shifted towards the good in which each country has the comparative advantage.

World production and consumption has increased as a result of trade. World production was 60C, 100R. After trade, it changes to 80C, 120R. The 'gain' of 20C, 20R, has been evenly distributed in this example, with country A gaining 10C, 10R in terms of consumption (was 30C, 50R; now is 40C, 60R). Similar numbers are found for country B when the relevant figures are examined. The numerical example has been simplified, but the principle that at least one party gains in overall consumption, is a result which is not conditioned on the precise examples used.

This section has been hard work for you. It is quite a difficult model to grasp, because of the number of assumptions used, and the 'hidden' nature of the economics on which it draws. The following paragraphs provide a succinct summary of the basic conclusions derivable from the analysis developed for Model 2.

1.  A country is endowed with a number of resources, some of which are more abundant than others. Saudi Arabia has an abundance of oil, Australia an abundance of minerals, the USA an abundance of capital. In each case, abundance is defined in relative terms, i.e. oil relative to capital, minerals relative to capital, etc.

2.  If competitive conditions prevail in every sector, and if technology is the same in these countries, each country will produce certain goods relatively more cheaply than other countries. The goods that they can produce cheaply will be those that use large amounts of the abundant factor. Thus the USA will export goods which involve large amounts of capital (relative to labour) because these will be the goods it can make relatively cheaply. India has a large amount of labour relative to capital. – therefore, it should export labour intensive products such as textiles and garments. Natural resource abundant countries, such as Saudi Arabia and Brazil, should export natural resources, according to this theory.

## 9.6.8  Implications and Limitations of the Theories of Comparative Advantage

A very important implication that arises from the models discussed above is that trade will be one directional. If Saudi has a comparative advantage in oil, it exports oil. It will import cars, luxury goods, etc. in exchange. If the USA has a comparative advantage in computer equipment, it will export such equipment, and import labour intensive goods such as textiles. This type of trade has been defined as Inter-industry Trade. But a significant proportion of the world's trade is now Intra-industry trade. The theory of comparative advantage does not explain this type of trade flow at all! For example, if it is observed that the USA imports computers and exports computers at the same time, (say from Japan or Singapore), which country has the comparative advantage? They cannot both have! Economists have developed additional theories to help analyse this trade type.

The predictions of the comparative advantage models were also based upon a number of crucial assumptions, the most important of which are listed below:

a)  Full employment of resources exists in both economies

b)  Model only explains balanced trade (Value of exports = value of imports)

c)  The model is of a barter economy. The role of money is not considered!

d)  The model is static – there is no explanation of growth.

e)  Economies of scale are not allowed for

f)  Each sector is competitive – no allowance for monopoly problems!

These assumptions should make it clear that the model is not terribly realistic; yet it has provided the basis for the liberal intellectual argument in support of Free Trade, because of the gains that have been demonstrated in the models discussed above.

## 9.6.9     Multinational Company Trade: The International Product Life Cycle

One key statistic noted in the section 1 was that Multinational Corporations are now responsible for a significant proportion of trade flows. There are two points worth noting here. The first is that trading between subsidiaries of the same MNC may help to explain the observed trade in computers between the USA and Japan say. Nippon IBM and IBM (US) may well be trading with each other, each specialising in a certain computer type and then trading. Such processes may help to explain Intra industry trade.

Secondly, Multinational Corporations can shift the profits that they earn to the country with the lowest rate of corporation tax by the use of 'Transfer Pricing'. Since all subsidiaries are usually wholly owned by the parent Multinational, the prices charges by one subsidiary to another are largely immaterial. It does not really matter if accounting profits are struck in Brazil or in the USA. But if tax rates are lower in Brazil, it would be better to ensure that the trading profit which arises is located, as far as possible, in the Brazilian subsidiary. This may sometimes be done by charging the US subsidiary artificially high rates for services provided; thus 'shifting' profit to Brazil. Transfer pricing is difficult to prove, since many of these transactions are internal to the MNC, and are never made public.

Thirdly, MNC's can locate production in the cheapest place, and serve global markets. A good example is to follow the history of the trade in pocket calculators. First designed and launched in the USA by Texas Instruments in the mid sixties, they were priced at around $500 and replaced mechanical adding machines that were then still widely used. The production facilities were located in the USA, with North America the first target market. After a few months, the same product was launched in Europe. This early market was met by exports for the USA. As the market expanded in Europe it became feasible to source the market from European Factories, as the production costs fell enough to make EC tariff barriers and the transport cost from the USA a more expensive option. Rapid technical change and increased competition drove down calculator prices. TI's response was to relocate production to Malaysia and Singapore, taking advantage of the global mobility of capital and low transport costs. Now the product is imported into both the USA and Europe from this source.

Not that this example generates three different trade flows. First, Calculators are exported from the USA, as technology leading products. Second, they are made in Europe and other markets, so that US exports decline. Finally, the same product is exported from the Far East (by TI) back into the USA, and into Europe. Such trade flows cannot be explained by comparative advantage!

## 9.6.10     Economies of Scale and Product Differentiation as Sources of Trade Advantage

The final economic theory of trade flows shifts attention from cost differences and allows for the fact that products are often generated by companies, not by industries. BMW cars are regarded as being superior to Minis by many consumers in Europe; Coca-Cola is different from Peps-Cola, and so on. The traditional comparative advantage model assumes that every company within an industry is identical, thus ignoring these differences. New theories of trade, especially those developed by Professor Paul Krugman, have shown how trade in similar goods can flow in both directions at once, if consumers show preferences for particular types of product, and if economies of scale exist. Under standard competitive assumptions, a trade equilibrium can be found which explains why the UK sell luxury cars to Germany, and Germany sells luxury cars to the UK. The explanation is simple. The individual markets in Germany and the UK are not sufficiently large to create efficient production levels for this type of car on their own – there are not enough consumers to create sufficient demand. In order to exploit economies of scale, each company has to sell abroad as well. If consumers view BMW's is slightly different from Rolls-Royces or Mercedes, this means that both BMW and Roll-Royce can sell in each other's home market and not take too much business away from each other; consumers view the product as being 'differentiated'. Under this assumption about demand, it is possible to arrive at an equilibrium position in which the combined UK and German market for luxury cars is served by several luxury, car manufacturers. Each manufacturer will sell some of its product in its home market, and some abroad. This gives rise to the trade in luxury cars going in both directions at once, because it is no one country that has a comparative advantage. The advantage is better understood in terms of each company creating a 'niche' for itself in both its home and export markets, by producing a similar, yet slightly different product.

## 9.7 THE BENEFITS AND COSTS OF FREE TRADE

The above models of trade have also been used to provide the basis for the debate over the benefits and costs of moving towards freer trade. The theory of comparative advantage illustrated that, in principle, everyone in society would be on balance better off than without trade. This conclusion is arrived at by assuming that every person in society has the same economic weight and importance as everyone else. Thus the loss to one member of society (say a producer who has to cut output because of import penetration) is regarded as being offset by the gains to consumers, who pay lower prices because of the extra competition. It can be shown that under certain special assumptions the net gains to consumers more than offsets the losses to domestic producers. The principal gains arise because consumers pay lower prices, and because domestic resources are redeployed to more efficient and productive uses, thus generating production efficiency gains.

It should appear then, that free trade is an unalloyed blessing. But in reality, many countries have deliberately created barriers to trade, to protect their domestic economy from external competition. Why the difference between theory and practice?

There are a number of reasons, listed below:

1.  The model of free trade assumes that resources displaced by the opening up of markets are redeployed in other sectors. In the real world, import penetration often leads to job losses and unemployment, so there are economic and political pressures generated by those who stand to lose in this process.

2.  One very significant group who stand to lose from free trade are the producers who currently survive behind relatively high domestic prices for their goods or services. Unlike the model, if they are few, in number, and large employers, they may well be able to exert significant political pressure on the government to resist free trade pressures.

3.  The major beneficiaries of free trade are domestic consumers. But there are many millions of them, and each will perhaps gain only a very small individual amount from lower prices. Thus consumers tend to have less political influence on the decision making process.

4.  There are some economically justified arguments which can be put forward by a country in support of a policy of limiting free trade, i.e. a policy of 'protecting' the domestic economy from import pressures. These will be discussed next.

## 9.8 FREE TRADE VERSUS PROTECTIONISM

There are five main economic arguments which can be employed in the support of government regulation of free trade. They are:

### 9.8.1 The 'Infant Industry' Argument

The Infant Industry Argument is very simple. It basically states that a country may protect a 'young', growing industry from the full rigours of global competition in order to permit the industry to develop in both size and technical knowledge, so that when mature, the industry would be capable of competing against foreign companies with no government support, (either via subsidy or by tariff barrier or by quota). The argument rests of the implicit assumption that small industries are unable to exploit scale economies open to large firms in other countries, and therefore operate at a competitive disadvantage. The 'playing field' is therefore being levelled by government support.

The objection to this argument is simple. When does an 'infant industry' become a 'teenage industry'? At what point, precisely, should subsidy be withdrawn? Once created, the industry may come to rely on the subsidy, rather than become more efficient and competitive.

### 9.8.2 'Smoothing the R4 Resources' Argument

A second argument, less popular now that many countries have industrialised, is that protection is required in certain sectors of the economy so that the transition of resources may be more smoothly carried out. The argument has been applied in support of protecting the agricultural sectors of many countries. In the past, rural farming, because of its low productivity, supported many workers. Governments feared that opening up their markets to open competition would generate large levels of rural unemployment, and would exacerbate the drift to the towns. This argument has less force for countries who have industrialised, as the proportion of their work force engaged in agriculture declines steadily. But it is still employed as a justification for support. In the European Community, the EC has a social fund which subsidises certain activities in the poorer parts of the community, for just this reason.

### 9.8.3 The 'Strategically Important' Industry Argument

The third argument employed in support of protecting an industry is that it is strategically vital for domestic production capability to be maintained. The obvious reason for this is to provide that capability for wartime conditions, when reliance on imported goods becomes a weakness. Many countries have justified support for domestic agriculture for this reason. Some also support their domestic shipbuilders for the same reason. It is hard to imagine the UK, Germany, or the USA ever allowing their domestic shiprepair and shipbuilding facilities to disappear, no matter how efficient the world's competitors become.

### 9.8.4 To Counter 'Dumping' Behaviour by Foreign Governments or Companies

The fourth argument put forward for protecting the economy from foreign competition is based on the observation that sometimes companies may sell products in overseas markets at a price that is less than real costs of making it. This undercuts even the efficient home producer, and can occur if the exporter deliberately cross subsidises the exported good from excess profits made in their protected home market. The fear is expressed that once the imported goods have captured the home market, they can use their monopoly position to drive prices up afterwards. The US government has accused Japanese DRAM[3] manufacturers of doing just this to its domestic market – it threatened to retaliate by imposing a 100% tariff on the offending product. The problem was resolved by the appreciation of the Yen, which raised the $ price of the chips concerned. The US also accused British Steel of 'dumping' steel on the US market in the early 1990's. Such disputes can be potentially damaging to all parties if retaliation actually takes place.

### 9.8.5 To Correct a Temporary Balance of Payments Disequilibrium

Protection for this reason is only justified if the disequilibrium is *temporary*, since a permanent disequilibrium represents a more deep-seated problem in the economy itself. The increasing openness of world trade, together with the formation of regional trading blocs such as the EC, which prohibits its members from using such tactics against other members, has meant that adopting protectionist measures to 'cure' a temporary problem is less and less common. In the 1960's, the UK government imposed a 15% import surcharge on goods; but at the time it was only a member of the European Free Trade Association, EFTA. Such an action would be illegal under EC rules if levied on other EC member countries' exports to the UK.

A number of other arguments are often put forward in support of protection, but they do not have much economic justification.

#### a) Retaliation

A government may be tempted to retaliate if a trading partner imposes a restriction on its exports. The threat of retaliation may be employed as a means of persuading the trading

---

[3] DRAM, or dynamic random access memory, is an integrated chip designed to store information.

partner to lift the proposed restriction. When the other EC countries announced a ban on all UK exports of beef, following the discovery that BSE can be transmitted to calves, the UK government tried to find non-retaliatory solutions to the problem, as it argued that British health standards had been improved enough to ensure that the disease would not be transmitted to Europe via the export of cattle.

Retaliation was widespread in the 1930's, when world trade volumes collapsed. Retaliation leaves both countries worse off than they were before; the World Trade Organisation now has a forum designed to allow the resolution of trade disputes before they reach this stage. It should be noted that the USA has often used the threat with Japan, in negotiations to reduce the huge trade deficit it has with that country; as noted in section 1 of this lesson, the USA would be less affected by such disputes than European countries, which have a higher proportion of trade to national income than has the USA.

### b)   The 'cheap foreign labour' argument

Often national businessmen complain about 'unfair' competition from companies located in low labour cost economies. There is an important distinction to be made between low wages and low labour costs. A low wage economy can in fact be a high labour cost economy, if labour productivity is also very low. Unit labour costs are determined by the unit cost of labour, divided by the unit productivity of labour. Low labour productivity and low wages often offset each other. If low labour unit costs do exist in one country rather than another, this may well reflect on the relative abundance of the factors of production.

It is interesting to note that Japan's labour force earns higher real wages than the UK's. This has been achieved after 30 years of fantastic growth, both in economic output, and in labour productivity. Japanese firms may well still have lower unit labour costs than a rival UK firm, if the growth in labour productivity has outpaced the growth in their wages.

The above arguments notwithstanding, many economists are convinced that 'freer trade' is a more desirable goal for the world community to aim for than 'regulated or restricted trade'. The principal reason for this has already been highlighted – free trade encourages innovation and competition, rewards the efficient, and involves less government intervention – the invisible hand of the market directs resources.

## 9.9   METHODS OF PROTECTION

There are six main ways of creating barriers to trade; these are tariffs, quotas, voluntary export restraints, exchange controls, embargoes, and production subsidies. All have effects which can be observed in the market place, via their effects on price. In addition, governments can influence trading patterns via a number of more subtle ways. These include public procurement polices, product quality standards, and health and hygiene regulations. Economists put these into two categories – tariff, and non-tariff, barriers to trade.

### 9.9.1   Tariffs

A tariff is a tax imposed on a commodity import. It may be levied in two basic ways; on an ad valorem basis or as a specific duty. More complex schemes exist, combining these two, but the basic blocks are ad valorem or specific tariffs.

### 9.9.2   *Ad Valorem*

This is a tariff which is levied as a percentage of the import price. For example, if computers from the USA are imported into the UK, an EC common external tariff of 5% might be levied. A £1000 computer costs the importer £1050, plus carriage, insurance and freight. If the price were to rise to £2000, the duty to be levied would rise to £100; the UK price thus varies in proportion with the world price if an ad valorem tariff is used.

### 9.9.3 Specific Duty

The amount of the tax to be paid is always fixed, no matter what the price of the imported commodity. It might be 10p per kilo of tomatoes. If the world price of tomatoes was 20p a kilo, the price in the UK would become 30p. If the world price doubled to 40p, the UK price rises to 50p, which is less than double. This is because the tariff is fixed in absolute terms, rather than being determined as a proportion of the import price.

### 9.9.4 Tariffs as a Source of Revenue

It should be noted that tariffs can generate significant revenues to the government that levies them. This assumes of course, that any tariff that is imposed is not set at such a high level that imports are completely eliminated. It would be pointless, from the revenue point of view, to set a tariff so high that the domestic market was served only by domestic suppliers. This would mean no imports, and no imports means no tariff revenues!

### 9.9.5 The Effect of a Tariff

The simple model of demand and supply can be used to illustrate the economic effects of a tariff. By imposing what is in effect an import tax, the government raises the domestic price level of a product, stimulates domestic production, reduces or eliminates imports, and raises revenues for the exchequer. All of these effects are measured relative to the free trade position. The model is drawn under the following assumptions. First, competition exists in the domestic market for the product. Secondly, the world supply of the product is perfectly elastic. This means that the domestic economy can obtain as much or as little as it likes of the product at the prevailing world price, which is constant. Variations in demand from the home economy have no effect on that price – it is too small an economy in the world scheme of things to have any impact. Under these assumptions, the world supply curve is given by WS, the domestic supply curve ST, and the domestic demand curve DD. In the absence of any government interference, and in the presence of free trade, the domestic market price must be the same as the world price, OW.

### Figure 9.5 – Free Trade Versus Protection

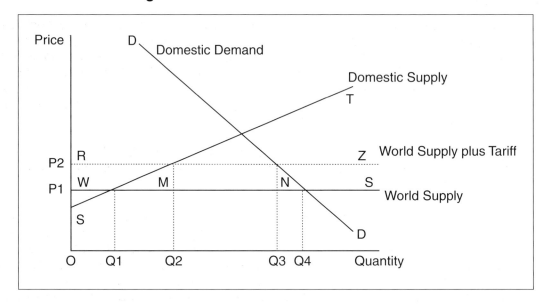

Given the market price is OW, market demand at that price is OQ4. This is met by producing OQ1 from domestic companies, because ST shows the amounts that domestic firms are willing to supply at any market price (See Chapter 1). The quantity Q1Q4 will be supplied by imports, as the world supply schedule implies that overseas companies can supply any amount at that price. Note the small domestic sector. Now a tariff is imposed. It is reflected in the vertical difference between the line WS and the line RZ, which represents the new price of imported goods *after* the tariff has been levied. This raises market price, which generates three principal effects. First, market demand declines slightly, so total sales fall from OQ4 to OQ3.

The precise size of this fall will depend on the slope of the demand curve, or the own price elasticity of demand. (See Chapter 2). The second effect is that domestic supply is increased, as domestic producers are willing to supply more at a higher market price. Thirdly, the importers suffer a decline in business, as import volumes fall to Q2Q3.

Does this mean that the economy is better off being protected? The answer is no. Two principal effects can be observed in the diagram. Firstly, consumers are worse off than they were in the free trade position. They have to pay higher prices, and as a consequence, they buy less of the product which is being protected. They are clearly worse off. Their precise loss is in fact measured by the triangle N, which measures their loss of consumer surplus. To see this, note that at the old price consumers bought OQ3. They also bought OQ3 when the price rose to OP2 from OP1. In a sense then, they were willing to pay OP2 even when the price was at OP1. This willingness to pay is measured by the vertical distance between the price actually paid and the demand curve, for each unit of output. The output range Q3Q4 generates the area shown by the triangle N as a result.

It appears that producers are 'better off' as they have expanded. In a sense they are, but this is a false impression. Remember that the comparative advantage model assumes full employment. This means that the resources that have been redeployed in the protected sector have been moved from elsewhere. It follows that output in another part of the economy must have fallen as a result. These two effects can be shown to lead to the economy being worse off overall. Look carefully at the triangle marked M. This shows the difference between what it 'cost' the economy to import the quantity Q1Q2, and what it now 'costs' to produce the same amount in the domestic economy (e.g., the Q2th unit used to cost OP1 as it was imported, but now, after the tariff is imposed, it costs OP2, a difference of P1P2 repeating the same process for all units between Q1 and Q2 generates a total resource cost of M).

Overall, there is a loss to consumers, and also an efficiency loss on the production side, as resources are redeployed in an inefficient manner. These two aspects lead to the argument that free trade is superior to no trade.

### 9.9.6 Quotas

These are quantity limits imposed on the amount of imports that can be landed in the country in a particular time period, usually a year. They operate by the simple device of the issuing of licenses, which are needed by any importer to bring their goods through customs. The most common form of quota is to determine the number of units to be permitted to enter the economy under license; but the quota limit might be set in value terms as an alternative. This second type might be used if the primary objective is to save a given quantity of foreign exchange, since the amount is predetermined.

The USA has quotas limiting the amount of sugar imported into the country. In Europe, the EC has sugar quotas for sugar produced by the West Indian economies, primarily to protect its own internal sugar beet industry.

The economic effect of a quota is identical to those generated by tariffs; domestic market price and production are increased. Instead of raising revenue from tariffs, the government can generate it from the sale of import licenses. Since the domestic market has been restricted, the higher price means that importers are willing to pay a 'premium' to obtain the licence. If the licenses are given away for nothing, the beneficiaries will be the importers, who receive the entire excess profit, because they pay the world price and receive the full domestic price. It is easy to see how corruption can creep in when governments determine who should receive the licenses.

Quotas are in some sense easier to monitor than a tariff, as they can be easily measured. The effect of a tariff on market price depends on demand conditions, which may be less easy to determine. On the other hand, quotas may lead to severe shortages if the product cannot be easily supplied by the home market. It may also be difficult to adjust the required quota amount to changes in demand conditions; what is appropriate this year may be inadequate next year, if demand grows rapidly.

### 9.9.7 Voluntary Export Restraints

In the 1980's, the growing openness of the world economy meant that individual countries found it increasingly difficult to use tariffs and quotas to protect their own economies, as these were regulated by the various trading rounds of GATT. What emerged in this period was the growth of what has become known as Voluntary Export Restraints (VERs) as a substitute. In the UK for example, the practice was first introduced in 1975, as a means of limiting the share that Japanese car manufacturers were taking of the domestic car market. The UK government and the Japanese car makers association entered an agreement whereby Japanese car manufacturers agreed to limit their exports to the UK to be no more than 15% of the total car market in any one year. This practice spread. The EC found that Italy had a limit of 11%, France 10% on the same product. The arrangement, being voluntary, was not illegal under the existing GATT rules, which explains its rise. The USA negotiated a similar agreement with Japanese car manufacturers when its domestic market suffered the same fate.[4]

### 9.9.8 Exchange Control

Exchange control refers to measure implemented by the government to ensure that there is a limited supply of the domestic currency (in the case of the UK, the pound) on to the foreign exchange markets. By limiting the amount available to be exchanged for foreign currencies, its value in terms of those currencies is also controlled. Many countries used to limit the amount of their domestic currency that could be taken abroad by tourists; the UK used to have such a limit.

This device is increasingly uncommon, as the trend towards greater liberalisation of the world's economies continues. For example, the UK government abolished all limitations on currency movements in 1981. Any UK citizen can enter any UK bank an open an account denominated in any currency they wish. This would not have been possible before 1981. The EC insists that any new member country abolishes its exchange controls vis-à-vis other members over a period of time, to permit the free movement of capital. For example, Greece liberalised its currency controls in 1996. Even Japan is moving in this direction. Many developing countries have found that support from the World Bank has been conditioned on a similar liberalising of their exchange controls.

### 9.9.9 Embargoes

Embargoes, or trade sanctions, prevent the export of all goods (or a range of selected) to a particular economy. It is the result of political events rather than economic ones, and can be very effective. For example no country permits the import of cocaine or other hard drugs. They are illegal substances, so unless they are required for medical purposes, they are not legally available. More spectacular cases have arisen in which trade with a particular economy is prohibited by one or more countries. The USA has embargoed all trade with Cuba since Castro's take over of that country. As many of you will be aware, the Cuban economy is now is some disarray, especially following the loss of trade with Soviet Bloc economies who had ignored the American sanctions.

Trade with South Africa was embargoed by the UN; Nelson Mandela actively encouraged the boycott of South African exports prior to the ending of the apartheid regime there. Iraq is the subject of another UN trade embargo, following on from their invasion of Kuwait in 1990.

### 9.9.10 Subsidies

A subsidy is a payment by the government agency to the domestic producers of goods which permits them to charge lower prices for their products. There are two types of subsidy, an *export subsidy*, and a *general subsidy*.

---

[4] The European VER with Japan's car makers became largely redundant with the setting up of the single European Market in 1992. They responded by setting up car plants inside the EC and producing from there. Such production is defined as domestic by the EC, and output is thus not restricted. It of course had implications for shipping demand, which the reader can work out on his/her own. The same process has developed in the North America, with Honda and others setting up car plants in the USA.

As its name implies, an export subsidy is received by producers selling products into overseas markets. A very good example is the use of cheap finance which was offered by Japanese shipbuilders to overseas shipowners who decided to place an order for a new ship in a Japanese yard. Before the OECD standard terms were agreed, which outlawed such practices, each shipyard would offer more and more attractive finance deals to overseas owners, as a means of competing. The Japanese government met the cost difference between the loan terms offered to the owner and the cost of the finance to the shipyard – in effect, a subsidy. Under OECD rules, all such finance is now offered under standard terms.

Subsidies can also be offered in the form of location grants, tax relief on profits, and subsidised raw materials. All these devices have the effect of lowering production costs and prices.

A general subsidy is any support which is granted to domestic producers irrespective of their export performance. Such subsidies drive down the domestic price of the products, thus limiting the market share taken by imports. The subsidy is funded by higher general taxation, so the consumer finds lower prices but higher taxes! The UK operated its own agricultural support scheme in the years 1947-1973, which allowed the price of food to be set at world price levels. This would have meant a very small domestic farm sector if there had been no subsidies. Instead, domestic production was stimulated by support in the form of efficiency related subsidies, which were funded from taxation. When the UK joined the EC. a period of three years transition was allowed, during which the price of food was raised quite sharply, as the EC policy is funded in effect, by high domestic food prices and a large external tariff.

### 9.9.11 Criticisms of the Free Trade Argument

Many economists have pointed up the limitations of the arguments underlying Free Trade. The main ones are listed below.

1. **The strong gain** – There is a general failure to analyse the way that gains from trade are distributed between the trading partners. Some have argued that only strong economies have gained, with weak ones losing out. The rise of the Asian Tigers may perhaps be seen as a counter to this position; these economies have demonstrated an ability to exploit trading opportunities to a greater extent than Europe or North America has in the past 15 years.

2. **Infant Industries** – It is argued that certain industries will always need to be protected or supported before they can become large enough to become competitive on a global basis. A good example is the rise of Airbus Industrie, the European consortium of French, German and British companies which by 1996 had obtained a 50% share of the world's large commercial aircraft market, formerly dominated by Boeing. It has achieved this with the aid of subsidies from the EC; who knows what will happen if and when those subsidies are phased out.

3. **Unemployed Resources** – The basic model of comparative advantage assumes that resources are fully employed. No economic model has been developed to ascertain the net effect if increased trade leads to permanently higher unemployment. However, it should be noted that the historically high levels of unemployment observed in the 1930's in Europe were associated with falling trade volumes – the general consensus is that trade stimulates jobs overall, rather than destroys them.

4. **Monopoly Elements** – It used to be argued that the free trade argument was flawed because the comparative advantage model is based on the assumption that all sectors of the economy are competitive. It is well known that many sectors of real economies contain monopoly or oligopoly elements. Their existence was argued to mean that the argument for free trade was weaker as a result. However, some of the modern theories of trade are based explicitly on the presence of oligopoly and economies of scale, and these theories have still demonstrated that 'more trade' is better than 'less trade'.

## 9.10  TRANSPORT COSTS AND INTERNATIONAL TRADE

The discussion of the benefits from trade has so far been conducted with the assumption that goods can be moved costlessly. What happens to the model if transport costs are introduced? The answer is that the presence of transport costs means that there is another potential barrier to trade – the size of the transport cost element itself. If transport costs are high, they act just as if the price of the import has been increased; after all, the consumer has to pay both the import price and the costs of delivery. If transport costs can be reduced then, it follows that trade can be stimulated. The size of, and trends in transport costs can thus influence the way the market develops.

Transport costs are defined here as any costs which are incurred in the act of transferring the commodity from its origin in one country to its final destination in another. This clearly includes seaborne transport costs, port loading and discharge costs, transfer costs, and land transport costs, as well as insurance premiums and interest costs arising from inventory or bank credit.

The presence of such costs explains why some goods are not traded in significant amounts.[5] A good example is brewing. There is very little exporting of beer, relative to domestic production and market size. The reason is simple. 95% of the product is water. Beer is a bulky and heavy product, which generates very high transport costs for road distribution. It is cheaper to build breweries near major consumption centres, and serve markets this way, than it is to develop a large international trade in beer. When major brewing companies achieve export success, they license a domestic brewer to make the product. Many successful 'European' lagers are actually made by UK brewers to meet UK consumption, rather than being exported from Denmark or the Netherlands.

Figure 9.6 below shows the effect that the incorporation of a constant transport unit cost has on prices and output. Transport costs have the effect of raising the price of the imported goods from OW, to OR, an increase in price of WR per unit. The inclusion of transport costs thus has exactly the same effect as a tariff – it raises the domestic price and helps protect domestic suppliers. It follows that falling transport costs actually help to stimulate world trade, as they make it easier for imported goods to compete with domestically produced ones. Shipping has played a role in this process over the past twenty years, with the use of larger ships, and the spread of containerisation. These two technical changes have helped to lower transport costs, and thus assist the development of world trade.

Another model of the effect of transport costs on trade is shown in Figure 9.7. This shows the effect in a slightly different way. It focuses on the market for imported goods. The demand curve, DD1 in the Figure, shows the demand for the imported good only, in contrast to the demand curve in the previous figure. If there were zero transport costs, equilibrium imports would be given by OQ, at price OPw. The addition of transport costs raises the domestic price of the import, and demand falls. Sales now run at OQ1. In this model, the supply curve is upward sloping, so that a fall in price discourages suppliers. The new equilibrium price is OPw+t, but suppliers only receive OP. The difference, PPw+t, represents the transport cost element. The model shows that this is divided between suppliers and consumers, as suppliers previously received OPw per unit, so they have lost PPw per unit to 'transport'. Similarly, consumers now pay the extra amount PwPw+t compared to the 'no transport case'. The distribution of the 'burden' of transport costs depends on the relative slopes of demand and supply. If you were to imagine that the demand curve was almost vertical, (perfectly price inelastic), there would be little or no change in the output sold, and the full amount of the transport cost element is passed on to consumers. If the demand curve was horizontal (perfectly elastic), the market price would not change, so suppliers would have to 'absorb' the transport cost element. This would entail the suppliers reducing output sufficiently, lowering production costs, to create the necessary margin to fund the transport element.

---

[5] It should be noted that certain services cannot be traded across frontiers at all, even if there are no transport costs. For example, how does one export a haircut? Motorbikes, easy – but personal services, such as house cleaning, haircuts etc, cannot be traded in this way.

**Figure 9.6 – The effect of transport costs on trade**

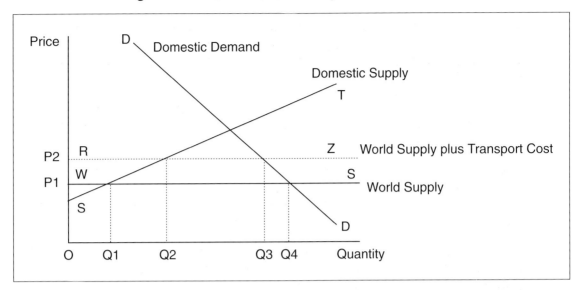

**Figure 9.7 – The effect of transport costs on the market for imported goods**

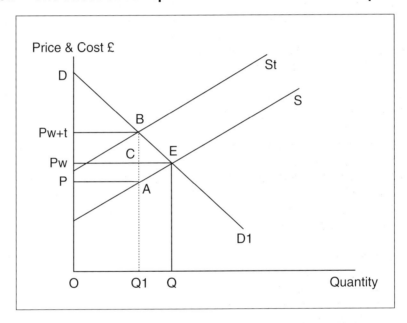

If shipping companies are able to reduce the size of transport costs relative to market demand, the effect is to stimulate output and lower prices.

## 9.11 DEVELOPING FREE INTERNATIONAL TRADE: THE ROLE OF THE WORLD TRADE ORGANISATION

The World Trade Organisation (WTO) came into being in 1995, replacing the General Agreement of Tariffs and Trade, which had been set up after WWII with the express purpose of reducing the size and extent of barriers to trade which had existed in 1939. It did this by meeting every few years to conduct a 'round' of negotiations between member countries, the aim of which was the lowering of external tariff barriers. The famous 'Kennedy' round made a significant contribution towards the lowering of tariffs on manufactured goods, which averaged 40% in 1947. By 1995, the Uruguay round had seen this figure drop to less than 5%. As manufacturing tariffs dropped, tariffs in the agricultural sectors, and barriers to trade in services became the centre of attention.

The WTO policy objectives in both the short and long run has been seriously questioned by demonstrations and protests in the example of Seattle (USA), and Genoa (Italy). Those serve to cast a shadow over its' activities, particularly in areas like the environment and the developing countries' trading potential. Based in Geneva, the WTO has as its own objective are to further liberalising of trade, and its focus has shifted towards the resolution of such problems as the non-recognition of American and European copyright and patent rights in some Far East countries. Also, the reduction of import restrictions imposed on textile manufacturers by the Multi-Fibre Agreement. In addition, trade conflicts, the determination of internationally accepted standards in for example, food hygiene are all current issues on their agenda. GATT oversaw a 12 fold increase in trade volume, and a 28 fold increase in trade value. The future growth of shipping markets will be shaped by the success of this organisation in further stimulating trade.

## 9.12 CONCLUSION

This chapter has provided information about the growth and pattern of world trade, which of course is the key driving force for shipping demand. Types of trade flows have been mentioned, economic theories of trade have been briefly outlined. The arguments for and against free trade policies were reviewed, as well as discussing the main forms of protection. The concepts employed have been introduced in other Chapters; if you have had difficulty with them, please refer to Chapter 1 for the production possibility frontier, Chapter 2 for demand, and elasticity of demand, and Chapter 3 for supply concepts.

## 9.13 SELF-ASSESSMENT AND TEST QUESTIONS

Attempt the following and check your answer from the text.

1. Work out the Opportunity Cost of an extra car in Country B. What is the opportunity Cost of an extra unit of rice in Country B? The opportunity costs for the two countries are shown in Table 9.7.

2. List the reasons put forward to justify protection. Explain any one of these in detail, in your own words.

3. Explain the different ways in which a tariff and quota are used to restrict trade.

4. Why might import licences become valuable when a quota system is employed?

5. What is meant by a 'Voluntary Export Restraint'. How might a foreign company get around such a restraint?

6. Draw a diagram, based on Figure 9.7, showing the economic effects of a reduction in the unit cost of transport from its existing level.

Having completed Chapter Nine, attempt the following and submit your essay to your Tutor.

"The theory of comparative advantage explains some, but not all, of the observed pattern of international trade flows."

Assess the validity of this statement, using examples from trades and countries of your choice.

# Chapter 10

# THE BALANCE OF PAYMENTS AND EXCHANGE RATES

## 10.1    INTRODUCTION

This Chapter is concerned with certain aspects of international trade; the balance of payments, exchange rates and the way that shipping activities are recorded in international transactions.

Balance of payment accounting is complex because of the numerous and different items that appear in international trade. There is one simple principle underlying the accounts which has to be grasped straightaway. The principle is that all transactions that involve *resources,* such as the export of cars from the UK to Zimbabwe, involves a *credit* to the exporting country. Most transactions that appear in the Balance of Payments accounts also involve a corresponding financial adjustment, which is entered in a separate part of those accounts. This procedure is called double-entry book-keeping, and explains why the overall Balance of Payments Account is expected to sum to zero. The reason is that the financial entry is entered with an opposite sign from the resource entry, so if all transactions were perfectly matched, they would sum to zero.

A simple example is given below, to make this fundamental point clear.

Suppose there was only one trade between the UK and Germany in the year. The UK exports £1mn worth of cars to Germany, and Germany exports nothing to the UK. Two transactions would appear in the Balance of Payments Accounts. The flows that relate to resources would appear on the current account, and are shown in Table 10.1 below.

In the case being considered at present, the payment for the cars would create a need for the German importer to buy sterling to settle the account. The UK has, by selling goods abroad, created an increase in the UK's holdings of overseas assets. There will be a demand for sterling from Germany in order to settle this debt, which will be funded by a supply of Germany's currency (the Euro) onto the foreign exchange market. Every resource transaction thus creates a matching change in the assets and liabilities position of the economy, and these changes are recorded in the second part of the Balance of Payments accounts, called Transactions in UK assets and liabilities.

Note that changes that increase a country's assets are, by convention, awarded a negative sign; those that increase a country's external liabilities are given a positive sign. This is very important to remember when studying the accounts.

The simple example in Table 10.1 highlights another important point. Basically, credit items on the current account create a demand for a country's currency while debit items create a supply of the country's currency seeking to purchase other currencies. Hence a deficit in the balance of payments means a country is losing reserve assets and a surplus means they are increasing these assets. There is a link between the balance of payments position and movements in the exchange rate, with countries which experience weak growth and persistent deficits finding that their currencies depreciate over time. Shipping is an important factor in the balance of payments calculations at a number of levels which will be discussed overleaf.

## Table 10.1 – Hypothetical Example of UK Balance of Payments Account

|  | £ million |  |
| --- | --- | --- |
| Current Account (measuring resource flows) |  |  |
| Exports of Goods | 1 |  |
| Imports of Goods | 0 |  |
| Current Account Balance | +1 | (1) |
| Transactions in UK Assets and Liabilities |  |  |
| UK's Overseas Assets | –1 | (2) |
| Balancing Item | 0 | (3) |
| Balance (1) + (2) + (3) | 0 |  |

## 10.2 DEFINITION OF THE BALANCE OF PAYMENTS

International trade will give rise to indebtedness between countries. Such indebtedness is the central element of the balance of payments. It may be defined as 'a systematic record of all economic transactions between the residents of the reporting country and the residents of all foreign countries over a given period of time'. The term 'resident' covers both individuals being permanently in a country and corporate bodies located therein, but not their overseas branches and subsidiaries. It does include government agencies and military forces located abroad. By the term 'permanent resident' is meant the intention to remain in a country for at least a year. The term 'economic transactions' must not be confused for it not only includes exchange of currency for goods and services but also the transferring of currencies and valuable assets abroad and exchange of goods for other goods involved. Care also must be taken of the word 'balance'. It is to be understood in the sense of a relationship rather than as an exact equality, since it is unlikely that goods and services bought by residents of a country from abroad will be exactly balanced by those sales and services to foreign countries.

To define the balance of payments from a slightly different point of view, rather than simply stating what it is, look at what it is for. From an economic point of view its object is to identify and record transactions between residents of the domestic economy and all other economies. It uses a method that is suitable for analysing the economic relationships between the domestic economy and the rest of the world. Such transactions may involve the movement of real resources, that is goods and services, or property incomes between the domestic economy and foreign economies as well as the change in the domestic economy's foreign assets, liabilities, or transfer payments.

It is usual to set out the economic transactions of the domestic economy with all other foreign economies as a series of credit and debits. These transactions are divided into three broad areas. They are:

1. Accounts relating to the flows of goods and services currently being produced by the domestic economy, or owned by residents of the domestic economy. All these transactions appear in the *Current Account.*

2. Accounts relating to *changes* in the stock of assets or liabilities of permanent residents of the UK. This part of the account records *changes* in the net wealth of the country and is called *Transactions in UK assets and liabilities.* It may be thought of as a *capital account,* recording *changes* in the wealth of the economy.

3. An account of the *total* holdings by UK residents of assets abroad, and of holdings by overseas residents of assets in the UK, is called the *International Investment Position.*

## 10.3  THE STRUCTURE OF THE BALANCE OF PAYMENTS

The Account headings listed above can be examined in greater detail:

i)  Current Account transactions cover trade in goods (visibles), trade in services, investment incomes and transfers (invisibles).

ii)  Transactions in UK Assets and Liabilities. This heading covers several important sections of the Balance of Payments accounts. It records changes in the flows of direct investment, changes in the flows of portfolio investment, transactions by both UK and non-UK banks, and the general government account. The latter records changes on official reserves, borrowing and lending of currencies, and the take up or repayment of loans from the International Monetary Fund (IMF).

iii)  Balancing item. This represents the net total of errors and omissions arising throughout the account. These arise mainly through timing errors in recording transactions and on recording capital flows. As in the hypothetical example in Table 10.1, the sum of all flows in i) and ii) above should equal zero. The balancing item ensures that this convention is met.

iv)  While the capital account (transactions in UK external assets and liabilities) covers the flows of overseas investments and capital assets, the International Investment position covers the *levels* of identified external assets and liabilities.

The structure of the Balance of Payments Accounts is presented in Figure 10.1. Details may vary from country to country, but in each case, it should be possible to identify the current account, some kind of capital account recording private sector transactions and government capital transactions, a balancing item, and a record of the present stocks of a country's overseas assets and liabilities.

Table 10.2 provides summary data for the UK's Accounts on this basis.

## Table 10.2 – Summary Account of the UK's Balance of Payments 1990-1995

| | £ million | | | | | |
|---|---|---|---|---|---|---|
| | **1990** | **1991** | **1992** | **1993** | **1994** | **1995** |
| **Current Account** | | | | | | |
| Trade in Goods | -18809 | -10284 | -13104 | -13460 | -10831 | -11628 |
| Trade in Services | 3689 | 3564 | 4950 | 5516 | 4747 | 6142 |
| Investment Income | 1269 | 150 | 3124 | 2197 | 8691 | 9572 |
| Transfers Balance | -4896 | -1383 | -5102 | -5007 | -5027 | -6978 |
| **Current Balance** | -18746 | -7954 | -10133 | -10756 | -2419 | -2892 |
| **Transactions in UK Assets and Liabilities*** | | | | | | |
| UK external assets | -80415 | -18683 | -81600 | -155611 | -35147 | -124045 |
| UK external liabilities | 96958 | 26128 | 86565 | 168691 | 32497 | 124491 |
| Net transactions | 16543 | 7445 | 4965 | 13080 | -2650 | 446 |
| EEA loss on forward commitments | | | | | | |
| SDR allocations | | | | | | |
| Gold subscription to IMF | | | | | | |
| **Balancing Item** | 2203 | 509 | 5168 | -2324 | 5069 | 2446 |

Source: Table 1.1, Summary of Balance of Payments, UK Balance of Payments 1996, CSO, London.
* Increases in assets are shown with a negative sign.

Note that the fourth item mentioned above is not shown in these accounts. The overall international investment position is shown elsewhere.

**Figure 10.1 – Outline of the Balance of Payments**

| | | | | | | |
|---|---|---|---|---|---|---|
| 1. | Current Account | | | | | |
| | 1.1 | Trade in Goods | | | | |
| | | Exports | (+) | | Imports | (-) |
| | | Net Position | | = | Visible Trade Balance | |
| | 1.2 | Trade in Services | | | | |
| | | Services Exports | (+) | | Services Imports | (-) |
| | | Net Position | | = | Services Trade Balance | |
| | 1.3 | Investment Income | | | | |
| | | Interest Payments | (+) | | Interest Payments | (-) |
| | | Profits | (+) | | Profits | (-) |
| | | Dividends | (+) | | Dividends | (-) |
| | | Net Position | | = | Investment Income Balance | |
| | 1.4 | Transfers | | | | |
| | | Govt receipts from abroad | (+) | | Govt payments abroad | (-) |
| | | Private receipts from abroad | (+) | | Private payments abroad | (-) |
| | | Net position | | = | Transfers Balance | |

Current Account Balance = sum of balances from 1.1, 1.2, 1.3, and 1.4.
*Note:* Services and Investment Income Trades are sometimes called *Invisible* Trades.

| | | | | | | |
|---|---|---|---|---|---|---|
| 2. | Capital Account/ Transactions in Assets and Liabilities | | | | | |
| | 2.1 | Direct Investment | | | | |
| | | UK companies investing abroad | (-) | | Foreign companies investing in UK | (+) |
| | | Net position | | | | |
| | 2.2 | Portfolio Investment | | | | |
| | | UK residents purchase of overseas stocks and shares | (-) | | Foreign residents purchase of UK stocks and shares | (+) |
| | | Net position | | | | |
| | 2.3 | UK banks and non-banks' lending and borrowing | | | | |
| | 2.4 | General government account | | | | |
| 3. | Balancing Item | | | | | |

Balance on Current Account = Balance on Capital Account + Balancing Item

**To Recap on the Basic Structure of the Balance of Payments**

Whatever the exact form the figures take in any particular country they will include payments which arise from i) visible trade, that is the sale and purchase of goods; ii) invisible trade, that is payments for interest, profits and dividends and services, of which shipping would be an example, and finally, iii) the transfer of capital from one country to another.

In addition there will be a category known as the Balancing Item which should be thought of as errors and omissions which arise throughout the period of the accounts.

In this Chapter, in order to highlight the factors influencing the Balance of Payments, the experience of the UK will be used as a general example. The points made will all, to a lesser or greater degree, apply to the balance of payments of other countries.

Throughout the lesson students should attempt to evaluate the extent to which the factors discussed apply to their own country. The basic headings of the UK Balance of Payments are:

i) Current Account
ii) Transactions in Assets and Liabilities Account
iii) Balancing Item
iv) The International Asset Position

Table 10.1 presents the net position for these flows, except for item iv. Students may find it useful to look at how the Balance of Payment figures are presented in their own countries.

The information provided in Table 10.1 is rather sketchy, showing only the net balances. This data hides the size of the flows recorded in the accounts, as many of the net balances are the difference between two very large numbers. Some of the account items are explored in more detail below.

## 10.4 THE CURRENT ACCOUNT

### 10.4.1 Trade in Visibles

The current account is the account of which the general public is usually made most aware, since it is concerned in part with actual goods exported and imported by a country. This includes raw materials, fuel, foodstuffs, semi-processed and finished manufactures. All items are important to the industrial base of a country and its standard of living. The official definition is 'Transactions in goods which are freighted into and out of a country'. This section of the Balance of Payments, the Visibles in the Current Account is known as the Balance of Trade or Trade Figures and often features in the national news. When figures are prepared for the Balance of Payments they are based on the Overseas Trade Statistics compiled from H.M. Customs and Excise records to which adjustments have been made. The most important valuation adjustment made is the deduction of the freight and insurance elements from the c.i.f. (cost insurance freight) valuation declared for imports to arrive at the required f.o.b. (free on board) valuation for the balance of payments. Freight and insurance are services and therefore included in the services section of the current account.

Tables 10.3 and 10.4 show an analysis of UK trade by commodity and by geographical area.

## Table 10.3 – Trade on a balance of payments basis: commodity analysis

| | | 1985 | 1990 | 1995 | 1996 | 1997 | 1998 |
|---|---|---|---|---|---|---|---|
| **EXPORTS** | | | | | | | |
| Food, beverages and tobacco | HCIV | 4937 | 6,995 | 11,161 | 11,343 | 11,094 | 10,231 |
| Basic materials | CGJX | 2,199 | 2,242 | 2,932 | 2,793 | 2,750 | 2,512 |
| Oil | BOPX | 16,115 | 7,484 | 8,687 | 10,943 | 10,229 | 7,039 |
| Other mineral fuels and lubricants | HDVE | 662 | 324 | 563 | 651 | 775 | 492 |
| Semi-manufactured goods | HCJK | 19,921 | 28,796 | 43,437 | 45,366 | 44,538 | 43,385 |
| Finished manufactured goods | HBTG | 32,219 | 53,613 | 83,783 | 94,353 | 100,454 | 98,576 |
| Commodities and transactions not classified according to kind | BOPF | 1,838 | 2,264 | 1,783 | 1,954 | 1,943 | 1,897 |
| **Total** | **CGJP** | **77,991** | **101,718** | **152,346** | **167,403** | **171,783** | **169,132** |
| **IMPORTS** | | | | | | | |
| Food, beverages and tobacco | HCJB | 8,660 | 11,606 | 15,237 | 16,840 | 16,214 | 16,258 |
| Basic materials | HCNN | 5,041 | 5,525 | 6,441 | 6,550 | 6,277 | 5,622 |
| Oil | BPAX | 8,014 | 5,955 | 4,457 | 6,120 | 5,680 | 3,980 |
| Other mineral fuels and lubricants | HDVN | 2,257 | 1,471 | 1,102 | 1,167 | 1,146 | 915 |
| Semi-manufactured goods | HBTK | 20,338 | 31,556 | 45,035 | 46,898 | 45,553 | 45,161 |
| Finished manufactured goods | HCJP | 35,667 | 62,500 | 90,180 | 101,199 | 107,163 | 111,144 |
| Commodities and transactions not classified according to kind | BPAF | 1,359 | 1,914 | 1,522 | 1,765 | 1,760 | 1,817 |
| **Total** | **CGGL** | **81,336** | **120,527** | **163,974** | **180,489** | **193,693** | **184,897** |
| **BALANCES** | | | | | | | |
| Food, beverages and tobacco | HBXU | -3,723 | -4,611 | -4,076 | -5,197 | -5,120 | -6,027 |
| Basic materials | HBUO | -2,842 | -3,283 | -3,509 | -3,757 | -3,527 | -3,110 |
| Oil | HBSD | 8,101 | 1,529 | 4,230 | 4,823 | 4,549 | 3,059 |
| Other mineral fuels and lubricants | HDVX | -1,595 | -1,147 | -598 | -516 | -371 | -423 |
| Semi-manufactured goods | HCHB | -417 | -2,760 | -1,598 | -1,482 | -915 | -1,776 |
| Finished manufactured goods | HDIU | -3,348 | -8,887 | -6,397 | -6,846 | -6,709 | -12,568 |
| Commodities and transactions not classified according to kind | HCLW | 479 | 350 | 261 | -189 | -183 | -80 |
| **Total** | **HCHL** | **-3,345** | **-18,809** | **-11,628** | **-13,086** | **-11,910** | **-20,765** |

## Table 10.4 – Trade on a balance of payments basis: geographical analysis

| | | 1985 | 1986 | 1987 | 1988 | 1989 | 1990 | 1991 | 1992 | 1993 | 1994 | 1995 |
|---|---|---|---|---|---|---|---|---|---|---|---|---|
| **EXPORTS** | | | | | | | | | | | | |
| European Union[1] | ENOF | 42,148 | 38,292 | 42,612 | 44,432 | 51,132 | 58,584 | 62,857 | 64,707 | 68,892 | 76,737 | 88,711 |
| Other Western European | HCJD | 3,186 | 3,478 | 3,905 | 3,723 | 4,019 | 4,647 | 4,542 | 4,281 | 5,617 | 5,617 | 6,282 |
| North America[2] | HBZQ | 13,498 | 12,275 | 13,150 | 12,971 | 14,741 | 15,296 | 13,489 | 14,587 | 17,524 | 19,267 | 20,364 |
| Other OECD countries | HCII | 2,791 | 2,793 | 3,126 | 3,433 | 4,369 | 4,687 | 3,917 | 3,847 | 4,644 | 5,430 | 6,477 |
| Oil exporting countries | HDII | 5,943 | 5,493 | 5,263 | 4,921 | 5,694 | 5,415 | 5,746 | 6,039 | 6,494 | 5,618 | 6,203 |
| Rest of World | HCHW | 10,425 | 10,296 | 11,097 | 10,865 | 12,199 | 13,088 | 12,862 | 13,882 | 18,600 | 21,997 | 24,309 |
| **Total** | **CGJP** | **77,991** | **72,627** | **79,153** | **80,346** | **92,154** | **101,718** | **103,413** | **107,343** | **121,396** | **134,666** | **152,346** |
| **IMPORTS** | | | | | | | | | | | | |
| European Union | ENOS | 44,900 | 48,401 | 53,831 | 60,168 | 68,612 | 70,327 | 65,250 | 69,700 | 74,315 | 82,399 | 92,892 |
| Other Western European | HBTS | 7,252 | 6,659 | 7,183 | 7,711 | 8,806 | 9,136 | 8,464 | 8,390 | 9,365 | 9,110 | 10,209 |
| North America | HCRB | 11,298 | 9,626 | 10,622 | 12,721 | 15,055 | 16,446 | 15,323 | 15,162 | 17,730 | 19,143 | 22,150 |
| Other OECD countries | HDJQ | 5,027 | 5,624 | 6,308 | 7,245 | 8,010 | 7,734 | 7,478 | 8,450 | 9,489 | 10,093 | 10,918 |
| Oil exporting countries | HCPC | 2,645 | 1,874 | 1,622 | 1,842 | 1,971 | 2,526 | 2,553 | 2,845 | 3,555 | 2,943 | 2,903 |
| Rest of World | HCIP | 10,214 | 10,002 | 11,169 | 12,142 | 14,384 | 14,358 | 14,628 | 15,902 | 20,408 | 21,809 | 24,902 |
| **Total** | **CGGL** | **81,336** | **82,186** | **90,735** | **101,826** | **116,837** | **120,527** | **113,697** | **120,447** | **134,858** | **145,497** | **163,974** |
| **BALANCES** | | | | | | | | | | | | |
| European Union | ENPF | -2,752 | -10,109 | -11,219 | -15,736 | -17,480 | -11,743 | -2,393 | -4,993 | -5,662 | -5,662 | -4,181 |
| Other Western European | HBZW | -4,066 | -3,181 | -3,278 | -3,988 | -4,787 | -4,489 | -3,922 | -4,109 | -3,493 | -3,493 | -3,927 |
| North America | HBYF | 2,200 | 2,649 | 2,528 | 2,528 | -314 | -1,150 | -1,834 | -575 | 124 | 124 | -1,786 |
| Other OECD countries | HBZC | -2,236 | -2,831 | -3,182 | -3,182 | -3,641 | -3,047 | -3,561 | -4,603 | -4,663 | -4,663 | 4,441 |
| Oil exporting countries | HBVG | 3,298 | 3,619 | 3,641 | 3,641 | 3,723 | 2,889 | 3,193 | 3,194 | 2,675 | 2,675 | 3,300 |
| Rest of World | HBXP | 211 | 294 | -72 | -1,277 | -2,185 | -1,270 | -1,766 | -2,020 | 188 | 188 | -593 |
| **Total** | **HCHL** | **-3,345** | **-9,559** | **-11,582** | **-21,480** | **-24,683** | **-18,809** | **-10,284** | **-13,104** | **-10,831** | **-10,831** | **-11,628** |

[1] Figures for all years relate to all fourteen EU countries
[2] Mexico is included under North America. In previous editions of the Pink Book it was included under Rest of World

## 10.4.2   Trade in Services

The transactions which are concerned with the import and export of services are recorded in this section. These are, of course, a vital part of international trade, and have played an important role in the UK Balance of Payments. Traditionally the UK has had a deficit on the visible trade part of her Current Account, that is she has imported more goods than she has exported, but this has often been compensated for by a surplus earned in services. This changed in the 1980's, as oil exports expanded, and the oil price peaked. The visible trade balance was in surplus between 1980 and 1982, after which it moved into deficit again. The traditional surplus on services, which reached £6bn in 1995, has not proved large enough to prevent a persistent deficit on the overall trade in goods and services since 1985.

The principal components of the trade in services account are:

a)   Sea transport
b)   Civil aviation
c)   Travel
d)   Financial Services

Items a) and d) are discussed below.

*The Sea Transport Account*
It is important to note that this is not the same as the value of shipping to the Balance of Payments, for two main reasons. Firstly, the transactions are recorded on an expenditure basis, and not adjusted to measure the value added of each sector. Secondly, transactions associated with Shipping, and the provision of shipping services, such as Marine insurance, cargo insurance, shipbroking services, are recorded elsewhere in the accounts. Thirdly, the figures do not allow for any 'knock on' effects that the earnings might create for employment and additional domestic jobs related to the shipping industry. They must be regarded as very 'rough and ready' measures of the role of shipping in the UK economy.

Appendix 10.1 reproduces the Sea Transport Account from the 1996 UK Balance of Payments, published by the CSO. The figures available for sea transport are sub-divided into dry cargo and tankers. Receipts include earnings from the country's merchant fleet, either owned by or chartered to residents of the home country, freight on UK exports, freights from cross trades, passenger revenue collected from abroad, time charter hire from abroad and payments of foreign ships in the ports of the home country. These are all Credits to the home (recording) country.

The payments on the debit side of the sea transport figures include home operators' payments abroad. The chartering of foreign vessels, freights and passenger payments to overseas operators and various disbursements such as canal dues, port charges and payments for tankers and other services to vessels.

In the case of the UK, tankers owned by oil companies are considered to be UK operated.

Table 10.5 shows that the Sea Transport account has run at a small net deficit for the past decade. Some £4.5bn of credit was generated, and £4.7bn paid out as debits. These flows are relatively small compared to the £12bn credit, £15bn debit, generated by Tourism, and a £12bn net surplus on financial services.

Students from countries other than the UK should endeavour to gain access to the shipping figures of their own country, and attempt to analyse what events have influenced these figures.

UK Shipping Balances – Suggested reasons for relative decline and imbalance over the last two decades.

1.   The heavy commitment historically to sterling area trade and its cross trade which has grown at a slower rate than international trade.

2.  The significant re-orientation of UK trade and movement away from the more distant markets towards the closer industrial regions, in particular Europe, has run counter to UK shipping which has traditionally concentrated on the long distance trades. Sixty per cent of UK merchandise trade is now with its European Union partners.

3.  Shipping freights are usually related to cargo weight rather than value. British export tonnage has been declining since 1914 with a movement away from the heavy staple industries, developed in the 19th century exporting coal, iron, steel and textiles, towards more technologically sophisticated exports of high value and low weights.

4.  The virtual disappearance of the re-export trade has been a depressive influence on the UK Shipping net contribution to the Balance of Payments, as most of this trade is now through Rotterdam or Antwerp.

*Trade in Financial Services – The Contribution of the City*

This category includes a wide range of financial and other services which generate foreign exchange earnings. This may be a very important item in the economies of certain countries, for example Hong Kong and Singapore and, of course, the UK. The Financial section includes receipts from and payments for insurance, banking, commodity trading, merchanting, brokerages, the earnings of investment trusts and pension funds. Details of these earnings are shown in Table 10.6 below. It is worth noting that earnings from the Baltic Exchange and Lloyds Register average 6% of all the City's net credits, a not inconsiderable sum. The credits from Marine and other types of insurance, which are also shipping related, are not separately recorded in these accounts.

It should also be noted that the government account in the Trade in services section is the location for debits arising from the maintenance of embassies and military establishments abroad. The UK government has had a persistent net deficit on this account because of its expenditures on military bases in Germany.

## Table 10.5 – Shipping in UK Invisible Trade Balances Contributions and Expenditure Annual Average £mn 1985-1998

| Years | 1985 | 1986 | 1987 | 1988 | 1989 | 1990 | 1991 | 1992 | 1993 | 1994 | 1995 | 1996* | 1997* | 1998* | A |
|---|---|---|---|---|---|---|---|---|---|---|---|---|---|---|---|
| Credit | 2986 | 28.59 | 2932 | 3276 | 3522 | 3444 | 3351 | 3525 | 3913 | 4246 | 4550 | 4284 | 4477 | 3996 | Export |
| Debits | 3515 | 3323 | 3219 | 3517 | 3779 | 3758 | 3634 | 3821 | 4225 | 4561 | 4715 | 4562 | 5161 | 4740 | Imports |
| Balance | -529 | -464 | -287 | -241 | -257 | -312 | -283 | -296 | -312 | -315 | -165 | -278 | -684 | -708 | Balance |

Source: Table 3.3 Sea Transport, United Kingdom balance of Payments 1996 and 1999 Table 3.2
* Classification was changed to end of column

**Table 10.6 – Earnings of Financial and Allied Institutions (net credits) – Selected Years £mn**

|  | 1985 | 1986 | 1987 | 1988 | 1989 | 1990 | 1991 | 1992 | 1993 | 1994 | 1995 |
|---|---|---|---|---|---|---|---|---|---|---|---|
| Baltic Exchange | 229 | 221 | 227 | 334 | 427 | 474 | 326 | 300 | 275 | 262 | 292 |
| Money Market Brokers | 57 | 58 | 59 | 56 | 73 | 85 | 84 | 92 | 107 | 130 | 112 |
| Securities dealing | 82 | 349 | 950 | 867 | 888 | 538 | 282 | 687 | 580 | 664 | 770 |
| Lloyds Register of Shipping | 25 | 24 | 22 | 18 | 23 | 29 | 33 | 39 | 45 | 48 | 57 |
| Insurance – Lloyds | 741 | 1331 | 1417 | 681 | 172 | -490 | -106 | -645 | 76 | 185 | 383 |
| Insurance – Companies | 793 | 1126 | 882 | 495 | 89 | 97 | 211 | 679 | 419 | 484 | 363 |
| Banks | 1105 | 1169 | 1285 | 1269 | 1469 | 1712 | 1569 | 1689 | 1721 | 1584 | 1735 |
| Commodity Traders, bullion dealers, and export houses | 551 | 440 | 368 | 415 | 325 | 431 | 412 | 455 | 471 | 576 | 556 |
| Total Earnings | 4207 | 5429 | 5927 | 4825 | 4183 | 3899 | 3961 | 4612 | 5221 | 5424 | 5778 |
| Baltic Exchange & Lloyds Register earnings as % of Total | 6.0 | 4.5 | 4.2 | 7.3 | 10.8 | 12.9 | 9.2 | 7.4 | 6.1 | 5.7 | 6.0 |

Source: Government Statistical Service – United Kingdom Balance of Payments 1988 HMSO

### 10.4.3 Investment Income

The third component of the Current Account, items which are recorded here have generated significant and growing surpluses in the past decade. The dramatic improvement in the UK's overall current account balance in 1994 and 1995 has been primarily due to a huge increase in the surplus on this account, rising from £2.2bn in 1993 to £9.6bn in 1995. The principal items on this account are the earnings from profits, dividends, and interest payments arising from the ownership of assets in the rest of the world, and the payment of similar items to overseas residents who own assets in the UK.

### 10.4.4 Transfers

These items differ from all others on the current account because they do not correspond to an underlying resource transaction – they relate to the transfer of funds from one country to another. Government transfers includes contributions and subscriptions to the EU, and bilateral aid to developing countries. Private debits would include the repatriation of salaries by Indian workers in the UK to relatives in India. Transfers are not included in the calculation of either GDP or GNP.

Summing the net credits in items i) to iv) above yields the Current Account Balance.

## 10.5 THE CAPITAL ACCOUNT, OR TRANSACTIONS IN UK ASSETS AND LIABILITIES

The Capital Account is that sector of the Balance of Payments concerned with investment and other capital transactions and will include the accounts measuring changes in the government's reserves, which may be used from time to time if exchange rate movements become excessive, or if there is a 'run' on the currency in the foreign exchange markets.

Two types of capital investments are recorded in this section of the accounts, *Direct* investment and *Portfolio* investment. Direct investment is the act of buying physical plant and equipment located in a different country. For example, the large investment by Nissan in setting up a car plant on Teesside in the UK would be direct inwards investment. Glaxo-Wellcome's setting up of a factory in Singapore to manufacture its drugs would be an outward direct investment. Portfolio investment refers to the purchase or sale of financial assets, such as stocks, bonds and shares. If a UK citizen decides to buy Microsoft shares, a capital outflow is created, as sterling is sold to pay for dollars to purchase the shares – but assets will increase. Other capital transactions cover the main borrowing and lending of banks and some other financial institutions in respect of non-residents.

An important distinction should be drawn between the current account and the investment sections of the Capital Account.

The current account refers to flows of expenditure which directly cause flows of goods and services and which are likely to be influenced by the level of income at home and abroad and by relative prices at home and abroad (that is of imports, exports and home produced goods and services).

Transactions in the UK Assets and Liabilities relate to changes in the national stock of assets and are likely to be influenced by relative rates of return and rates of interest in particular. For example, a UK company looking for development opportunities may choose to invest in factories abroad if the profits it is likely to earn (the rate of return) will be higher than could be earned in the UK. Increases in the rate of interest in the home country may result in foreigners investing in that country rather than in their own because they will earn more interest. This may have important implications for the rate of exchange which will be discussed below.

The recordings of movements in the Capital Account may give some difficulty to students. It may seem strange, for example, that a capital outflow is recorded as a debit when it actually makes the country a creditor.

But it must be remembered:

An INFLOW of capital (foreign direct or portfolio investment) is an immediate credit to the Balance of Payments. (This would have the same effect as an inflow of funds paying for exports).

An OUTFLOW of capital (direct or portfolio investment overseas) is an immediate debit to the Balance of Payments. (This would have the same effect as an outflow of funds paying for exports).

A net inflow of direct or portfolio investment might well be advantageous as it could result in a surplus on the balance of payments. However, it is important to remember this may only be a short run advantage, for in the long run the profits, interest, etc. resulting from this investment will be a debit on the investment income section of the current account. This latter disadvantage would however also have to be weighed against the extent to which foreign investment significantly affects job opportunities for the home country's workers.

A net outflow of direct or portfolio investment may result in an initial deficit for the home country, but in the long run this will be compensated for by credits to the invisibles of the current market. This has historically been an important factor in the UK balance of payments. On the other hand, if the direct investment abroad takes jobs away from home country workers then it may have serious implications for the national economy.

Since the liberalisation of capital controls in 1981, the UK has steadily accumulated a large portfolio of overseas assets. In the early 1980's the outflow of funds was financed by the surpluses on the current account.

## 10.6 ACCOUNTING FOR GOVERNMENT INTERVENTION IN FOREIGN EXCHANGE MARKETS

An important section of the Trading Account in UK Assets and Liabilities measures the degree of intervention used by the domestic monetary authorities, (Central Banks) in stabilising the exchange rate of their currency. In the case of the UK, the Bank of England monitors the par value of the pound, and from time to time, may intervene to try to stabilise it. The movements of funds required to finance these transactions are recorded in several accounts, which will be discussed in more detail in the section on Exchange rates. The principal means of intervention is the use of Official Reserves. The official definition of Official Reserves states that this item:

> "consists of the sterling equivalent, at current rates of exchange, of drawings on, and additions to, the gold, convertible currencies and Special Drawing Rights (SDR's) held in the Exchange Equalisation Account, and, from July 1972, changes in UK reserves in the IMF. From July 1979 it also included reserves of European Currency Units".

The Bank of England sells these reserves on the foreign exchange market when it wants to increase the demand for sterling, and buys foreign currencies to add to its reserves when there is upward pressure on the pound. Intervention of this type is much less common than it used to be, because for most of the past 18 years, the pound's value has been driven by market forces. This is discussed in more detail below.

The absence of any persistent intervention by the UK government, and its repayment of loans taken out in the 1970's from the IMF, mean that many of the account entries are zero, as can be seen in Appendix 10.1. Transactions involving the Exchange Equalisation Account (EEA), allocations of SDR drawing rights, and IMF gold subscription account have all been non-existent. When the UK government has intervened, its intervention has shown up in borrowings from other European Central Banks, and its use of Official Reserves. All of 'the action' revolved around the UK's relationship with Exchange Rate Mechanism of the European Community, which is a forerunner to the intended single European Currency.

## 10.7    THE INTERNATIONAL MONETARY FUND (IMF)

The IMF was one outcome of the Bretton Woods Agreement which came into operation in 1947. The agreement was intended to encourage international co-operation in respect of the stabilisation of foreign exchange rates in the post war period. When a country becomes a member of the IMF, it is given a quota which is based on the member's national income, its stock of foreign exchange reserves, and other signs of its economic importance. The quota is directly reflected in terms of the voting and drawing rights of that country. A subscription is paid by each member, 25% in gold and the remainder in the country's own currency. Thus the IMF has a reserve of currencies from its members which it may later lend to countries with balance of payment deficits. A country may borrow up to 75% of its quota, and any loan plus service charges has to be repaid usually within 3 to 5 years. Further drawings above the 75% may be made, but these normally result in the IMF imposing increasingly severe conditions on the country concerned in terms of economic policy it should pursue. These additional drawings are not normally included in the balance of payments in terms of currency reserves because they are only lent under certain conditions.

### Special Drawing Rights (SDRs)

These were agreed by the Fund in 1967 and came into operation in 1970. These are completely new reserve assets, inconvertible paper money which is issued to members in proportion to their quota. Any member has free access to SDRs, but it must maintain 30% of its initial allocation over a five-year period. Drawings may be used to purchase foreign exchange from other members.

SDRs are charged at a rate of 5% interest, and since they are never repaid they make a net addition to world reserves and so differ from ordinary drawing rights which have to be repaid.

## 10.8   EXCHANGE RATES AND THE BALANCE OF PAYMENTS

In the previous sections, the exchange rate has been taken as given. But any glance at the financial press reveals that there are very wide fluctuations in currency values, a situation that has developed from the early 1970's. After discussing some different measures of exchange rates, this section gives a brief outline of the post war changes that have occurred in the way that the international monetary system has evolved since the Second World War. A simple model of exchange rate determination is then developed, and its limitations discussed.

There are a number of different ways of defining the rate of exchange. The *spot* rate is the rate for immediate delivery of a currency, which is usually two or three days. Most of the discussion in this Chapter is focussed on this rate. The *forward* rate is the name given to a contract which promises to deliver a fixed amount of foreign exchange a certain period of time in advance, usually one or two months. Both of these rates are for specific currencies. Measuring the relative value of a currency against another is easily done with the spot rate, but countries trade with hundreds of partners. Economists now use a trade weighted index to measure the overall performance of one currency against its trading partners, the weights being given by the relative shares of trade. For the UK, the relevant index is the Sterling exchange rate index, and is set at 100 for 1990. In 1992 the index stood at 96.9, and in 1993, 88.9[3]. This means that the pound's value fell by about 9% against all its trading partners currencies (88.9/96.9), reflecting an overall devaluation of the currency. This is sometimes called the *effective exchange rate*, because it reflects the currency's value against all of its trading partners.

Between 1945 and 1971 most world economies operated a 'fixed exchange rate system'. Under these arrangements, each country's currency was given a par value, which was guaranteed by the Central Bank within a band of 2.5% either side. The central bank thus needed to intervene to maintain this rate. Suppose there is a greater supply of sterling onto the foreign exchange market than there is demand for it, at the current par value. The Central Bank, in this case, the Bank of England, would intervene by buying its own currency from traders, which it would finance by running down reserves of gold and foreign currencies held for that purpose. If there was an excess demand for sterling, it would sell its own currency, and purchase dollars, yen etc., to be placed back into its reserves.

Providing that there was, over time, a broad balance of demand and supply, this kind of arrangement worked quite well. But if there is a persistent excess supply of sterling, there would be a persistent drain on reserves. This cannot be sustained indefinitely, so the government would have to intervene to try to eliminate the cause of the problem. There is thus scope for government policy action of the sort discussed in the next section.

One major disadvantage of the above system was that par values were not changed to reflect differences in the underlying economic performance of the major trading economies. The rise of Japan, the decline of the UK as economic powers were not reflected in the relative values of the two currencies. The UK, in particular, found it had persistent problems on its balance of payments at the par value of £1=$2.40, a rate which persisted from 1949 until 1967.

Why should such problems arise? One way of understanding them is to study the model developed below. Assume for the moment, that all currency flows are driven by trade. Portfolio and direct investment are set to zero. Suppose there are two trading countries, the UK and the USA. The UK exports goods and services to the USA, and the USA does the same to the UK. Consider three different exchange rates. £1 = $1, £1 = $1.50, and £1 = $2.00. A UK car costing £5000 will sell at $5000, $3,333, and $2,500 respectively. At the lower dollar price, more cars will be sold to the US. As a result, there is a greater demand for sterling from US exporters. This is shown as schedule DD in Figure 10.2. Now consider the effect of these exchange rates on the sterling price of a US export priced at $5,000. This translates into sterling prices of £5000, £3,333 and £2,500 respectively. As the pound 'appreciates' against the dollar,

---

[3]   Source: Table 8.1. Exchange Rates, United Kingdom Balance of Payments 1996 CSO.

199

the sterling price of US dollar exports falls, and demand will rise. This means that the supply of sterling onto the foreign exchange market will rise as the value of the pound rises[4]. This relationship is drawn as SS in Figure 10.2.

If the market is allowed to find its own level, an equilibrium rate of exchange is determined. In this example, it is £1 = $1.50. At this rate the demand for sterling from US exporters equals the supply of sterling from UK importers. Since they are both using the same rate, it follows that the value of exports to the US must equal the value of imports, at that rate of exchange. In other words, equilibrium in the foreign exchange market coincides with equilibrium in the value of international merchandise trade.

Now suppose the US manages to sell far more goods to the UK, as the result of launching a new product. There will be a sharp rise in the sales of US exports at every possible rate of exchange. This is shown by a rightward shift in the SS curve as UK importers supply more sterling at every possible exchange rate. In a free market, the value of the pound would fall against the dollar, to £1.00 = $1.00 in this example. At this new rate of exchange, UK exports are cheaper in dollar terms, and imports from the US become more expensive in sterling terms. This will reduce US import volumes and increase UK export volumes, with a new equilibrium at point B.

If, on the other hand, the Government is unwilling to permit the pound to fall in value, it would have to step in. It does this by providing an additional source of demand, sufficient to maintain the rate at £1=$1.50. It would have to run down its reserves to fund this process. Note that if the problem persisted next year, it would again have to run down its reserves. This solution is thus only temporary in nature; there are limits to the degree of support.

## Figure 10.2 – Free Market Equilibrium in the Foreign Exchange Market

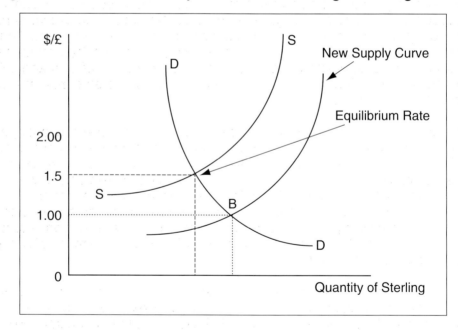

After 1971, this kind of intervention became less necessary. Exchange rates have now been left to find their own levels, that is, they have been permitted to 'float'. The government can still influence the free market rate, but nowadays the intervention is usually achieved via the manipulation of interest rates. The reason for this is that a very large proportion of currency movements are now driven by portfolio investment, which are not directly related to trade. These currency flows are affected by the rates of return earned, which itself is driven by levels of interest

---

[4] For the interested reader, the model developed here assumes that the Marshall-Lerner conditions apply. These state that the sum of the own price elasticities of demand for exports and imports must exceed unity, for a fall in the currency value to generate an increase in the demand for it. Note that the model from which this is derived assumes that all currency movements are trade related. The model is therefore less relevant to today's trading conditions than when it was first developed.

rates. In the context of the above example, the UK governments can raise the rate of interest, which has the effect of increasing the demand for sterling from abroad. Such rate rises also reduce domestic demand, so governments have to use them with care.

A recent example may help to illustrate the ideas mentioned above. In the late 1980's, the UK was shadowing the DM, with a target rate of £1= DM2.95, as part of its anti-inflation strategy. During 1991 and 1992, US interest rates fell, and German rates rose, as reunification was financed. As a result, a large amount of portfolio funds, and banking assets, were moved to Germany. This caused a wave of selling of the pound, which the UK authorities met by raising domestic interest rates. A wave of speculative selling then triggered several currency re-alignments in Europe. The UK borrowed £7.25bn in foreign currency to assist its defence of the £. By the 16th September the currency was trading at its 'floor' level. On that day, two successive rises in interest rates were announced, from 10 to 12, and then from 12 to 15%. Neither had any effect on the selling wave of sterling, so the pound was allowed to 'float' – it fell from 2.95 to 2.36DM in one month, a devaluation of about 20% against that currency.

In this case, neither interest rate increases or government announcements were sufficient to prevent a change in the value of the currency against the German mark.

## 10.9 DEALING WITH A BALANCE OF PAYMENTS DEFICIT: FIXED EXCHANGE RATES

The way in which a balance of payments deficit is dealt with by a government will depend to a large extent on the cause of the deficit and whether it is a long or short term trend.

A deficit may arise on the part of the private transactions recorded in either the current or capital account of the balance of payments. In effect, this creates an excess supply of the domestic currency on the foreign exchange markets, since the demand for sterling say, generated by its credits, is less than the supply of sterling generated by private sector debits. If the government is committed to maintaining the present rate of exchange, it will have to find a means of supplying the difference between these two amounts, in order to maintain the target exchange rate.

It may do this by running down its stock of reserves of foreign exchange. In effect, it enters the foreign exchange market and buys back its own currency, creating an additional source of demand. But it can only do this as long as there is a positive stock of reserve currencies. Persistent deficits will drain these reserves, and so their use can only be a temporary device. Alternatively, the government may try to reduce the deficit by the use of domestic monetary policy, namely, raising domestic rates of interest. This has two effects; it encourages an increase in holdings of portfolio investments of UK assets from abroad, and it reduces domestic demand, thus slowing the growth of imports. Both these effects will reduce the size of the private sector deficit.

In extreme circumstances, additional financial support may be obtained from the IMF or other international banks, primarily to back up the official reserves. The 'price' of such arrangements often means that national governments have to run their economic policies in line with IMF recommendations, and these may not be very comfortable.

In addition to intervening in the foreign currency markets, or using interest rate policy, governments may use the following policy instruments to try to reduce the deficit.

They may try to raise tariff barriers, or grant export subsidies. They may impose exchange controls, or quotas on imports. All of these have been discussed in Chapter 9. Note that many countries now recognise that these devices do not cure the underlying reason for exchange rate re-alignments, which are driven by changes in the relative economic competitiveness of the world's economies. The only way of ensuring a strong currency is to have a strong economy. In the long run, policies designed to ensure that the economy remains competitive are far more likely to be successful than those designed to deal with what is a symptom, not a cause, of a problem.

## 10.10 DEALING WITH A BALANCE OF PAYMENTS DEFICIT: FLOATING EXCHANGE RATES

Under a regime of floating exchange rates, government intervention should not be required, at least in theory. This is because any private sector deficit will generate economic forces which will help to restore equilibrium to the account. Two examples are given here.

Firstly, suppose there is a deficit in trade in goods and services on the current account, and a balance on the private transactions of the capital account. There will be an excess supply of sterling at the present rate of exchange as a result. If sterling's value is determined by supply and demand, its 'price' will fall against other countries currencies. This will make exports become cheaper in overseas markets, and imports dearer in the UK. Provided that certain conditions are satisfied[5] exports will rise, generating and increase in demand for sterling, and imports will fall, reducing its supply. Both of these processes will lead to a reduction in the excess supply of sterling. Thus the rate falls until it finds its equilibrium level, at which point exports and imports are also rebalanced.

Alternatively, the deficit may be on the capital account. But this means the same process will evolve. The difference being that lower currency values raise rates of return to outside holders of currency, and start to make sterling look more attractive as a home for portfolio investment.

## 10.11 EXCHANGE RATES AND SHIPPING

One of the most obvious examples in shipping is that of brokers who earn their commission in US Dollars. This is the currency in which their business is done, but their expenses must be met in their home currency. Thus as the exchange rate alters so does their income. For example, sometime in late 1990 the £ was worth US $1.93, whereas at the end of 1995 it was worth US $1.55. Therefore an income of US $100,000 was worth only £51,813 in 1990, but £64,516 in 1995. The fall in the value of the dollar generates a sterling capital gain in this case.

As you may imagine this could create problems as all the UK brokers' own expenses will normally have to be met in sterling and not US dollars. For this reason, brokers may very well opt for a US dollar rather than a sterling mortgage when buying a house.

We can look very simply at the business side for a moment and consider the cost of bunkering a vessel. This is a dollar cost. Let us say that in late 1990 the price in Rotterdam of 1000 tons of bunkers would be US $125,000 ($125 per ton) giving a total of £64,250, using the current exchange rate of US $1.9455 = £1. Four months previously the exchange rate was such that the cost would have been £71,921 (assuming the dollar cost was the same).

This volatility in exchange rates can be dealt with in a number of ways. Firstly, all transactions can be measured in dollars, where possible. Secondly, one can use the forward exchange market to hedge some of the currency risk. This works by entering into contract to buy dollars say, at a rate fixed today, for three months forward delivery. If a UK importer had a contract to settle with a US trader three months forward, they could hedge against currency risk in this fashion. There is of course, a cost to the hedge.

The increased volatility of exchange rates has led to the development in sophisticated financial products which are designed to permit shipowners and ship charterers limiting

---

[5] See Footnote 2

their degree of currency risk exposure. These are called financial derivatives, or options. An analysis of this market is beyond the scope of this Chapter.

## 10.12 CONCLUSION

The rate of exchange evidently has a strong influence on the balance of payments and is vital in considering prices in international trade.

The individual and the company in international trade, and related services, must therefore be conversant with what is happening on the exchange market and the balance of payments of their country.

## 10.13 SELF-ASSESSMENT AND TEST QUESTIONS

Attempt the following and check your answers from the text:

1. Identify the main account items in the Balance of Payments.

2. Explain the difference between Trade in Visibles and Trade in Invisibles.

3. Using either Table 10.3 or 10.4, Analysis of UK Trade by Commodity and Geographical area, or similar figures from your own country, write brief notes on the main changes that have taken place in the last decade.

4. Write brief notes on the components of the Balance of Payments.

5. What is meant by a balance of payments disequilibrium?

6, Does a balance of trade deficit necessarily mean that there is a Balance of Payments Problem?

Having completed Chapter Ten attempt the following and submit your essay to your Tutor:

Explain why a deficit on a country's current account might lead to a devaluation of its currency. Explain why this may not be the case, if the country also has a large net inflow of portfolio and direct investment during the same period.

## Appendix 10.1 – Sea Transport Account of the UK's Balance of Payments 1985-95

| | | £ million | | | | | | | | | | |
|---|---|---|---|---|---|---|---|---|---|---|---|---|
| | | 1985 | 1986 | 1987 | 1988 | 1989 | 1990 | 1991 | 1992 | 1993 | 1994 | 1995 |
| **Credits** | | | | | | | | | | | | |
| Ships owned or chartered-in by UK residents | | | | | | | | | | | | |
| Dry Cargo | | | | | | | | | | | | |
| Operating earnings | | | | | | | | | | | | |
| Freight on UK exports | HECV | 494 | 393 | 411 | 466 | 462 | 411 | 378 | 366 | 384 | 406 | 421 |
| Freight on cross-trades | HDVI | 608 | 696 | 775 | 839 | 974 | 863 | 867 | 902 | 1,127 | 1,269 | 1,354 |
| O/seas passenger revenue | HCOD | 499 | 514 | 470 | 495 | 486 | 507 | 479 | 586 | 588 | 594 | 723 |
| Time charter receipts from O/S | HDPZ | 131 | 115 | 115 | 179 | 214 | 162 | 115 | 137 | 155 | 128 | 176 |
| Total | HEDS | 1,732 | 1,718 | 1,771 | 1,979 | 2,136 | 1,943 | 1,839 | 1,991 | 2,254 | 2,397 | 2,674 |
| Wet Cargo | | | | | | | | | | | | |
| Operating earnings | | | | | | | | | | | | |
| Freight on UK exports | HEIX | 63 | 47 | 61 | 70 | 56 | 44 | 46 | 50 | 45 | 67 | 61 |
| Freight on cross-trades | HECX | 377 | 320 | 322 | 377 | 411 | 443 | 470 | 383 | 415 | 501 | 465 |
| Time charter receipts from O/S | HDUS | 128 | 119 | 89 | 90 | 96 | 150 | 123 | 104 | 127 | 169 | 187 |
| Total | HEIH | 568 | 486 | 472 | 537 | 563 | 637 | 639 | 537 | 587 | 737 | 713 |
| Ships operated by overseas residents | | | | | | | | | | | | |
| Disbursements in the UK | HBUD | 686 | 655 | 689 | 760 | 823 | 864 | 873 | 997 | 1,072 | 1,072 | 1,163 |
| Total credits | CGJW | 2,986 | 2,859 | 2,932 | 3,276 | 3,522 | 3,444 | 3,351 | 3,525 | 3,913 | 4,246 | 4,550 |
| **Debits** | | | | | | | | | | | | |
| Ships owned or chartered-in by UK residents | | | | | | | | | | | | |
| Dry Cargo | | | | | | | | | | | | |
| Disbursements overseas | HDNR | 1,190 | 1,060 | 993 | 1,033 | 1,134 | 959 | 906 | 903 | 1,056 | 1,241 | 1,354 |
| Charter payments overseas | HCMW | 127 | 145 | 158 | 170 | 213 | 182 | 189 | 209 | 231 | 254 | 270 |
| Total | HDPT | 1,317 | 1,205 | 1,151 | 1,203 | 1,347 | 1,141 | 1,095 | 1,112 | 1,287 | 1,495 | 1,624 |
| Wet Cargo | | | | | | | | | | | | |
| Disbursements overseas | HDSI | 221 | 188 | 231 | 212 | 239 | 179 | 202 | 201 | 198 | 196 | 201 |
| Charter payments overseas | HCMW | 203 | 160 | 160 | 155 | 179 | 247 | 260 | 285 | 277 | 266 | 256 |
| Total | HDUL | 424 | 348 | 391 | 367 | 418 | 426 | 462 | 486 | 475 | 462 | 457 |
| Ships operated by overseas residents | | | | | | | | | | | | |
| Freight on UK imports – dry | HCJO | 1,277 | 1,243 | 1,229 | 1,405 | 1,460 | 1,437 | 1,354 | 1,519 | 1,686 | 1,763 | 1,789 |
| Freight on UK imports – wet | HCNJ | 248 | 275 | 175 | 227 | 199 | 340 | 287 | 195 | 237 | 221 | 193 |
| Freight on UK coastal routes | HFAA | 51 | 51 | 45 | 66 | 73 | 75 | 80 | 81 | 97 | 98 | 100 |
| UK passenger revenue | HDJK | 198 | 201 | 228 | 249 | 282 | 337 | 356 | 428 | 443 | 522 | 552 |
| Total | HCPH | 1,774 | 1,770 | 1,677 | 1,947 | 2,014 | 2,189 | 2,077 | 2,223 | 2,463 | 2,604 | 2,634 |
| Total debits | CGGW | 3,515 | 3,323 | 3,219 | 3,517 | 3,779 | 3,756 | 3,634 | 3,821 | 4,225 | 4,561 | 4,715 |
| **Balances** | | | | | | | | | | | | |
| Ships owned or chartered-in by UK residents | HDOS | 559 | 651 | 701 | 946 | 934 | 1,013 | 921 | 930 | 1,079 | 1,177 | 1,306 |
| Ships operated by o/s residents | HBVD | -1,088 | -1,115 | -988 | -1,187 | -1,191 | -1,325 | -1,204 | -1,226 | -1,391 | -1,492 | -1,471 |
| Overall balance – sea transport | HBTO | -529 | -464 | -287 | -241 | -257 | -312 | -283 | -296 | -312 | -315 | -165 |

# MOCK EXAMINATION

**Do not turn to the next page until you have followed the suggestions below.**

Overleaf is a sample examination paper. In your own interest do not look at it yet but instead, do the same revision of the course as you would do for any examination.

On completing your revision, put away your notes, have pen and paper ready and set aside three hours when you will not be interrupted. In other words create as near as possible examination room conditions.

It is recommended that you hand write this mock examination. You will have to write the actual examination and many students find that it is difficult to write legibly for three hours without practice. If your writing is illegible you will lose marks. Examiners cannot mark what they cannot read.

Carry out the instructions on the question paper and send your answers to your course tutor for marking (Note your start and finish times on the front of your answer paper).

# THE INSTITUTE OF CHARTERED SHIPBROKERS

# MOCK EXAM

## ECONOMICS OF SEA TRANSPORT AND INTERNATIONAL TRADE

Time allowed – Three hours

Answer any FIVE questions – All questions carry equal marks

**Candidates should use diagrams where applicable to enhance their answers**

1  During the second half of 2003 dry bulk freight rates reached all time record high levels. This was attributed to continuous growth in Chinese demand for iron ore and steel whilst at the same time the supply of ships to carry these cargoes was limited. With the aid of diagrams explain the development of this situation making reference to elasticity.

2  What is the effect of the imposition of a tariff on an imported good. Use diagrams to explain your answer.

3  Exchange rates between countries adjust continuously. At the same time most shipping transactions are concluded in US dollars. Explain: a) What factors are behind these movements, and b) How can the exchange risk be minimised by both parties in the transaction?

4  The Theory of "Economies of Scale" is widely applied in the shipping industry. Explain the principles of the theory and discuss how it is applied in a) ports, b) the liner industry and c) the shipbuilding industry.

5  Using examples explain the concept of "opportunity cost" as it applies to the shipping industry from the point of view of an owner, a charterer and a port agent.

6  In the second half of 2003 dry bulk freight rates rose to a level such that for some commodities the fob price of the cargo was less than, or close to, the freight rate.

   Discuss the implications of this for world trade and shipping patterns.

7  Discuss the structure of the tanker market drawing out the differences between crude and products trade.

8  Fleet supply at any one time is governed by many factors. Discuss how these factors influence the freight market in both the short and long-term especially with regard to newbuilding deliveries from the shipyard and scrappings / demolition.

# THE PURPOSE AND SCOPE OF THIS BOOK AND COURSE GUIDE

## ECONOMICS OF SEA TRANSPORT AND INTERNATIONAL TRADE

*NB. Students are expected to use appropriate graphs, diagrams, examples and modelling to illustrate economic concepts and changes.*

*Throughout the syllabus students should be able to relate the theory to empirical evidence.*

*This syllabus does not require an understanding of statistical techniques or methods*

### BASIC ECONOMIC CONCEPTS

Understand the basic definitions of economics and maritime economics.

Understand the distinction between the micro economic theory of shipping and macro economic factors affecting international trade and shipping and the differences between them.

Thoroughly understand: factors of production, utility and price, opportunity cost.

Thoroughly understand price mechanism and the relationship between demand, price and quantity.

Be aware of competitive models and demand factors.

### THE DEMAND FOR SHIPPING

Thoroughly understand how the demand for shipping arises.

Understand the basic measures of economic activity (GNP and GDP)

Thoroughly understand derived demand, elasticity of demand and the relevance of elasticity.

Understand demand measurement – distance, ton/miles and tonnes/kilometres.

### THE SUPPLY OF SHIPPING

Thoroughly understand the factors influencing the supply of shipping – tonnage, number and flag.

Understand the trends in development of the world fleet, newbuildings and scrapping.

Thoroughly understand productivity and supply trends - surplus tonnage, active fleet, market segments.

Understand short and long run supply, supply responsiveness and the concept of elasticity.

## COST ANALYSIS AND ECONOMIES OF SCALE

Understand basic economic cost concepts - conventional cost analysis in shipping, specific factors affecting the relationship between costs and shipping output.

Thoroughly understand economies of scale in shipping and optimal ship size.

Understand factors affecting costs including fiscal regimes and flag of registry.

Be aware of the relationship between costs and quality.

Understand factors affecting costs including fiscal regimes and flag of registry

Understand empirical testing of theory against trends in ship size and the factors involved over the last two decades.

## COMPETITIVE MARKETS – TRAMPS

Thoroughly understand the dry cargo market structure and characteristics.

Understand market demand structure and the concept of perfect competition.

Understand the use of voyage estimating, breakeven analysis in determining minimum freight rates and the lay up decision.

Thoroughly understand the cost structure of tramp ships.

## COMPETITIVE MARKETS – TANKERS

Thoroughly understand the structure of the tanker market and the seaborne trade in crude and products.

Understand the imbalance of ownership, identical service, freedom of entry and exit, full information and segmented supply

Be aware of the relationship between the tanker and dry markets.

Understand the effect of political and environmental factors.

Thoroughly understand recent changes in the tanker fleet and; fluctuations in freight market indices.

## LINER TRADES – OLIGOPOLY AND THE COMPETITIVE MARKET

Thoroughly understand characteristics and demand for liner services.  Understand trends in liner markets and ship types.

Understand pricing behaviour including price discrimination and profitability and the empirical evidence of lower profits than other shipping markets.

Understand the relationship between profit maximisation and optimal utilisation.

Understand the role and function of conferences, alliances and consortia and the differences between theses structures

Be aware of the effect of international regulation.

Understand customer demand, the ability to meet customer demand and maximise utilisation.

## PORTS, CANALS AND WATERWAYS

Understand the functions of ports, canals and waterways.

Understand the relationship between efficiency and cost and the importance of ship/port time.

Understand investment, criteria and economic factors including cost and tariff structure.

Be aware of arguments for and against public ownership.

## SHIPPING AND INTERNATIONAL TRADE

Understand the patterns of world trade; be aware of world trade statistics.

Understand the demand for shipping.

Understand types of trade flows; inter-industry and intra-industry; absolute and comparative advantage.

Thoroughly understand global trading; the arguments for free trade versus protectionism in its many forms; the role of the World Trade Organisation and G8.

## EXCHANGE RATES AND BALANCE OF PAYMENTS

Thoroughly understand how exchange rates are determined; free floating and regulated markets.

Understand the effect of exchange rate fluctuations on shipping.

Understand the components of a balance of payments with particular reference to shipping.

Understand the relationship between exchange rates and the factors affecting their fluctuations and a country's balance of payments.

Lyndon B. Johnson School of Public Affairs
Policy Research Project Report
Number 138

# Maritime Transportation in Latin America and the Caribbean

Project directed by

Leigh B. Boske

A report by the
Policy Research Project on
Multimodal/Intermodal Transportation
2001

The LBJ School of Public Affairs publishes a wide range of public policy issue titles. For order information and book availability call 512-471-4218 or write to: Office of Publications, Lyndon B. Johnson School of Public Affairs, The University of Texas at Austin, Box Y, Austin, TX 78713-8925. Information is also available online at www.utexas.edu/lbj/pubs/.

Library of Congress Catalog Card No.: 2001095022 ✓
ISBN: 0-89940-751-X ✓

Cover design by Doug Marshall
LBJ School Publications Office